T0313488

DESIGN

History, Theory
and Practice
of Product Design

Bernhard E.
Bürdek

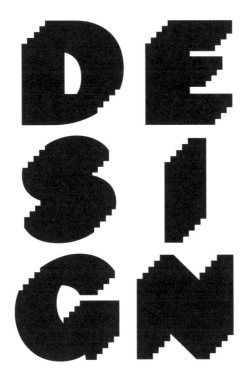

History, Theory
and Practice
of Product Design

Second revised edition

Birkhäuser
Basel

Preface   7
Design as a Concept   11

Design and History   15

Retrospective   17
The Bauhaus   27
The Ulm School of Design   37
The Example of Braun   48
German Democratic Republic   52
From Good Design to the Art of Design   57

Design and Globalization   67

Design and Methodology   75

Epistemological Methods in Design   80
Semiotics and Design   83
Phenomenology and Design   98
Hermeneutics and Design   102
Developments in Design Methodology   108

Design and Theory 125

The Information Aesthetics Approach 129
The Influence of Critical Theory 130
On the Road to Disciplinary Design Theory 131
Aspects of a Disciplinary Design Theory 135
On the Communicative Function of Design 148
The Formal Aesthetic Functions 154
The Marking Functions 164
The Symbolic Functions 169
From Product Language to Product Semantics 177

Design and its Contexts 187

From Corporate Design to Service Design 189
From Design Management to Strategic Design 196
Architecture and Design 202
Utopias, Visions, Concepts, and Trends 216
Design and Society 226

Design and Technology 239

Microelectronics and Design 245

Outlook 259
Bibliography 262
Index of Names 281
Subject Index 286
Picture Credits 295

View of the paternoster elevators "Perpetual Motion of the Present"
Permanent design exhibition in Pinakothek der Moderne, Munich (2002)
Die neue Sammlung

Preface

Ten years after publication of the third edition of this book (and the first English translation) in 2005, it is high time to outline and reflect the incisive changes design has witnessed since the turn of the century. To summarize, design has branched off in two directions:

An industrial path, known in the twentieth century as industrial design (product design),

a non-industrial path with less specific contours, referred to very generally as "design."

The latter is strongly represented in – and conveyed by – the media. Overall, it is fair to say that design has shifted from product design to lifestyle design. And it has at least partly left behind the industrial traditions that shaped the twentieth century, moving instead backwards to a new – often craft-influenced – mode of one-offs and small series (bricolage design).

Design historian Thomas Hauffe (2014) puts his finger on an interesting parallel here: The protagonists of new German design in the 1980s sought to take charge of the design, production, and marketing of their own products (largely furniture and simple household objects). But that route proved to be largely a dead end, perhaps with the exception of the few design galleries and craft collections that acquired individual objects. The growing technical complexity of industrial products, driven especially by the digitalization of all spheres of life and work, and their mass dissemination, mitigate undeniably against DIY manufacture. Moreover, global product marketing is today an exceptionally complex undertaking.

This phenomenon was also observed after the Milan-based Memphis group presented its first collection (to coincide with the 1981 Milan furniture fair) (Radice 1981, 1985). The media sensation they caused kicked off a global design boom that has lasted to this day. Corporations and institutions increasingly acknowledge the publicity value of design, but also its strategic business value – and cultivate it to a high degree of perfection. Design has become an instrument of the formation and differentiation of identity (to cite Martin Heidegger, and also Pierre Bourdieu). In that sense, design is today one element of a global culture in a manner that lends it great importance – especially economically, unfortunately rarely ecologically.

Peter Sloterdijk (2004) describes the phenomenon with great clarity: "If one wanted to say in one sentence, using a minimum of expressions, what the twentieth century – alongside its incommensurable achievements in the arts – has contributed to the history of civilization in the way of unique characteristics, three criteria would suffice for a response. To understand the originality of the epoch, one must consider the practice of terrorism, the concept of design, and the idea of environment." One need only equate "incommensurable" with "irrational" to understand very well how Sloterdijk comes to use the term in connection with design.

Today there is a never-ending flow of publications (periodicals, books, catalogs, online, etc.), media reports, product presentations at trade fairs, competitions (generally rather modestly rewarded, but apparently possessing great publicity value for the organizers), and galleries, exhibitions, even whole museums dedicated to the discipline of design. The best-known include the Design Museum in London, the Neue Sammlung in Munich, the Red Dot Design Museum in Essen, the Museu do Design e da Moda in Lisbon, and the Cooper-Hewitt, Smithsonian Design Museum in New York.

On top of this come numerous conferences where the theoretical and academic implications of design are presented and discussed, in a process driven by the hundreds of doctoral programs now offered worldwide. The primary objective of these conferences is to offer the upcoming generation of academics a platform upon which to present their ideas. The impact of such contributions on practiced design, it must be said, remains largely indiscernible. So-called design science is often autopoetic in nature.

First of all, we should note that the traditional concept of the "product" is in the process of being transformed. Today designers concern themselves not only with the hardware (the objects themselves), but also increasingly with the software, in the form of interfaces and user environments. The example of the digital media underlines how today's focus is increasingly on services – which need to be designed if they are to meet with the acceptance of potential users.

The idea of event design goes even further. At trade fairs and exhibitions, products are elaborately staged and celebrated. New cars, for example, are launched at exorbitant expense in order to impact on globalizing markets.

The Zollverein project in Essen provides a nice example of staging. For more than a century (from 1847 to 1986) Zeche Zollverein was a major coal mine in the German industrial city of Essen. Today it has been transformed into a culture and exhibition center with UNESCO World Cultural Heritage status. It includes a design museum of its own, as well as offices and studios for working designers. The plant and buildings of the erstwhile mining facility now function as nothing more than a symbol recalling the region's industrial heritage. Today Zeche Zollverein is a gigantic center for the experience society, where design acquires a whole new meaning: Design becomes a creative service in the experience society; the clients and projects have changed dramatically.

Making matters even more interesting, design and art have apparently become cultural equals, as confirmed by the rise of design museums across the globe. Their *raison d'être* is not the use of the products but their presentation in a museum setting. They seek to raise design to the rank of art, which is one of the central misunderstandings of the contemporary design discourse.

Today, most people's lives would be unimaginable without design. It accompanies us from dawn till after dusk: at home, at work, in our leisure time, in education, in health services, in sports, in the transport of people and goods, in the public sphere; everything is designed, intentionally or not. Design can be very close (fashion) or far, far away (space travel). Design determines not only existence, but also self; through products we communicate with other people, define ourselves in social groups, and thus mark out our individual place in society. In a notable development, Bernd Guggenberger's "be or design" (*Sein oder Design,* 1987) has given way to "design or die."

So it is certainly time to revise this volume: to update, cut, and expand. After its first publication in German in 1991, translations into Italian (1992), Spanish (1994), Dutch (1996), and Chinese (1996) soon followed. The third edition in 2005 appeared simultaneously in English, which has turned out to be especially fortuitous for the global design discourse, where language barriers meant that very few German-language books on design made any impact at all on the international debate. It was therefore also very gratifying to see the third edition translated into Portuguese (2006), Chinese (2007), and Italian (2008).

This edition, now the fourth, contains a number of significant changes, specifically the decision to omit the country-by-country overview. The speed with which digitalization has progressed means that there are now numerous internet platforms supplying reliable up-to-the-minute information on new products and projects (for example www.designboom.com, www.core77.com, www.stylepark.com).

Instead the central question during the planning and preparation of this new edition has been which topics within the current flood are durable enough to deserve space in a printed book. There has been change in another sphere too. Today nobody would dispute that design possesses core competences and is definitely on the road to becoming a discipline (Bürdek 2012). This new edition describes and reflects these significant developments.

I am especially grateful to Christa Scheld, the librarian at the Offenbach School of Design, who was again an enormous help in researching information, sources, and references.

Obertshausen, June 2015

Design as a Concept

The manifold currents and directions of design are reflected in the very use of the concept of "design," up to and including sometimes rather diffuse definitions of the word. A number of these interpretations will be introduced at the outset of this essay.

From a historical perspective, it is popular to regard Leonardo da Vinci as the first designer. In addition to his scientific studies on anatomy, optics, and mechanics, to name but a few, he performed pioneering work in the elementary science of mechanical engineering, producing a *Book of Patterns of Machine Elements*. As a glance at his machines and devices reveals, this involved more a technical than a creative understanding of design. In his application to Ludovico Sforza Duke of Milan, in 1482, da Vinci concentrated on his talent for constructing bridges and in particular machines of war, mentioning his ability to design weapons of supreme functionality and great beauty. Leonardo da Vinci thus decisively influenced the idea of design at a very early stage: The designer as an inventor.

The sixteenth-century painter, master builder, and literary author Giorgio Vasari was one of the first to plead in his writings for the autonomous character of works of art. He designated the principle to which art owes its existence as *disegno,* which translates directly into "drawing" or "sketch." At that time, *disegno* referred to the artistic idea. Accordingly, even back then, people differentiated between the *disegno interno,* the concept for an emerging work of art (the sketch, the draft, or the plan), and the *disegno esterno,* the completed work of art (such as a drawing, painting, or sculpture). Vasari himself pronounced drawing, or *disegno,* to be the father of the three arts: painting, sculpture, and architecture (for more information, see Bürdek 1996).

According to the *Oxford Dictionary* the concept of "design" was used in 1588 for the first time. Its definition reads:

a plan or scheme devised by a person for something that is to be realized,

a first graphic draft of a work of art, or

an object of the applied arts, which is to be binding for the execution of a work.

Later, Sigfried Giedion (first edition 1948, see also 1987) significantly described how the industrial designer appeared in the twentieth century: "He fashioned the housing, saw to it that the visible machinery (of the washing machines) disappeared, and gave the whole, in short, a streamlined shape like the train and the automobile." In the US, this clear separation of technical work from artistic work on the product led to the discipline's increasing orientation toward styling, and thus to purely superficial fashioning.

The concept of "industrial design" can be traced back to Mart Stam, who supposedly used the term for the first time in 1948 (Hirdina 1988). For Stam, an industrial designer was someone who drafted, sketched, and planned. In his opinion designers should be employed in every area of industry, especially in the production of new kinds of materials.

The definition of design had long been a matter of intense concern in the former German Democratic Republic. This regime always understood design to be a component of social, economic, and cultural policy. Horst Oehlke (1978), in particular, pointed out that shaping affects more than the sensually perceptible side of objects. On the contrary, the designer must be concerned with satisfying the needs of societal and individual life.

A broad and therefore quite useful definition of design was worked out by the Internationales Design Zentrum Berlin in 1979 in the context of an exhibition:

Good design may not be a mere envelopment technique. It must express the individuality of the product in question through appropriate fashioning.

It must make the function of the product, its application, plainly visible so that it can be understood clearly by the user.

Good design must allow the latest state of technical development to become transparent.

Design must not be restricted to the product alone; it must also take into consideration issues of ecology, energy conservation, recyclability, durability, and ergonomics.

Good design must take the relationship between humans and objects as the point of departure for the shapes it uses, especially taking into account aspects of occupational medicine and perception.

This complex definition clearly takes into consideration not only the functional aspects (practical functions), but also the product language (semantic) and ecological aspects of design. In the same sense, but in a quite compressed form, Michael Erlhoff undertook a clear and current delimitation of design on the occasion of *documenta 8* in Kassel (1987): "Design, which – unlike art – requires practical justification, finds this chiefly in four assertions: being societal and functional and meaningful and concrete."

There was no problem with such an open description of design well into the 1980s. However, the age in which a uniform – and thus ideologically cemented – concept of design could predominate now appears to be over once and for all. The reflections of the postmodern age have promoted the dissolution of totality in a variety of disciplines. Anyone who continues to regard this as a loss is thus, in the Lyotardian sense, stuck in the "discussion condition" of a modern age which has since become history (Welsch 1987).

With that in the meantime superseded by a metamodernity, design is today separating into two very different categories:

a traditional one, to which the term "industrial design" continues to apply;

a regressive form, in the sense of a retrograde move back to the arts and crafts. This reflects in particular a critical stance toward the advancing industrialization of Western countries.

The diversity of concepts and descriptions is not a sign of postmodern arbitrariness, however, but rather a necessary and justifiable pluralism. In the transition from the twentieth to the twenty-first century I have therefore proposed, instead of yet another definition or description, listing a number of the tasks design is supposed to fulfill (Bürdek 1999). Thus, for instance, design should:

visualize technological progress,

simplify or make possible the use and operation of products (hardware or software),

make transparent the connections between production, consumption, and recycling,

promote and communicate services, but also – pursued energetically enough – help to prevent products that are senseless.

However, this latter aspect appears increasingly dubious in an era of global hyperconsumption (especially in Asia). All the same, there are diverse attempts, not least at design schools, to understand design as a "world-bettering" discipline. While this does no end of good to the consciences of the protagonists, it changes nothing in the technological, economic, and social circumstances under which design is practiced.

On the one hand, design is today anything from urban design to nail design. Everything is design. On the other, much thought is now being devoted to developing and describing design as a discipline. The latter is the topic of this volume.

Design

and

History

17   Retrospective

27   The Bauhaus

37   The Ulm School of Design

48   The Example of Braun

52   German Democratic Republic

57   From Good Design to the Art of Design

Retrospective

This chapter can in no way substitute for a comprehensive history of design. Instead, it outlines the developments that have shaped the history of industrial design, briefly covering the products, companies, and designers that mark the significant events and their repercussions. Readers seeking greater depth and detail are encouraged to turn to the many standard works on the history of design. These include John Heskett (1980), Guy Julier (2000), Penny Sparke (1986), History of Industrial Design (1990/1991), Gert Selle (1978, 1987, 1994), John A. Walker (1992), Jonathan M. Woodham (1997), and Thomas Hauffe (2014). From the perspective of design theory, Walker's contribution is especially significant. He argues for a "disciplinary" development of design history that places the meaning of objects (semantics) front and center: "Designers can, therefore, be said to be engaged in 'a discursive practice'." Semiotics (↗ p. 83 ff) is particularly important here.

Victor Margolin's *World History of Design* (vols. 1 and 2: 2015; vol. 3: 2016), which spans an arc from the very beginnings of human history through to the present day, must also be mentioned: it is without doubt the ultimate work in the twenty-first century on the history of design.

The Beginnings of Design

The origins of functionally optimized product design can be traced all the way back to classical antiquity. The writings of the Roman artist, architect, and military engineer Vitruvius (ca. 80–10 BC) are among the oldest surviving architectural documents. His comprehensive *De architectura libri decem (Ten Books on Architecture)* comprised the first handbook of planning and design. Here, Vitruvius describes the close relationship between theory and practice, saying that an architect has to be interested in art and science, as well as being versed

Henry Cole, drawings of simple objects for rising children (1849)

in rhetoric and having a good knowledge of history and philosophy. In chapter three of his first book, Vitruvius names a guiding principle that has found its place in design history: "all buildings must satisfy three criteria: strength (firmitas), functionality (utilitas), and beauty (venustas)" (Bürdek 1997b). It could be said that Vitruvius laid out the basic tenets for the concept of functionalism, whose time did not come until the twentieth century, when it was to define modernism in design across the world.

It is actually only since the mid-nineteenth century, the age of the Industrial Revolution, that we can speak of industrial design in the modern sense. Since then, increasing division of labor has meant that the design and manufacture of a product are no longer carried out by one and the same person. Over time, the process of specialization has progressed to such an extent that today a designer in a large company is only responsible for one specific part of a product. In the 1970s a reaction to this division of labor led younger designers in particular to attempt to undertake design, production, and marketing as a unified whole.

In the mid-nineteenth century a number of English designers rebelled against the grandiloquent interiors of the Regency style. In Europe the room itself had been steadily losing importance since the Middle Ages, whereas the furniture in the room increasingly became the center of attention. Sigfried Giedion (1987) has vividly described how a medieval room always appeared furnished; it never seemed bare, even when empty of furniture, as it came alive through its proportions, materials, and forms. A trend that treated the furniture as if it were the room itself reached its zenith in the Regency period (approx. 1811–1830). The declining significance of the room as a space was only recognized in the twentieth century, by the architects and designers of the Bauhaus. They responded by designing very simple, reductionist furniture in order to direct attention back to the meaning of the room.

In England, Henry Cole aspired to influence applied design educationally through his modest and short-lived publication, *The Journal of Design and Manufactures,* which appeared from 1849 to 1852. Cole's work focused on the practical and functional aspects of design, to which he felt the representative and decorative elements should be secondary. Cole also proposed holding a Great Exhibition in London, where all nations would be given the opportunity to present their manifold products. At the heart of his thought was the idea of "learning to see, seeing by comparing," which was taken up by the German Werkbund in the twentieth century.

Joseph Paxton won the commission to design the building for the 1851 Great Exhibition in London. His Crystal Palace, which Friemert (1984) refers to as a "glass ark," was prototypical of the industrialized construction methods of the nineteenth century. The structure was built in just four and a half months, all the parts being manufactured elsewhere and assembled at the site. Furthermore, the building was dismantled several years later and re-erected at a different location (Sembach 1971).

The first World's Fairs – among them 1873 in Vienna, 1876 in Philadelphia, and 1889 in Paris (with Gustave Eiffel's tower) – were gigantic collections of products and expositions of design, where the technical and cultural developments of the age were put on show.

It was an era of new materials and technologies: cast iron, steel, and cement were no longer processed in small-scale workshops, as mechanized industrial enterprises replaced older modes of production. Automated looms, steam engines, industrial carpentry, and prefabricated construction methods utterly transformed the conditions of life and work. The social consequences of industrialization were plain to see. A large part of the population fell into poverty and became the proletariat, while the environment was transformed by the advent of mass accommodations and extensive industrial zones. The real fathers of design were contemporaries of this Industrial Revolution: Gottfried Semper, John Ruskin, and William Morris. They, like Henry Cole, reacted against the superficial embellishment of the new industrial products. This reform movement was strongly influenced by John Stuart Mill's philosophy of utilitarianism, which stated that the moral quality of human acts depended solely on their usefulness (or harmfulness) to society. This criterion, incidentally, can be traced right through to the present as a determining category in design. Wend Fischer (1971) even saw it as the foundation of rational design: "In considering the nineteenth century we have also learned something about our own century. We recognize ourselves in the efforts of reason to establish the idea of functional design against the arbitrariness of historical formalism, in order for the world of people, their houses, rooms, and utensils to be given a characterful form in which the expression of life can be found."

German architect Gottfried Semper emigrated in 1849 to seek political asylum in England, where he pushed for the reform of industrial design activities, advocating that the form should be appropriate to the function, the material, and the manufacturing process. Semper worked together with Cole on the Great Exhibition of 1851 and taught at the newly founded drawing school in London. At the turn of the twentieth century Semper's ideas exerted a strong influence on the German Arts and Crafts movement, which also placed the pure function of the object in the foreground.

John Ruskin, art historian and philosopher, attempted to revitalize medieval production methods in a countermovement to the Industrial Revolution. Craft production, he believed, would make better living conditions possible for the workers and represent a counterweight to the aesthetically impoverished world of machines.

William Morris founded Morris, Marshall, Faulkner & Company in 1861 with the aim of reinvigorating the arts and crafts. The British Arts and Crafts Movement that formed around Morris worked for social reform and to rejuvenate style. Revoking the division of labor and reuniting design with production, the Arts and Crafts revival directed its energies especially against the aesthetic of the machine, but was thwarted by the tumultuous industrial developments of the second half of the nineteenth century.

Joseph Paxton, London's Crystal Palace (1851)

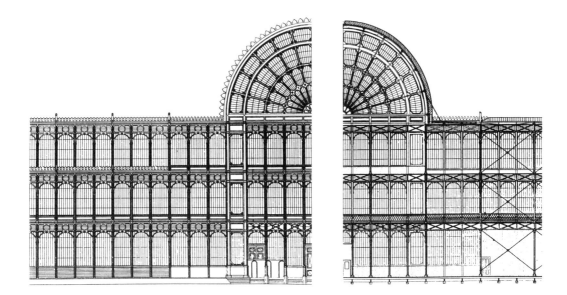

One typical product from this early phase of design is the Singer sewing machine, whose annual production volume had already surpassed 400,000 by 1879.

This period also saw the development of the bentwood chair by the Thonet brothers, first in Germany, then in Austria. Their method of steaming wood to make it pliable was patented in Vienna, and became the basis for worldwide success. These chairs were already on display at the Great Exhibition of 1851 in London. The principles of standardization (using only a small range of identical components) and mass production meant that a reduced language of form had to be used. The Thonets' chairs thus embody an important keynote of design – high production volume with reductionist aesthetic – that was to remain ascendant in that form until the 1970s. It is said that fifty million units of Chair No. 14 had been made by 1930, and it is still in production today.

New movements emerged in Europe toward the end of the nineteenth century: Art Nouveau in France, Jugendstil in Germany, the Modern Style in England, and the Secession Style in Austria. What they all shared was an artistic *joie de vivre,* which was reflected especially in the visual appearance of everyday products.

1 **Gebrüder Thonet,** chair, canapé, half-armchair, armchair
   Catalog of the furniture factory Gebrüder Thonet in Vienna (around 1895)

2 **Henry van de Velde,** desk (1899)

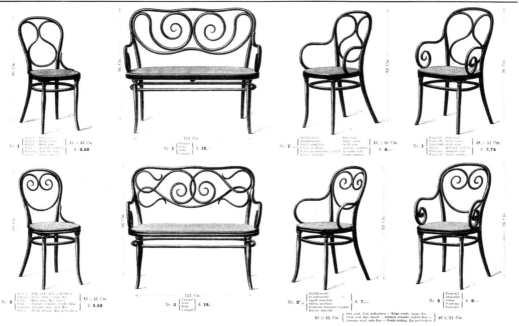

1

2

The leading proponent of this movement, the Belgian Henry van de Velde, designed furniture, implements, and interiors, but the ideas of social reform formulated by William Morris were forgotten. All that the two had in common was the arts and crafts renaissance. Van de Velde was an elitist and an individualist; a combination we shall meet again in the early 1980s in the Memphis group and new German design (↗ p. 60 ff).

In Austria Josef Hoffmann, Joseph Olbrich, and Otto Wagner joined together to form the Vienna Secession, establishing a group of artists whose work prominently featured geometric ornaments and a reduced language of form. In the Vienna Workshops, which were set up at this time, craftsmen designed furniture for the upper middle classes.

From Werkbund to Bauhaus

The German Werkbund was founded in Munich in 1907. It was a society of artists, craftsmen, industrialists, and journalists, who set themselves the goal of improving mass-produced goods through cooperation between industry, the arts, and the craft trades, and by means of education and publicity work. Leading members of the Werkbund at the turn of the twentieth century included Peter Behrens, Theodor Fischer, Hermann Muthesius, Bruno Paul, Richard Riemerschmid, and Henry van de Velde. Both leading currents of the time were represented in the Werkbund: industrial and product standardization on the one hand, expression of artistic individuality *à la* van de Velde on the other. These were, in fact, to be the two decisive tendencies in twentieth-century design.

Werkbund organizations sharing the same central tenets were set up in other countries, too: the Austrian Werkbund in 1910, the Swiss Werkbund in 1913, the Swedish Slöjdforenigen (1910–1917), and the English Design and Industries Association in 1915. The goal they all shared was to popularize a holistic good taste among manufacturers and consumers of products, working educationally in the tradition of Henry Cole.

The high point of the German Werkbund's work after World War I was an exposition held in 1927 in Stuttgart: the Weissenhof project. Under the leadership of Ludwig Mies van der Rohe, more than a dozen of the most famous architects of the time – including Le Corbusier, Hans Scharoun, Walter Gropius, Max Taut, Jacobus Johannes Pieter Oud, Hans Poelzig, Peter Behrens, and

Mart Stam – were invited to put their new ideas about architecture and design into practice in houses and apartment buildings.

The application of new construction materials made the design of new housing concepts possible, and the intention was to restore significance to the room itself, as mentioned earlier. The Weissenhof project represented an attempt to subject everything – from the house itself right down to the coffee cup – to a fundamental design concept. The apartment as a gesamtkunstwerk was intended on the one hand to propagate new aesthetic models (reduction to the elementary functions, utilitarianism), and on the other to offer affordable furnishings to a broad section of the population. Giedion credits the Dutch architect Oud with being the first to treat the working-class apartment as an artistic challenge. The holistic ideas expressed in the Weissenhof exposition corresponded to the basic ideas of the Bauhaus (↗ p. 27 f.).

In hindsight, Weissenhof represented the first visible expression of the so-called International Style in architecture. But in contrast to the superficial formal manifestations we know, for example, from the satellite towns built round the major conurbations since the 1960s, Weissenhof embodied a well-thought-out, meaningful unity of social conditions using new materials and forms (Kirsch 1987).

In Scotland a group centered on Charles Rennie Mackintosh formed in opposition to Jugendstil. His purist utilitarian forms stood in the tradition of medieval Scottish furniture, as well as demonstrating a severity that was to resurface in constructivism.

Peter Behrens was one of the key pioneers of modern design. Behrens, a German architect and advertising expert, was appointed as artistic adviser to AEG (Allgemeine Elektrizitäts Gesellschaft) in 1906–1907. His responsibilities there included designing buildings and electrical domestic appliances. Because he designed mass products for general consumption, he is regarded as one of the very first industrial designers. The rationale of industrialized manufacturing led him to turn his back on Jugendstil and concentrate on products that were economical to manufacture, simple to operate, and easy to service.

The De Stijl group in the Netherlands formed in 1917. Its most important representatives were Theo van Doesburg, Piet Mondrian, and Gerrit T. Rietveld, all of whom put forward aesthetic and social utopias that were futuristic rather than backward-looking like those of Ruskin and Morris. Doesburg rejected the crafts in favor of the machine, and spent time in Weimar in 1921–

1 **Jacobus J. P. Oud**
Weißenhofsiedlung
Stuttgart (1927)

2 **Ferdinand Kramer**
Interior furnishing (1927)

1

2

Peter Behrens, table fan "Type NGVU2", AEG, Berlin (around 1910/12)

1922. His concept of "mechanical aesthetics" was identical to the technical aesthetics of the Russian constructivists.

The reductionist aesthetic of De Stijl was characterized on the two-dimensional plane by simple geometric elements such as circles, squares, and triangles, and in the three-dimensional world by spheres, cubes, and pyramids. This specific use of formal elements created enduring design categories, some of which are still valid today. The Bauhaus and its successors, such as the Ulm School of Design and the New Bauhaus in Chicago, looked to this tradition, especially in their foundation courses. The geometric principles of De Stijl are also reflected in the sparing use of design elements found in Swiss graphic art, and the oft-quoted catchphrase of Dieter Rams, Braun's long-serving head designer, that "less design is more design" can also be traced back to the same origins.

In Russia a group known as the constructivists formed after the October Revolution of 1917; the most famous of them were El Lissitzky, Kazimir Malevich, and Vladimir Tatlin. They made social aesthetics their top priority; satisfying the basic needs of the general population was the primary goal of their work. The basic principles of constructivism developed by Tatlin were based on the real material conditions of production: technology, materials, and processes. Style was to be replaced by technology. Malevich drew up guiding principles for the Vkhutemas which was a kind of Russian Bauhaus (↗ p. 172).

The ideas of this group, too, can be followed through to the present. Design in the 1960s and 1970s, especially, was characterized by themes of social relevance, and, because of the crippling lack of basic consumer goods, the rigid concentration of technology continues to govern design in most countries of the Third World today.

The Bauhaus

In 1902 Henry van de Velde established an arts and crafts seminar in Weimar, which was expanded to form the School of Arts and Crafts under his directorship in 1906. The School merged with the Academy of Arts in 1919 to form the Staatliches Bauhaus Weimar, with Walter Gropius as its director. The Bauhaus was to become the flagship for the subsequent development of design (Wingler 1962).

With the exception of sculptor Gerhard Marcks, Gropius appointed only representatives of abstract and cubist painting to teaching posts at the Bauhaus. These included Wassily Kandinsky, Paul Klee, Lyonel Feininger, Oskar Schlemmer, Johannes Itten, Georg Muche, and László Moholy-Nagy.

The unity of design and execution that had existed in the craft trades had been torn asunder by the advance of industrial modes of production during the nineteenth century. Gropius was guided by the idea that the Bauhaus should bring together art and technology to form a new, modern unity. Technology might not need art, but art certainly needed technology, was the motto. This idea was associated with a fundamental social objective, namely to anchor art in society.

The Bauhaus drew on the ideas of the life reform movement of the turn of the twentieth century, which had taken a particular interest in housing issues. The fustiness of the nineteenth century with its dark furniture in dark rooms was to be blown away, supplanted by new forms of accommodations. The idea was that the modern twentieth-century individual, housed in clear bright rooms, would develop new ways of living (Becher 1990).

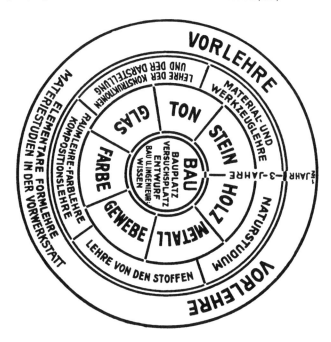

Walter Gropius, diagram of the structure of instruction at the Bauhaus school (1922)

The Foundation Course

The foundation course at the Bauhaus represented the heart of the program of basic polytechnic artistic education. Introduced in 1919–1920 by Johannes Itten, it was a significant component of the curriculum and was obligatory for all students. The twin purposes of the course were to encourage students to experiment and to explore their own creative talents, and to teach fundamental design skills through an understanding of an objective science of design.

The foundation course was conducted first by László Moholy-Nagy and later by Josef Albers, whose goals were "inventive building and observational discovery." Methodologically Itten, like Albers, took an inductive approach to design, allowing the students to investigate, explore, and experiment. In this manner, cognitive skills were fostered indirectly. Theory did not lead the way; instead the conclusions drawn from analysis and discussion of experiments were progressively distilled into a generalized "theory of design."

In 1925 the Bauhaus moved from Weimar to a new building in Dessau designed by Gropius, where it stayed for seven years before being forced to close under pressure from the Nazis. A small group of Bauhaus teachers and students kept the school going in 1932–1933 in Berlin under extremely difficult conditions as a private school, which Mies van der Rohe finally closed down in summer 1933.

Development Phases

According to Rainer Wick (1982) the Bauhaus period can be divided into three developmental phases:

The Founding Phase 1919–1923 The most important educational element was the foundation course described above. Students who had completed it then chose from a number of specialist workshops: printing, pottery, metalwork, mural painting, stained glass, carpentry, stagecraft, weaving, bookbinding, and woodcarving.

Each workshop had two supervisors: a master of form (an artist) and a master craftsman. The intent of this dualism was to promote the students' manual and artistic skills equally, but in practice it soon became clear that the craftsmen were subordinate to the artists. Pervasive social tensions arose, because in the end the autonomous artist was the center of attention, even at the Bauhaus. In the field of design mostly one-offs were produced during this phase, representing the first moves toward a product aesthetic.

The Consolidation Phase 1923–1928 The Bauhaus increasingly became a teaching and production facility for industrial prototypes, which aimed to meet both the realities of industrial manufacturing and the social needs of the general population. From our perspective today, the most successful Bauhaus workshop, apart from metalworking, was carpentry. Marcel Breuer, who had studied at the Bauhaus since 1920, took over the carpentry workshop as "young master" in 1925. In developing his tubular steel furniture, Breuer achieved a breakthrough: functional furniture capable of exploiting the opportunities offered by mass production. Probably inspired by the curved form of his bicycle handlebars, Breuer made a mental leap to the Thonet chairs. Combining the strength and stability of steel tubing with lightweight coverings (wickerwork, fabric, leather), he succeeded in creating a completely new category of seating (Giedion 1948); the same principles were soon being applied to tables, cabinets, shelves, desks, beds, and combination furniture.

The Bauhaus Building in Dessau (1925)

The aim of the design activities at the Bauhaus was to develop affordable products for the populace, while maintaining a high degree of functionality. During this second phase much theoretical and practical work was conducted on the concept of function, which always involved a social perspective in its aim to "govern the circumstances of life and labor" (Moholy-Nagy) and take "questions of mass demand" seriously. Function always meant a combination of two factors in design, marrying the conditions of industrial manufacturing (technology, construction methods, materials) with the social conditions, in the service of the needs of the broader population and the requirements of social planning.

Accordingly, during this second phase of the Bauhaus, undirected artistic experimentation retreated in favor of applied design tasks. To some extent as a result of assignments that gave rise to industrial commissions, the Bauhaus became a "university of design." Standardization, series manufacturing, and mass production became the backbone of all Bauhaus activities. The principal force behind these developments was Swiss architect Hannes Meyer, who be-

came head of the Department of Architecture in 1927 and set up a systematic, scientifically grounded architecture program.

The Phase of Disintegration 1928–1933 Hannes Meyer was appointed director of the Bauhaus in 1928. On his watch new subjects and workshops were introduced, including photography, sculpture, and psychology. Meyer energetically promoted a social purpose for architecture and design. The designer should serve the people, he said, which meant providing adequate products to satisfy their basic needs, for example, in the field of housing. This meant giving up for good the original concept of an art academy. Many artists left the Bauhaus, among them Schlemmer, Klee, Moholy-Nagy. In 1930 Meyer, too, left the Bauhaus, emigrating to Moscow with twelve students to escape the political pressure in Germany.

Ludwig Mies van der Rohe was named the new director, but in 1932 the Nazis closed the Bauhaus in Dessau. Mies attempted to keep it going as an independent institute in Berlin, but the Bauhaus disbanded just a few months after Adolf Hitler seized power in Berlin, on July 20, 1933 (Hahn 1985).

The Goals of the Bauhaus

The Bauhaus had two central aims:

to achieve a new aesthetic synthesis by integrating all the artistic genres and craft trades under the primacy of architecture, and

to achieve a social synthesis by aligning aesthetic production with the needs of the general population.

Both of these aspects became central categories of design activity over the course of the subsequent decades. Aside from its purely educational contributions, the Bauhaus was also a "school of life," where teachers and students practiced a shared constructivist philosophy of life (Wünsche 1989), and which, during the Weimar phase at least, resembled a "closed community," as Moholy-Nagy put it. This common identity was certainly crucial in building the almost missionary zeal with which the Bauhaus idea was transported all over the world.

This is evidenced in a range of public collections: in Weimar (Klassik Stiftung Weimar, Abteilung Bauhaus-Museum), Dessau (Stiftung Bauhaus Dessau), and Berlin (Bauhaus-Archiv / Museum für Gestaltung). The China Academy of Art (CAA) has established a Bauhaus collection with more than seven thousand objects in Hangzhou near Shanghai. For this, the City of Hangzhou acquired the collection of Torsten Bröhan, son of the renowned Berlin art collector Karl Bröhan, for about 60 million euros in 2012 and built a dedicated design museum to house it.

Jeannine Fiedler and Peter Feierabend (1999) demonstrated in detail how the Bauhaus was a living community as well as a working one, as illustrated by the legendary parties held in Weimar and Dessau.

More recent research (see Wagner 2009) reveals a fertile strand of esotericism alongside the strong rationality of the architects and designers at the Bauhaus. Whether freemasonry, anthroposophy, astrology, or para-scientific beliefs, there was certainly a place for the esoteric at the Bauhaus. The most serious interest was shown by artists such as Johannes Itten, Wassily Kandinsky, and Paul Klee. It is reported that the architect and designer Marcel Breuer and the weaver Gunta Stölzl created an African chair that may have been intended as a "throne" for Bauhaus director Walter Gropius. Nothing, however, is known of his response.

A comparable melding of work and life arose again after World War II at the Ulm School of Design (↗p. 37). These hitherto neglected aspects of Bauhaus are addressed in the voluminous contribution by Fiedler and Feierabend (1999), which has quickly joined Wingler (1962) and is seen as the second standard work on the topic.

The Influence of the Bauhaus on Product Design Culture

Walter Gropius's postulate, "art and technology – a new unity," was aimed at producing new experts in industry who would be competent both in modern technology and in the corresponding language of form. Gropius thus laid the groundwork for the transformation in vocational practice that turned the traditional artisan craftsman into the modern industrial designer.

The methods of eidetic inquiry, functional analysis, and a nascent science of form were to be used to elucidate the objective conditions for design. In 1926 Gropius formulated this as follows: "A thing is determined by its nature. In order to design it so that it functions properly, whether it be a vessel, a chair, or a house, its nature must first be investigated, because it should serve its purpose perfectly, meaning that it fulfills its functions practically, is long-lasting, inexpensive, and attractive" (Gropius 1925).

In a dissertation on the logic of design prepared at the Offenbach School of Design, Florian Arnold points to a revealing tangent connecting the ideas of Walter Gropius and Martin Heidegger. While hard evidence of a concrete link is lacking, a search for their "essence" turns up commonalities produced by their time (Werner Marx 1961). Both Husserl's phenomenology (↗p. 98 ff) and Heidegger's fundamental ontology enriched the thinking of Walter Gropius – in the sense of a reaction to the rationalization of the modern lifeworld (Arnold 2012).

Whereas Bauhaus sought to design and produce more or less prototypical furniture, Heidegger was driving at the fundamental questions of human nature. The concept of "eidetic marks" (Fischer and Mikosch 1983) also stands in this tradition, denoting as it does that every product has typical marks, or visualizations of practical functions, that point to the specifics of a product class.

This social stance is particularly apparent in the work of Bauhaus student Wilhelm Wagenfeld, who was adamant that mass-produced goods should be both cheap and excellently designed and made. His designs for the Lausitz Glassworks and WMF (Württembergische Metallwarenfabrik) have become so widespread that they occupy an almost anonymous position in everyday culture, because Wagenfeld as a designer gave prominence to his products rather than his person (for his lifework see Manske and Scholz 1987).

It should, however, be pointed out that the Bauhaus designs had no influence on the mass culture of the 1930s. Purchasers of Bauhaus products came from intellectual circles, which were open to new design concepts. Nonetheless, looking back from today's perspective, we can certainly speak of a "Bauhaus style" that was a formative influence in twentieth-century design (Bittner 2003).

Bauhaus and Furniture Design

Design at the Bauhaus was largely shaped by a generation of young architects whose main interest was the functions of products and the surroundings of those who lived in buildings. In a radical break with the nineteenth century, and with the predominant ideas that produced the plush decor of the upper-middle-class home, designers turned their attention to technological questions. Fascination with new construction methods led to functionally reconceived "type furniture." At this early stage the allure of technology was already giving rise to a symbolism of its own. Steel tubing in the apartment became a trademark of the intellectual avant-garde. However, the market potential of such furniture was not exploited properly until the 1960s, for example, by Cassina and other Italian furniture manufacturers.

Carpeting by "Frauen am Bauhaus" (women at Bauhaus) (1929)
Classic, design: Gertrud Arndt, Vorwerk Teppichwerke (1994)

The Influence of the Bauhaus on Design Training

When political developments forced many Bauhaus students and teachers into emigration, the pioneering Bauhaus concepts were carried across the world and developed further in research, teaching, and practical application:

1926: Johannes Itten founds a private art school in Berlin.

1928: the "Budapest Bauhaus" (Mühely) is set up in Hungary with Sándor Bortnik as its head.

1933: Josef Albers goes to Black Mountain College in North Carolina, where he teaches until 1949.

1937: the New Bauhaus with Moholy-Nagy as its head is founded in Chicago.

also in 1937: Walter Gropius is appointed head of the Department of Architecture at the Harvard Graduate School of Design. Marcel Breuer also teaches there until 1946.

1938: Mies van der Rohe is appointed head of the Department of Architecture at the Armour Institute of Technology in Chicago, which joins with other institutes in 1940 to form the influential Illinois Institute of Technology.

1939: Moholy-Nagy founds the School of Design in Chicago, renamed the Institute of Design, with college status, in 1944.

1949: under Moholy-Nagy's successor, Serge Chermayeff, the Institute of Design merges into the Illinois Institute of Technology and gains university status. Under Chermayeff special departments are set up for visual design, product design, architecture, and photography. Many design schools across the world subsequently adopt this same structure.

1950–1959: Albers teaches at Yale University in New Haven, Connecticut, where he prepares his famous investigation of color, *Interaction of Color* (Albers 1963, 1977), which is still used in color courses, especially in foundation courses for designers.

Above all in Latin America, foundation courses at many design schools continue to build on the insights gained through the German Bauhaus.

And there is another completely different field where the impact of Bauhaus still lives on. In the 1970s the now legendary German music group Kraft-

Kraftwerk
Die Mensch-Maschine (1978)

werk invented "electropop" and opened the doors to a whole new genre of music. Their composition was influenced by Russian constructivism (↗ p. 26) and the Bauhaus. Hüetlin (2014) argues that the aesthetic reorientation of twentieth-century modernism (shaped by figures like Walter Gropius at Weimar and Dessau) also served as a model for the music of Kraftwerk.

The Ulm School of Design

The most significant new institution to be founded after World War II was the Ulm School of Design. Just as the Bauhaus put its decisive stamp on the architecture, design, and art of the 1920s, the Ulm School of Design also exerted such manifold influences on the theory, practice, and teaching of design and visual communication that a direct comparison of the two institutions would seem legitimate. The Swiss Max Bill, who himself studied at the Bauhaus from 1927 to 1929, was involved in setting up the Ulm School of Design and was its rector until 1956. Former Bauhaus staff who taught as visiting lecturers in Ulm included Albers, Itten, and Walter Peterhans. The School's curriculum, too, initially adhered closely to the Dessau Bauhaus model.

Continuity is also apparent in Walter Gropius's inaugural speech of 1955. He spoke of the significant role of the artist in an advanced democracy, and rejected the charge that the Bauhaus had promoted a one-sided rationalism. In his work, Gropius said, he was searching for a new equilibrium between the practical and the aesthetic, psychological demands of the age. Gropius understood functionalism in design to mean providing the products to satisfy the physical and psychological needs of the population. Gropius saw questions about the beauty of form, especially, as being psychological in nature. He believed that the task of a college was not only to educate the intellect by teaching the acquisition of knowledge, but also to educate the senses.

Max Bill, Ulm school of design building (1967)

In the wake of a growing interest in its history, the Ulm School of Design has been the subject of increased attention since the 1980s. In 1982 the HfG-Synopse working party presented a history of the School using documents arranged in a synchronous visual presentation (Roericht 1982, 1985). This presentation was used as the basis for an exhibition about the Ulm School of Design (for the documentation published at the same time, see Lindinger 1987). Several dissertations have been written from an art history perspective, including a quite controversial one by Hartmut Seeling (1985), one by Eva von Seckendorff (1989), and an extremely meticulous one by René Spitz (2001), who dealt in particular with the institutional processes and political and social context of the Ulm School of Design.

A traveling exhibition was staged in 2003 to mark the fiftieth anniversary of the founding of the Ulm School of Design. The catalog, *ulmer modelle – modelle nach ulm* (Ulmer Museum and HfG-Archiv 2003) is especially interesting on questions of theory and methodology. The volume confirms the uniqueness and historical significance of the Ulm School of Design model in the 1960s, and its attempt to unite theory and practice.

The Six Development Phases

We can identify six distinct phases in the history of the Ulm School of Design:

1947–1953 To commemorate her brother and sister – Hans and Sophie Scholl, who had been executed by the Nazis – Inge Scholl proposed setting up a foundation with the objective of starting a college where vocational skills and cultural creativity would be allied with political responsibility. On the initiative of John McCloy, the American High Commissioner for Germany, the Geschwister Scholl Foundation was set up as the institution responsible for the Ulm School of Design.

    Inge Scholl, Otl Aicher, Max Bill, and Walter Zeischegg led the development work on the concept for the school, and in 1953 construction of the building, designed by Bill, began.

1953–1956 The first students at Ulm were taught in temporary accommodation by former Bauhaus teachers Helene Nonné-Schmidt, Walter Peterhans,

Josef Albers, and Johannes Itten. The teaching represented a direct continuation of the Bauhaus tradition, although there were no painting or sculpture classes; in fact, there was no free or applied art at all. The first newly appointed lecturers had an artistic educational background, but the Ulm School of Design actually only had an instrumental interest in the knowledge of art, for instance, in its application in foundation course projects.

In 1954 Max Bill was appointed the first rector of the Ulm School of Design, and the official opening of the new building on the slopes of the Kuhberg followed on October 1 and 2, 1955. In his opening speech Bill set out the institution's lofty ambitions: "Our goal is clear. All activities at the School are directed to participation in building a new culture, with the aim of creating a way of life concomitant with the technical age we live in…. Our culture today has been too deeply shaken for us to start building again, so to speak, at the top of the pyramid. We have to begin at the bottom by examining the foundations" (Spitz 2001).

Otl Aicher, Hans Gugelot, and Tomás Maldonado were appointed as the School's first lecturers.

1956–1958 This phase was characterized by the inclusion of new scientific disciplines in the curriculum. The lecturers, Aicher, Maldonado, Gugelot, and Zeischegg in particular, pointed out the close relationships between design, science, and technology. Max Bill left the School in 1957 because he no longer agreed with the direction it was taking. This phase was also marked by the preparation of an educational model for the School, which Maldonado countersigned in 1958 with a clear statement: "As you can see we have spared no effort to put the work of the School on a precise footing" (Spitz 2001).

1958–1962 Disciplines such as ergonomics, mathematical techniques, economics, physics, politics, psychology, semiotics, sociology, and theory of science grew in importance in the curriculum. The Ulm School of Design thus stood clearly in the tradition of German rationalism, trying as it did to demonstrate "scientific character," in particular through the application of mathematical methods. At the same time, the selection of disciplines to be included in the curriculum was also heavily influenced by the choice of visiting lecturers willing to come at a particular time, and was therefore rarely characterized by continuity. Despite upholding its avant-garde, intellectual claims, the School ultimately proved unsuccessful in rigorous theoretical work. Hence, the claim by Michael Erlhoff that the last well-founded design concept was developed at the School (1987), appears problematic to me, because what was discussed in Ulm – and was integrated into teaching and research – was a series of rather random theoretical fragments and chance discoveries (Bürdek 2003). Equally, the ideas of Ulm alumni such as Reinhart Butter, Richard Fischer, and Klaus Krippendorff have laid viable foundations for the field of product semantics (↗ p. 178).

Walter Zeischegg, Horst Rittel, Herbert Lindinger, and Gui Bonsiepe were appointed as lecturers in the Product Design Department. During this time particular emphasis was placed on developing design methods; modular design and system design came to the fore in design projects.

1962–1966 During this phase equilibrium was achieved between theoretical and practical disciplines in the curriculum. Teaching itself was very strongly formalized and became a reference model for many other design schools throughout the world.

Increasingly, projects for industrial clients were handled by independent development groups (institutes), while at the same time industry's interest in exploiting design for its own ends became ever clearer. German corporations were quick to recognize that the principles applied at the Ulm School of Design could be used to realize rational manufacturing concepts that were particularly well suited to the technologies of the time. From outside, the Ulm School of Design itself was no longer regarded as a university-level institution in terms of research and development, and as a result, using the justification of "no research, no funding," the German government stopped financing the School (Spitz 2001).

1967–1968 During the final two years, attempts to preserve the School's autonomy sparked a search for new ideas and institutional structures, which, however, never came to fruition. The demands of the state parliament of Baden-Württemberg for new concepts were not met, not least because of internal disagreements among the staff and students, and as a result the School of Design closed its doors at the end of 1968 (Spitz 2001).

Quite apart from all the often-cited political reasons, the School also failed because after the mid-1960s it was unable to generate modern concepts and ideas. The critique of functionalism that arose at that time and the debate over

1 **Nick Roericht**
   Stackable tableware TC 100 (1958/59),
   Diploma project HfG Ulm
   Fa. Rosenthal AG (1961–2008),
   Fa. HoGaKa (since 2010)

2 **Klaus Krippendorf**
   Motor grader (1960)
   Diploma project HfG Ulm

1

2

ecological questions that took off a little later fell on deaf ears at the School. The institutes, in particular, had become so strongly commercialized through industrial projects that many lecturers could no longer be said to possess independence and critical detachment. Once the Ulm style had finally been established, it proved impossible to resist the temptation to reap the rewards in industry. These entanglements made it impossible to find solutions that would have satisfied the massive demands made by students at the same time: demands for work to be socially relevant and for colleges and universities to maintain academic independence.

The Institute for Environmental Planning In 1969 Stuttgart University opened an Institute for Environmental Planning in the buildings of the Ulm School of Design. The intention was to continue the former School's work while opening up its narrow definition of design. The Institute increasingly dedicated itself to social and political issues, which the students' movement of 1967–1968 had brought to the awareness of designers (Klar 1968; Kuby 1969). Losing the freedoms of an autonomous university left the Institute heavily dependent on Stuttgart University, which shut it down in 1972. It should be mentioned, however, that a working party at the Institute in this period sketched out the groundwork for a reorientation of design theory.

Ulm graduate Gerhard Curdes was appointed lecturer at the Institute for Environmental Planning in 1969. His meticulous *Gestaltung oder Planung?* (Curdes 2015) describes the problems of this period at the Ulm School of Design. In particular the dominance of planning over design (with the latter more or less neglected) spotlights the zeitgeist of the nascent 1970s.

The Departments of the Ulm School of Design

A brief examination of the School's individual departments also shows where its work was focused.

Foundation Course As at the Bauhaus, the foundation course was taken very seriously at Ulm. Its goal was to teach the general fundamentals of design, theoretical and scientific knowledge, and to introduce students to the practical work of design (including model-making and techniques of representation). Here, too, the teaching method aimed to sensitize the faculties of perception through experimentation with the elementary tools of design (colors, forms, Gestalt laws, materials, surfaces). Initially strongly influenced by Bauhaus, over time the foundation course moved in the direction of a visual methodology with a precise mathematical and geometrical basis (Lindinger 1987).

The ultimate intention of the foundation course at Ulm, however, was to achieve intellectual discipline by training students in manual precision. Cartesian thought dominated scientific theory. Thinking was governed by the wish for rationality, for strict form and construction. Only the "exact" natural sciences were truly accepted as reference disciplines. Mathematical disciplines, especially, were investigated with respect to possible applications in design (Maldonado and Bonsiepe 1964), including:

combinatorial analysis (for modular systems and problems of dimensional coordination),

group theory (in the form of a theory of symmetry for constructing networks and grids),

curve theory (for mathematical treatment of transitions and transformations),

polyhedral geometry (for constructing bodies), and

topology (for problems of order, continuity, and neighborhood).

Students were trained to carry out conscious, controlled design, and taught a way of thinking that mirrored the task definitions that they would later have to work through in the fields of product design, industrialized construction, or communication (Rübenach 1958–1959, 1987).

Architecture The Department of Architecture concentrated on prefabricated construction methods, with training focusing on construction elements, connection techniques, production management, and modular design. These methods were to be applied primarily in order to create affordable accommodation for a large section of the population. In its approach to design, the Ulm School took up the ideas of Hannes Meyer at the Bauhaus, which also fitted seamlessly with the trend for prefabricated design in the construction industry at that time.

Film A separate Film Department was set up in 1961. As well as learning the required practical and technical skills, students also developed new experimental forms of film. The lecturers were Edgar Reitz, Alexander Kluge, and Christian Straub. The Film Department set itself up as the independent Institute of Film Design in October 1967.

Information Studies The aim of this department was to train students for new professions in the press, film, radio, and television. The three most influential lecturers were Max Bense, Abraham A. Moles, and Gerd Kalow. The Information Studies Department also attempted to apply information theory to other areas of design.

Product Design This department's interests were centered on developing and designing industrially mass-produced products to be used in everyday contexts, offices, and factories. Special emphasis was placed on a design method that takes into consideration all the factors that determine a product: functional, cultural, technological, and economic.

Interest focused less on individual products than on questions of product systems, through which a unified image could be achieved, for example, a corporate design for a business. Appliances, machines, and instruments were the dominant product sectors. Objects that possessed an artistic or craft character were more or less taboo, nor was the design of prestige and luxury items part of the task definition of the Product Design Department.

Visual Communication The problems of mass communication were the main interest of this department. Design projects here covered the whole spectrum from typography, photography, packaging systems, and exhibition systems right through to technical communications, designing displays, and developing sign systems.

The Educational Impact of the Ulm School of Design

Like the Bauhaus, the Ulm School of Design remained exceptionally influential even after its closure, despite its relatively short existence of just fifteen years. The School's graduates also benefited from a fortunate circumstance. Many public-sector employers (for instance in Germany) prefer job applicants to hold a university degree. Until well into the 1960s only graduates from Ulm were able to meet this condition in the field of design. With their internalized rigid Cartesian thought they guaranteed that "deviating tendencies" were nipped in the bud or prevented from germinating in the first place. This also explains the very clear demarcation between design on the one hand, and arts and crafts on the other, during that period. In the end this provoked the post-modernist countercurrent of the 1980s, which attracted a great deal of attention to design but remained ultimately counterproductive, because little progress was made in the fundamental science of the discipline. In fact, today, at those universities where both free and applied arts are taught, we find that the much-trumpeted interdisciplinary dialog of the subjects fails in the face of an insistence on status by the supposedly "free" and apparently "independent" artists, among whom ways of thinking that date right back to the independent art academies of the nineteenth century are still very widespread. So it appears that design schools are especially successful when they demonstrate active, broad involvement in cultural contexts, which does not necessarily mean only the free arts, but can also include architecture, stage design, production and event design, film, photography, literature, fashion, music, pop culture, urban and regional planning, and theater.

The field of design methodology, in particular, would be unimaginable without the work of the Ulm School of Design. Dealing systematically with problems, using methods of analysis and synthesis, and justifying and selecting design alternatives, are today all part of the common repertoire of the design profession. Ulm was the first school of design to place itself absolutely and intentionally in the intellectual tradition of modernism.

Just as the members of the Bauhaus saw themselves not only as artists, architects, or designers, but also as a residential and intellectual community (Fiedler and Feierabend 1999), the "Ulmer" also saw themselves as a group with a similar character. Although a total of 640 students studied there, only 215 left the School with a degree, so it is certainly correct to speak of a "Mayflower effect" (Bürdek 1980). Today, having studied at Ulm has taken on the same kind of importance for a designer as being able to trace one's ancestry back to the Mayflower does for Americans.

A rough overview shows that about half the Ulm graduates work in design agencies or corporate design departments. Many product designers went to Italy, while the architects generally settled in Switzerland. The other half work, or have worked, in higher education. It is down to this second group and their participation in the curriculum reform of the 1970s (which produced new university regulations and examination rules) that the Ulm ideas have been incorporated into the respective curricula.

Aside from the official histories, the personal recollections of former students represent a valuable source. *hfg ulm: Die Abteilung Produktgestaltung: 39 Rückblicke,* edited by Achim Czemper (2008), supplies authentic insights into the Ulm experience. Contributions by Rido Busse, Andries van Onck, Klaus Krippendorff, Horst Diener, Hans-Jürgen Lannoch, Alexander Neumeister, Bernhard E. Bürdek, among many others, paint a vivid picture of study and daily life on the campus.

And because many teachers and students from Ulm went out into the world to seek new challenges, the influence of the Ulm School of Design has also been felt abroad:

In the 1960s designers from Ulm played a crucial role in setting up the Escola Superior de Desenho (ESDI) in Rio de Janeiro.

At the beginning of the 1970s an Institute of Environmental Design was founded in Paris, although it only existed for a few years.

At the same time in Chile attempts were made to develop products for basic needs. The design concepts were very strongly influenced by Ulm (Bonsiepe 1974).

The influence of Ulm is apparent in India at both the National Institute of Design in Ahmedabad and the Industrial Design Center in Mumbai.

The same applies to the Oficina Nacional de Diseño Industrial (ONDI) in Cuba, the postgraduate course for designers at the Universidad Autónoma Metropolitana (UAM) in Mexico City, and the former Laboratorio Associado in Florianopolis, Brazil.

The Influence of the Ulm School of Design on Product Culture

The Ulm design principles were applied quickly in an exemplary industrial context in the 1960s through the School's cooperation with the Braun brothers. Braun became the fulcrum of a movement that gained worldwide attention as "good design," which ideally matched the manufacturing possibilities of industry while also gaining rapid market acceptance when it was applied to consumer and capital goods. Over a span of two decades, good design, *el buen diseño, bel design,* and *gute Form* have become more or less international trademarks of German design. The concept met its first serious challenge in the 1970s (critique of functionalism), and an even stronger one in the early 1980s (postmodernism). Nonetheless, many German businesses have applied its principles with considerable success.

As well as Braun, which was very quick to join a collaboration with teachers at Ulm, the list includes Bulthaup, ERCO, Gardena, Hewi, Interlübke, Lamy, Rowenta, SSS Siedle, Viessmann, and Wilkhahn. Their company histories – as well as their products – clearly acknowledge the traditions of the Ulm School of Design. Here again, we see the special significance of this institution for German product culture in the twentieth century. No other design school can claim any comparable impact.

In 1993 the archives of the former Ulm School of Design passed to the custody of Ulm Museum. They include donations from numerous students and the artistic estates of Otl Aicher, Tomás Gonda, and Walter Zeischegg. The School of Design buildings were used for many years by Ulm University. In 2011, after it moved out and Bill's building was restored, the archives were able to move into their own rooms there. In 2013 a new permanent exhibition about the history of the Ulm School was unveiled there.

The Example of Braun

No other company has had such a decisive influence on the development of design in Germany as Braun in Kronberg near Frankfurt. An unbroken tradition of modernism guides Braun's business and design policies to this day. For many decades Braun was a model for many other companies, and not only in Germany.

The Beginnings

Following the death of founder Max Braun in 1951, his sons Erwin and Artur Braun took over the company. At that time, the company produced electric razors, radios, kitchen appliances, and electronic flash equipment.

Wilhelm Wagenfeld, Braun Combi (phono portable radio) (1954/55)

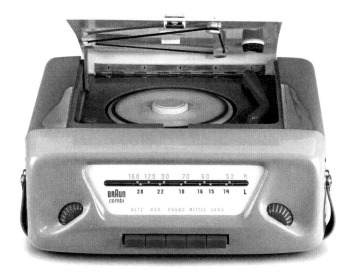

At the beginning of the 1950s Fritz Eichler, who was responsible for the company's design policies, initiated a collaboration with the Ulm School of Design to develop a new product line. Hans Gugelot, then a lecturer at the Ulm School, played a decisive part in this work. In 1955 Dieter Rams – who incidentally studied not at Ulm but at the School of Arts and Crafts in Wiesbaden – started as an architect and interior designer at Braun, where he was already taking on his first product design tasks by 1956 (Burkhardt and Franksen 1980). Hans Gugelot and Herbert Hirche worked with Rams to create the first substantive basis for Braun's corporate image.

The Principles

The implementation of functionalist principles is extremely clear in Braun's products (Industrie Forum Design Hannover 1990). Their characteristic features are:

high fitness for use,

fulfillment of ergonomic and physiological requirements,

high functional order of individual products,

painstaking design down to the smallest detail,

harmonious design, achieved with simple means,

intelligent design, based on innovative technology and the needs and behavior of the user.

Firmly in the tradition of classical modernism, Dieter Rams followed the motto "Less design is more design," a direct reference to the "Less is more" of Mies van der Rohe, whose affirmation of the International Style was so influential for architecture after World War II. Although Robert Venturi had already aptly parodied Mies with "Less is a bore" in 1966, that discussion had almost no influence on Rams.

In the example of Braun, it is clear how the unity of technological concept, controlled product design, and strictly ordered means of communication (as in letterheads, brochures, catalogs) produces an overall visual appearance for the company, one that is exemplary in its stringency. This kind of coordination of all design elements is known as a business's corporate design.

Although Braun was taken over by the US corporation Gillette in 1967, the change in ownership did not affect its design strategy. Globalization of its design began in earnest after control passed to the US corporation Procter & Gamble in 2005.

An eight-hundred-page volume on the lifework of Dieter Rams (Klemp and Ueki-Polet 2011), published in connection with an exhibition (in 2008/09) in Osaka clearly demonstrates how Rams succeeded in realizing design at the highest level over a period of forty years, while still preserving a personal stance.

Braun after Dieter Rams

The ramifications of the postmodernist design of the 1980s were not felt in Braun's product culture until the second half of the 1990s. The great success of firms like Alessi, Authentics, Koziol, and Philips, who flooded department stores and boutiques with product lines adorned with the style elements of a new pop culture, did not go unnoticed at a corporation like Braun. As head of the Design Department until 1997, Dieter Rams had been one of the most tenacious advocates of German functionalism (Klatt and Jatzke-Wigand 2002),

Products by Braun, Kronberg (1960–1980)

so when he left in 1997 his decisive – but also rigid – influence on Braun's product designs came to an end. The growing influence of marketing strategies increasingly based on global design led to a loss of uniqueness in many product sectors too (Braun Design 2002).

But under Oliver Grabes, head of design at Braun since 2009, the company has developed a new design stance and a design language to match: "Strength of Pure" (Terstiege 2012). "Retro is not an option for us. We build on the Braun design tradition, but translate it for the present age" (Braun Design Team 2012).

In 2012 Braun sold the rights to its household appliance brands to the Italian firm of De'Longhi, which in return established its own design department in Neu-Isenburg (near Frankfurt am Main). However, Thomas Edelmann (2014) describes the products developed there as "visions of yesteryear". For the moment it remains an open question whether the takeover can generate a new product identity culture.

German Democratic Republic

From 1949 until reunification in 1990 design in the German Democratic Republic (GDR, or East Germany) was characterized by three main features:

intensive state patronage, beginning right after World War II,

clear long-term social policy objectives, and

intensive theoretical consideration of questions of functionalism and product semantics, starting in the early 1980s.

Developments in East Germany were based on completely different social conditions than those in West Germany. During the first phase, design was oriented primarily toward tasks in the public sphere. Work, transport, residential, and leisure facilities were the most important fields of work for designers. Originally a largely agricultural economy, East Germany put great effort into building up heavy industry, principally to produce capital goods. It was not until the mid-1960s that the emphasis began to shift to consumer goods.

A serious historical assessment of the consumer goods design sector did not even begin until many years after reunification. Günter Höhne, who had been an editor on the journal *form + zweck* during the 1980s, collected and meticulously documented all the objects that made up East German product culture, and his search for the design classics produced astonishing insights (Höhne 2001). For example, many of the products were in fact absent from everyday life in eastern Germany, having been manufactured exclusively for major mail-order firms in West Germany. Their design was consequently modeled directly on the American, Italian, and Scandinavian products that filled the catalogs in the West. Thus Penti (compact viewfinder camera), Erika (mechanical typewriter), and Bebo Sher (electric razor) represent significant product designs from the former East Germany.

State promotion of design was upgraded considerably in 1972 through the establishment of the Office of Industrial Design (AIF). It reported directly to the East German Council of Ministers – its head (Martin Kelm) held the rank of under-secretary – and possessed far-reaching powers in all branches of the economy. It drew up directives, decrees, and legislation that laid down the law for product design across the country and applied to exports as well as to the domestic market. With more than two hundred staff, the AIF was one of the world's largest state-run design institutions at the time. Martin Kelm (2014) rightly notes in his confident memoir: "If one compares East German design promotion with other countries, a rather unique aspect becomes apparent: In no other country were there similar support structures. And this was valued and recognized internationally... . East German design promotion has often been held up as a model."

The relationship between design and art was important, and apparently largely unproblematic. For example, from 1958 on, the major Dresden art exhibitions had a design section where machines and appliances, vehicles and interiors, and designs for textiles and glass were presented alongside painting, sculpture, and free graphic art. The state "Good Design" award for "superbly designed products" was presented at the international trade fairs in Leipzig which, economically, were extremely important events for East Germany.

One important characteristic of East German design was the "open principle" (Hirdina 1988). Karl Clauss Dietel, who became president of the East German Association of Visual Artists in fall 1988, is regarded as the founder of the "open principle." He called for the existing objective and spatial environment to be treated with responsibility, saying that the repertoire of design should be continuously improved, but not thrown overboard for the sake of short-lived fashions (such as postmodernism, for example). "Openness" referred both to

Combine Harvester, design: Gunter Schober, Rüdiger Laleike, Erhard Noack,
VEB Erntemaschinen Singwitz (1982)

changes resulting from scientific and technical progress and to the changing
needs and requirements of users. People, in particular, should be allowed to
develop freely, and the design of things should assist them. "Openness" also
applied (at least in theory) to internationalization, but at that time it was almost impossible to put into practice.

    Karl Clauss Dietel (whose life work was honored at the 2014 German De-
sign Awards) and Lutz Rudolph were two of the best-known East German designers (Kassner 2002); their work often swam counter to the currents of the
ruling ideology and aimed to put people at the center of design. By influencing
the outer form of objects through design they wished to change the inner state
of society as well, hoping that their products would enable their users to interact democratically. East Germany was a particularly good example of how the
power of form becomes a form of power, or in other words: how the powerless-
ness of design can be a special (political) form of power.

    At the beginning of the 1950s functional design was more or less banned;
designers were to follow the traditional petty-bourgeois values of the years
preceding World War II. For a long time the traditions of the Bauhaus – geo-
graphically within East Germany – were almost taboo. Not until the end of the

UB 1233 Hydraulic Excavator, design: Georg Böttcher, Gerhard Bieber, Peter Prusseit,
VEB NOBAS Nordhausen (1986)

1960s did East Germany declare itself the only legitimate heir to the Bauhaus tradition and seize on the principles of functionalist design as a national resource for its manufacturing sector.

The International Bauhaus Colloquiums were initiated in 1976 in Weimar, and continued in 1979, 1983, and 1986. The papers for these colloquiums dealt with the historical, social, educational, and international repercussions of Bauhaus, and were published in the academic journal of the College of Architecture and Construction.

This openness to theoretical questions of design became particularly clear at a seminar on functionalism held in 1982 at the Office of Industrial Design (AIF) in Berlin (for more on this see the series of articles in *form + zweck,* 1982–83). Functionalism was declared to be the design principle that most closely corresponded to the living conditions of a socialist society. Functionalism, in this case, was understood not as a category of style (gray, angular, stackable), but as a "method of work" (Blank 1988).

In a series of lectures on "Postmodernism and Functionalism," Bruno Flierl (1985) pointed out that the functionalist program – theory and practice – often lacked unity of material and ideal functionality. Criticism of functionalism –

for example, in West Germany and Italy – he said, quickly turned into blind antifunctionalism, and was thus antisocial and reactionary.

Heinz Hirdina (1985) said that postmodernist design was reactionary because the designed object was merely inflated – styled – and subjected to the same mechanisms that applied in advertising and packaging. Hirdina believed that the crucial factor was not that postmodernist design abandoned the use-value discourse, but that it was obviously integrated into the capitalist principles of commodity aesthetics – manipulation by means of commodities that quickly go out of fashion.

Horst Oehlke (1982) made important contributions to design theory. His profound study of the semantics of design objects – the language of objects under conditions of socialism – was a decisive influence behind the reorientation of design in East Germany (↗ p. 182 f).

While the products documented by Heinz Hirdina (1988) – in hitherto unknown detail – largely fall into the traditional functionalist design categories, his short chapter on "Exploration and Experimentation in the 1980s" reveals new tendencies, as documented, for example, by a writing stand by Herbert Pohl that was shown in the *Design in East Germany* exhibition held in 1988 at the Stuttgart Design Center.

The strong export orientation led, on the other hand, to autonomous design for products for the domestic market, whose exotic character was documented in summer 1989 in an exhibition *(SED – Stunning Eastern Design)*. Just a few months before the fall of the Berlin Wall, this show revealed a concentration of products whose particular product–semantic significance lay in their rigid simplicity: "An independent identity arose, partly deliberately, partly unplanned, whose meagerness is a permanent irritation. One could almost say that the commodities suffer from a lack of fetish" (Bertsch and Hedler 1990). One former East German designer, Karl Clauss Dietel, saw that quite differently: The "denunciatory book SED – Schönes Einheits-Design," he said, "contributed absolutely nothing in the way of constructive criticism to the discussion of design in East Germany" (Kassner 2009), which is still awaited and can only be touched upon here.

As late as summer 1989 Karl Clauss Dietel was making the case that East Germany should do more for its "image" and get itself a new corporate identity (Zimmermann 1989). Nothing, however, was to come of this, because the loss of a separate identity progressed more quickly than anyone had imagined. In a little more than a year, East Germany had ceased to exist. The mechanisms of the market spread through the eastern part of Germany just as quickly as they had in the western half since the 1960s.

The "closed chapter" of East German design is reviewed in two publications by Günter Höhne (2007, 2009): *Das große Lexikon DDR-Design* (Encyclopedia of East German design) documents the country's designers, products, and companies, while *Die geteilte Form* (Form divided) contains essays by contributors from East and West, including a detailed analysis and assessment of Horst Oehlke's theory and methodology, which represents a major contribution to German theory development (Bürdek 2009).

One of the few companies that continues to exist with its own product identity is the porcelain manufacturer Kahla. Targeting younger consumers and purchasers of hotel china, Kahla established a new image and succeeded in the market economy. The company's definitive breakthrough came in 1998 with the Update combination service, which comprises just a few pieces but offers a wide range of patterns.

Glashütte Uhren was a small-scale East German producer of high-end functionally classic clocks. Since reunification it has prospered as NOMOS Glashütte in the luxury watch sector, which has become a global supplier of status symbols. Today the company belongs to the Swiss Swatch Group.

From Good Design to the Art of Design

It All Began with Sullivan

For a long time the commonly used definition of function was based on a glaring misunderstanding of the theses of American architect Louis H. Sullivan (1856–1924), who was actually interested not only in the practical function of buildings, but also in the semiotic dimensions of the objects: "All things in nature have a shape, that is to say, a form, an outward semblance, that tells us what they are, that distinguishes them from ourselves and from each other" (Sullivan 1896). What Sullivan wanted was for life and form to correspond and harmonize completely but that has hardly been reflected in "good design" as practiced in the twentieth century.

Adolf Loos, author of *Ornament und Verbrechen (Ornament and Crime,* 1908), initiated the development of rational design in Europe, which spread largely through the rapid expansion of industrial methods of production. Loos failed, however, to recognize that the everyday needs of the population were complex and generally shaped by traditional aesthetic models. Even before the work of the Bauhaus, Ernst Bloch attempted to wedge a little dialectical openness into the rigid dictum of ornamentlessness: "Obstetric forceps have to be smooth, a pair of sugar-tongs not at all" (1918).

Loos's ideas had their first heyday during the Bauhaus period. The design approach and methodology developed there was understood as overcoming styles, although in fact, their strict application gave rise to a new style, which became the symbol of a small intellectual and progressive stratum of the population, who demonstrated it in their houses and apartments through tubular steel furniture and spartan bookcases.

Functionalism's real boom came after World War II in the Federal Republic of Germany, and a few years later in East Germany, too. As mass production started up again, it was seen as a suitable tool for standardizing and rationalizing manufacturing. That applied to both design and architecture. This concept was developed systematically and refined – in theory and practice – during the 1960s, especially at the Ulm School of Design.

The Radical Sixties

The first signs of crisis appeared in certain European countries in the mid-1960s. The lengthy economic upturn that had followed World War II was almost at an end. The long Vietnam War gave rise to student protest movements in the United States, which were soon taken up in Europe in the Prague Spring, the May uprising in Paris, and demonstrations in Berlin and Frankfurt am Main. Their shared foundation was their critique of society, which is subsumed under the term "New Left" in Western Europe. In Germany this movement took its fundamental arguments from the theoretical works of the Frankfurt School: Theodor W. Adorno, Max Horkheimer, Herbert Marcuse, Jürgen Habermas, and others.

The work of Wolfgang Fritz Haug proved to be particularly important for design. His *Critique of Commodity Aesthetics* investigated, from a Marxist perspective, the dual nature of commodities (products), which can be defined by their use value and exchange value. In several examples, Haug demonstrated how design functions as a means of increasing exchange value or, in other words, how aesthetic design cannot increase the use value of objects (↗ p. 129 f).

The critique of functionalism had a particularly incendiary effect on architecture and urban planning. The International Style, which had been demonstrated very clearly in the Stuttgart Weissenhof project (Hitchcock and Johnson 1966), reappeared in a perverted form in the satellite towns around many conurbations. In Germany these included Märkisches Viertel in Berlin, Nordweststadt in Frankfurt, Neu-Perlach near Munich, and the Marzahn district of East Berlin. Later, this type of mass-produced environment was even accused of representing repression and violation of the human psyche (Gorsen, 1979).

The work of Alexander Mitscherlich (1965), Theodor W. Adorno's 1965 lecture "Functionalism Today," and the contributions of Heide Berndt, Alfred Lorenzer, and Klaus Horn (1968) were especially important milestones in the scientific criticism of functionalism.

Criticism of functionalism was much slower to surface within design. Abraham A. Moles (1968) saw instead the problems of an affluent society rearing their heads, and drew from the crisis of functionalism the conclusion that functionalism had to be interpreted even more rigidly. His Magna Carta of functionalism produced an outlook on life based on frugality and the rational use of existing means for clearly defined purposes.

Architect Werner Nehls responded with polemical irony, shocking the design scene with his opinion that the rational and functionalist understanding of design was completely outdated. Designers were producing wrong design, Nehls said, to exactly the extent that they were trapped in the ideas of the Bauhaus and the Ulm School of Design. Right angles, straight lines, geometric or objective forms, open forms, lack of contrast, and colorlessness all had to go. "Furthermore, the planar-optical approach to design must be done away with, the cube, the design of the masculine. Today's design comes from a feminine stance, the emotional is emphasized. Feminine, irrational design prefers organic forms, contrasting colors, random attributes" (Nehls 1968) This understanding of design was practiced to excess by Luigi Colani (Dunas 1993). He, in particular, exploited in exemplary fashion the freedoms offered by inexpensive new plastics and expressed them in design.

Distinguishing between the functionalism of the Bauhaus and of the Ulm School of Design, Gerda Müller-Krauspe (1969) advocated an "expanded functionalism," defined as an interpretation of design whose proponents attempt to discover as many product-determining factors as possible and include them in the design process. The role of the designer as coordinator was already featured in theory and practice at the Ulm School of Design.

The First Ecological Approaches

At the beginning of the 1970s *The Limits to Growth* burst into public consciousness in the form of a report for the Club of Rome on the state of humanity (Meadows 1972). The authors stated clearly that continued exponential growth would cause industrialized nations to lose the basis of their existence within the foreseeable future. Rapid depletion of natural resources, rising population densities, and increasing pollution would lead to destabilization or a complete collapse of industrialized societies. Ecological demands were made for design, too, but they were largely disregarded.

Responding to such considerations, a working party entitled des-in at the Offenbach School of Design developed the first attempts at "recycling design" in 1974 for a competition run by the Internationales Design Zentrum Berlin (IDZ). This early model, which involved the group designing, producing, and marketing its products itself, was doomed to failure by the group's lack of business acumen. Nonetheless, des-in was probably the first group in the field of design to attempt to connect new theoretical concepts with an alternative design practice.

The Eclecticist Countermovement

In design, however, a movement in the opposite direction was to gain the upper hand. The influence of the eclecticist movement of postmodernism (or neomodernism), which had formed principally in Italy in the Memphis group, became increasingly noticeable in Germany. By 1983 Rolf-Peter Baacke, Uta Brandes, and Michael Erlhoff were already proclaiming the "new shine of things," in a book which gave a huge boost to design's change of course – in the sense of overcoming the doctrine of functionalism. Not only in Italy, and especially in Germany, there were a large number of designers who worked outside the framework of functionalist design ideology.

The architect, sculptor, designer, and artist Stefan Wewerka designed mutated chairs that could not be sat on (see Fischer and Gleininger 1998; Herzogenrath and Wewerka 2010). His one-legged cantilever chair takes up the tradition of the Bauhaus classics and pokes fun at them at the same time. In fact, Tecta, itself a manufacturer of furniture classics, saw Wewerka's chair as an important addition to its product range (Wewerka 1983).

Cover of exhibition catalog for "Italy: The New Domestic Landscape," Museum of Modern Art, New York (1972)

In 1982, the Hamburg Museum of Arts and Crafts showed the first cross-section of new German design. Progressive furniture shops and galleries (for example, Möbel Perdu and Form und Funktion in Hamburg, Strand in Munich, and Quartett in Hanover) offered the designers – who caused a furor like the Neue Wilden of 1980s painting – a platform on which to present their objects (Hauffe 1994).

The young designers worked in groups like Bellefast in Berlin, Kunstflug in Düsseldorf, and Pentagon in Cologne. Solo designers such as Jan Roth, Stefan Blum, Michael Feith, Wolfgang Flatz, Jörg Ratzlaff, Stiletto, and Thomas Wendtland experimented with materials, forms, and colors, which they combined apparently at random. Discarded items found in refuse were mixed together with industrial, half-finished (or semi-manufactured) products (Albus and Borngräber 1992). A comprehensive retrospective on new German design in the 1980s was published in 2014 in conjunction with an exhibition in Berlin (Hoffmann and Zehentbauer 2014).

Alchimia Poster, Milan (1983)

Media components stand, Designwerkstatt Berlin (1988), design: Joachim B. Stanitzek
Computer desk for waiting areas, Designwerkstatt Berlin (1988), design: Gabriel Kornreich

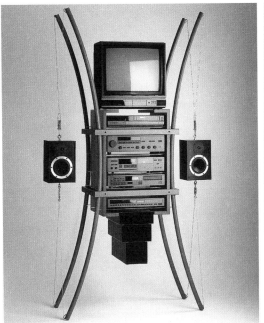 

In the process, designers intentionally adopted artistic working methods, but they were interested in discovering new qualities and expression in things rather than in founding some kind of elevated do-it-yourself movement. The separation of art and kitsch was dissolved too, and shops, boutiques, and galleries were created, as well as interiors for cafés and restaurants. The climax and swan song of the new German design came in the summer of 1986 in the Düsseldorf exhibition *Gefühlscollagen – Wohnen von Sinnen (Feeling Collages – Living Madness)* (Albus et al. 1986).

Design on the Throne of Art

After design had finally thrown off its functional shackles in the apparent radicalism of the 1980s, it was only a matter of time before it would finally metamorphose into apparently pure art. The parallels here are obvious. During the 1980s art had largely subscribed to Jean Baudrillard's theory of simulation,

Tobias Rehberger, "Was du liebst, bringt dich auch zum Weinen", Biennale di Venezia (2009)

presenting itself as the art of spectacle and facade. This was demonstrated impressively in the summer of 1987 at the *documenta 8* in Kassel. There, design was practically seated on art's throne, where, as Michael Erlhoff (1987) insisted, it neither belonged nor wanted to be.

As well as a number of architects, the design section of *documenta 8* had invited about fifteen designers to present objects and environments, including the Spaniards Javier Mariscal and Oscar Tusquet Blanca, the Italians Lapo Binazzi, Paolo Deganello, Guglielmo Renzi, Denis Santachiara, and Ettore Sottsass, London-based Ron Arad, the Germans Andreas Brandolini and Florian Borkenhagen, and the Pentagon group. The displayed objects were largely one-offs and were suited to be neither prototypes nor models for any kind of series production whatsoever. Whether modernism, postmodernism, or post-postmodernism modernism, the displayed designs fitted perfectly into the new obscurity of the 1980s.

From Design to Art and Back Again?

It would therefore be an obvious step to take a closer look at the transitions from art to design and vice versa. For more than a century the separations of art from craft, and design from art and craft, were clearly defined.

Naturally there were also considerable misunderstandings in the reception of design, specifically concerning the terms "free" and "applied" art.

The design historian Herbert Read (1958) points out that ornaments are often added (or applied) to products and buildings. Over time, imprecision crept in and "applied ornament became applied art." This is how "applied art" (including design) became a central misunderstanding that has endured since the 1930s (Bürdek 2012). And of course the term continues to thrive in the media in general and design reporting specifically.

However, just as designers had entered the territory of (supposedly applied) art in the 1980s, so had many artists long beforehand dedicated themselves to working on utility objects. Furniture and household objects were particularly popular objects for artistic reflection and production: Gerrit T.

Rietveld's chairs, Constantin Brancusi's *Table of Silence,* Marcel Duchamps's ready-mades, René Magritte's surrealist objects, Salvador Dalí's *Mae West sofa,* Meret Oppenheim's *Table with Bird's Feet,* Allen Jones's *Green Table,* the installations of Kienholz and Segal. Claes Oldenburg and David Hockney, Timm Ulrichs, Wolf Vostell, Günther Uecker, Daniel Spoerri, Joseph Beuys, Richard Artschwager, Mario Merz, Franz Erhard Walther, Donald Judd, Franz West, Edwin Wurm, and many others, have worked on utility objects. Frankfurt-based Tobias Rehberger is probably the most contemporary artist to operate in the realm between art and design. His cafeteria for the 2009 Venice Biennale, for which he received the Golden Lion for best artist, represented both interior design and a revival of the Op-Art of the 1960s (Menne 2010). Sabine Foraita, whose dissertation represents an important contribution to this topic, calls these artists "borderliners" (Foraita 2005/2011).

However, none of these projects was interested in reconciling art with design, but rather in alienating the products, calling the objects into question in paradoxical transformations, paraphrases, breaks, and fragments. "Furniture by artists contains the possibility of use, but that is not its primary intention. Its quality depends not on the degree of comfort, the space offered by shelves, or the ergonomics of the form" (Bochynek 1989). Franz Erhard Walther, one of the aforementioned artists, who also works in the field of objects, was once asked what he could learn from design. His simple reply was: "Nothing." From the perspective of industrial design one could say that design can learn nothing from art either, although they do share aesthetic questions. In the case of art these are primarily individual questions, in industrial design they are technological, economic, and social.

Design

and

Globalization

No issue has shaped design in this century more decisively than globalization. Yet few design-specific publications seriously address the topic. In German-speaking countries these would include Kerstin Plüm's dissertation (2007) and the exhibition catalog *Global Design* by Angeli Sachs (2010). The fields of economics and ecology, engineering and politics, sociology and ethnology, to name but a few, are hotly debating the repercussions of globalization for world society.

America-Europe-Asia is the principal axis along which this topic unfolds. Asian companies, particularly from China, Japan, South Korea, and Taiwan, were very quick to recognize the economic importance of design for their export-led marketing strategies. Enormous container ships loom in the great seaports of Hong Kong, Shanghai, and Tianjin, leaving no doubt as to where the goods originate from: "If the computer and the container are the backbone of globalization, then communication is its nervous system" (Sachs 2010). Philip Ursprung (2010) underlines the key role played by containerization: "The container is the key object within the design of globalization, the planning and execution of a flow of products and services unrestricted by national borders. And it is intimately connected with globalized design, with the forms we give our consumer goods."

It is the multi-level interaction of digitalization that is decisive for globalization: Industry 4.0, the internet of things, networked production, new forms of online commerce, etc.

Mobility of people and transfers of culture and knowledge are by no means new phenomena; they have been an aspect of global cultural development for millennia (Sachs 2010). Thus, while the Roman forays into Asia and North Africa were initially about power and control, expanding the flow of goods also played a role. And the thirteenth-century travels of the Venetian trader Marco Polo can certainly be subsumed under the term "globalization," for he, too, was seeking to open the way for international trading relations and ensuing economic power games.

Peter Sloterdijk (1999) rightly points out that in that sense the European states in particular have been globalizing for more than five centuries, and names Columbus's voyage of 1492 as the dawn of the age of globalization. But now we are entering a second phase, where the countries of Asia globalize the West (America and Europe). "From this point on the Europeans were no longer only discoverers but also the discovered, no longer just explorers but also the explored."

Here "internationalization" as a projection of economic interests beyond national borders can be understood as a precursor of globalization. Corporate export activities have steadily internationalized to transcend the bounds of national markets. In the last third of the twentieth century it was recognized that design had a prominent role to play in this process (as a promise of product quality and increasingly also as marker of social status).

The term "globality" (Beck 1997) is also used to designate the world society in which we find ourselves since the twentieth century. The concept also encompasses the negation of national characteristics, in a manner which is significant and obvious in design. Under "globalization" we then understand the processes through which globe-spanning networking is realized. Angeli Sachs (2010) pins the beginning of globalization in a narrower sense to the 1971 abolition of the gold standard, under which currencies had been exchangeable against gold at a fixed rate. At that point a hitherto stable value system had ceased to serve its purpose. But globalization was not truly unleashed until the end of the twentieth century.

In the process design has become a dominating factor in economic terms: "Being becomes design – worldwide. People are what they (are able to) buy. This law of cultural globalization applies – so it is argued – even where purchasing power tends to zero. The end of purchasing power is where social existence ends and exclusion begins. 'Exclusion!' is the fate of all those left out of the equation 'being equals design'" (Beck 1997).

Globalization is characterized by two opposing poles: the preservation and intensification of (national) cultural identities – overcoming them. Wolfgang Welsch (1996) applies the term "transcultural," which he believes characterizes the internal differentiation and complexity of modern cultures: "Today's cultures are generally characterized by hybridization." Yet for all the advances of globalization, national identities and associated sociocultural differences (between German, Italian, Japanese, Swiss, Scandinavian design, etc.) still remain meaningful.

Container ship, Maersk Line, Copenhagen

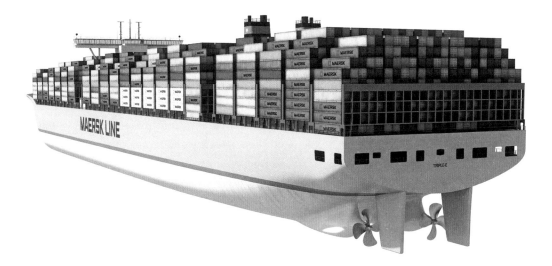

In the 1980s and 1990s Asian companies (especially from Japan) began establishing contact offices in Europe, to function as probes in the respective markets. As a result, design agencies from Europe and the United States were hired to develop products for Asian businesses, to be marketed to Europe and North America. In the 1990s major agencies like Design Continuum, frog design, and IDEO progressed to opening their own offices in Asia in order to work more directly with their respective clients; in other words, to have contacts on the ground for the companies they work with. Thanks to global data networks it was now possible to process the actual design and development projects in their offices in Europe and the United States.

The rapidly growing Chinese market offers diverse opportunities for design firms from all over the world if they can gain a foothold among the businesses there – and will continue to do so. So design firms themselves are increasingly globalizing in the course of globalization. In fact, the issue of "globalization" only really acquired its actual meaning after China entered the world markets at the end of the twentieth century. China's reforms following the death of Deng Xiaoping in 1997 made it the "the factory of the world." And the very low level of industrial wages led to massive investment in European and American subsidiaries.

One labtop per child
Courtesy of fuseproject (Ives Behar)
San Francisco (2007)

Globalization strategies are having other ramifications too. In 2014 the Japanese holding company LIXIL (with a turnover of about 11 billion euros) took over the German sanitary manufacturer Grohe, which already produces part of its range in China (for about 2.6 billion euros). The goal is to create a global supplier with a presence in the international housing construction and outfitting markets. Such a strategy naturally has consequences for product design: The very different needs and expectations of Asian populations can now be handled strategically in a globally operating corporation.

At the same time this example spotlights the differences between industrial design and design in the general sense. While the former is oriented on the terms and conditions of industry, the latter follows the possibilities of new technologies. Although much talked-about at the moment, individualized 3-D printing is suitable only for producing the smallest of series. As Hartmut Esslinger shows in his recollections of Apple's early years (2014), the success of frog design was based not least on its designers always being present in the manufacturing plants. That impetus is naturally lost with 3-D printing, where production can be accomplished right beside the desk.

European companies (especially in the electronics and automobile sectors) have increasingly been opening offices in Asia and the United States ("advanced design studios") in order to more closely follow the social and technological trends developing there; lifestyle trends too have to be investigated on the ground, in order to integrate them more rapidly into product development in the home countries. The AUDI TT is said to have been created on the drawing-boards of the company's Californian office in the early 1990s; it was a spectacular success in both Europe and North America (Bürdek 2011).

Another form of globalization consists in the exploitation of differences in conditions of production. For example, Apple has its products manufactured in China by the Taiwanese company Foxconn, which is also used by the likes of Dell, Hewlett-Packard, Microsoft, Nintendo, and Sony. Today Foxconn employs a workforce of about 1.2 million. The designs are developed in the home

Blue diversion toilet
Eawag – The Swiss Federal Institute of Aquatic Science and Technolgy Zürich and EOOS, Vienna (2014)

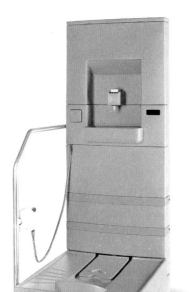

countries of its clients (Apple: "Designed in California"), but the manufacturing is outsourced ("Assembled in China"). The iPhone 5 neatly illustrates the advantages of globalization. Experts estimate the cost of the components and materials used to produce one in 2013 at about 152 euros, the labor costs at just six euros. At the time the sale price was about 600 euros (Der Apple-Check 2013).

According to the latest reports, however, change is on the way, especially in relation to wage costs. Foxconn planned to install ten thousand robots by the end of 2014 ("Foxbots"), including for a new iPhone for Apple. In this way the company hopes to become less dependent on its workers and it is envisaged that "the age of endless labor in China is coming to an end" (Siemons 2014). That would quickly put an end to the "factory of the world," after which the revolution of intelligent automation will greatly lower manufacturing costs and raise productivity, leading in turn to a considerably larger service economy – at least according to Chinese economist Yang Heqing. And when the era of cheap labor ends, some manufacturing sectors will move on to other low-wage countries.

The textiles branch has long been familiar with this principle. In the low-end sectors, production is conducted in Pakistan or Bangladesh, while in the high-price sector standardized prototypes secure quality standards in Italy and France. These days brands like "Made by Zegna" no longer identify a country of origin, but only a promise of quality. And such luxury brands enjoy great prestige in Asia, where Brioni, Cerruti, Gucci, Hermès, Prada, Zegna, and co. operate exquisite boutiques and galleries with great success in the major cities.

Since the beginning of the twenty-first century globalization has also been making the national variants of design obsolete. Intense design knowledge transfer is blurring the national identities that were visible in design until the end of the twentieth century. Perhaps with one exception: Designers based in Switzerland and the generally medium-sized companies producing there have ridden the storm of the international markets to retain and cultivate their "Swissness." In terms of product design this means preserving values from the era of "Good Design" (the 1950s), but also improving it intelligently with precision, functionality, well-chosen materials, and so on (Leuschel 2009). But even the so-lauded Swiss design may be ailing: Commenting on the exhibition *One Hundred Years of Swiss Design* (Brändle, Menzi, and Rüegg 2014) in Zurich, Urs Steiner (2014) spoke of the "end of design." Even in Switzerland current design trends are creating knick-knacks – unmistakable in the Louis Vuitton stool that folds into a handbag, or a leather hammock. One cannot avoid the question: "Is that it?" And anyway, why should Switzerland be immune to the current trend for bricolage?

Further aspects driving globalization include the untrammeled belief in progress and the myth of never-ending innovation, both felt so strongly in Asia. After the dominance of Europe in the nineteenth century and America in the twentieth, the twenty-first will undoubtedly be the Asian century (Naisbitt 1995). Put another way, the new leading culture will be Asian.

In view of these global developments, the overview of the history and present situation of design in selected countries has been omitted from this new edition – especially in light of the number of monographs published in the interim.

Design
and

Methodology

80   Epistemological Methods in Design

83   Semiotics and Design

98   Phenomenology and Design

102   Hermeneutics and Design

108   Developments in Design Methodology

Design is an activity associated with creativity and creative fantasy, the spirits of invention and technical innovation. The design process is often seen as a sort of act of creation.

It is certainly a creative process. However, design does not take place in a vacuum, with a completely free choice of colors, shapes, and materials. Each product is the result of a development process influenced by various – not only artistic – conditions and decisions. Socioeconomic, technological, and cultural developments, in particular, along with the historical background and the conditions of production technology, play just as important a role here as ergonomic and ecological demands, economic and political interests, and artistic-experimental aspirations. Dealing with design therefore also always entails reflecting on the conditions under which it emerged and visualizing their effect on the products.

The theory and methodology of design like to lay claim to a certain objectivity, because ultimately their efforts are directed toward optimizing the methods, rules, and criteria to be used in order to investigate, evaluate, and even improve design. Upon closer observation, however, it becomes apparent that the development of theory and methods is itself also shaped by cultural, historical, and social conditions. Thus the first step in dealing with design theory is to turn one's attention to epistemology. This focus then leads to recognizability, which, in the sense of Ernst Bloch (1980), also means that the world can be changed on the basis of this recognition, and on the basis of the difficult path which humanity has had to travel and which it is far from completing.

Just as in every other discipline, the theory and methodology of design develop on the basis of certain fundamental assumptions and requirements, most of which are self-evident and remain subconscious. Dealing with design theory therefore must also involve confronting the ideas underlying the methodological approaches and creative concepts. This ultimately leads to the study of philosophy.

After World War II, a major economic upswing began in Europe and later spread to certain Asian countries such as Japan, South Korea, Taiwan, and China. In those countries characterized by a market economy, competition quickly intensified to become the international business rivalry known today as globalization. In this situation, design, too, had to adapt to the changed conditions. It was not possible to continue practicing the subjective and emotional methods of design which originated in the tradition of the Werkkunst arts and crafts while industry was rationalizing design, construction, and production. It was thus an obvious step for designers to try to integrate scientific methods into the design process so that they could be accepted as serious partners in the sphere of industry. The Ulm School of Design played a pioneering role in this process (Ulmer Museum and HfG-Archiv 2003).

It was not until this intensive confrontation with methodology that design became in any way teachable, learnable, and thus communicable (Bürdek 2003). Today, the continuing importance of design methodology for instruction lies in its special contribution to training designers in logical and systematic thinking. As a result, methodology has more the character of didactic meaning than of a patented recipe – although the latter misunderstanding has proven persistent.

Claudia Mareis's meticulous dissertation on this topic (2011) is also very useful, although the conclusion she draws about the "design methods movement" of the 1960s (that it failed; Mareis 2014) simply does not stand up. One of the reasons for the necessity and success of classical design methodology was that it established product design as a serious and comprehensible factor in industrial processes (product planning and product development). Those who abandon that tradition in favor of bricolage naturally have no need for such methods.

Bruce Archer, one of the most important and influential proponents of the "design methods movement" in 1963/64 (who had, however, by the end of the 1960s become quite critical of the movement) describes the continuity of methodology and research very succinctly: "Design methodology is alive and well, and living under the name of design research" (Archer 1979). For him the question had always been whether design could become an independent discipline. He was also interested in how design differed from the sciences and humanities: Could there be some kind of third category of knowledge for design?

Derivation of methodology

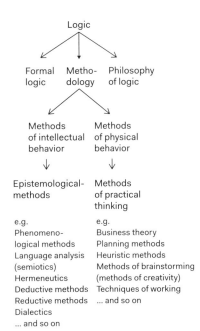

By the 1960s (and even more so today) it was already nigh on impossible for any single designer to comprehend all of the facets of the increasingly complex world of technical products (keywords: microelectronics and digitalization). Systems theory was recognized as an important discipline that could be helpful for design. This approach is growing even more relevant today as theorists of design proceed from Niklas Luhmann's considerations and attempt to proclaim systemic – holistic, networked – thinking for design. Increasingly, questions of meaning are shifting into the foreground of design (Bürdek 2001a); thus, from the methodological perspective, the question is not so much *how* to design products as what the products mean to their users in different sociocultural contexts and what they wish to communicate through the products (↗ p. 148 ff).

From the scientific and theoretical perspective, methodology – the science of method – covers significantly more territory than the concept of design methodology, as it is usually too narrowly applied. The Polish philosopher Józef Maria Bocheński (1954) proposed a scientific derivation of methodology, which serves as a reasonable framework for the above observations. Based on his description, it can be said that traditional design methodology was nearly exclusively concerned with the methods of physical behavior, which have certainly been documented sufficiently (Bürdek 1971, 1977), whereas methods of intellectual behavior in design have received scant attention. On the basis of this continuing imbalance, the former will be outlined only briefly, whereas the latter will be discussed in greater detail. This appears all the more urgent as ever more semiotic (emblematic), hermeneutic, and phenomenological methods are being applied in discussions about new tendencies in design. (Interestingly, the cultural sciences are also beginning, finally, to take an interest in design (↗ p. 91 ff).)

The view of design from the perspective of the humanities was enhanced by a number of crucial concepts in the 1990s. The focus on design management even lent design a sort of strategic importance. Of course, the broad discussions about branding are, at their core, semiotic processes as well. On the other hand, an increasing demand in practice was to check before production to see whether the new product concepts would find any resonance among potential users: empiricism had entered the methodology of design. This brought with it a new spectrum of methods largely borrowed from the social sciences. But as so often in matters concerning design, much of it was adopted uncritically (Brandes, Erlhoff, and Schemmann 2009), without even knowing or questioning how useful they really would be for the practice of design. Here too, design research would find existing shortcomings to rectify.

Epistemological Methods in Design

The humanities take on a special role in the development of the methodology and theory of design. The discipline's constant crisis of meaning is in fact an expression of its increased need for theory and reflection – that is, for philosophy. For this reason, the next section will discuss which aspects of design theory, or design methodology, have their origins in European philosophy.

A Few Aspects of Greek Philosophy

Socrates (470–399 BC) can be designated as the first real theorist of epistemology who developed and practiced a theory of method. Never concerned with the collection or conveyance of the content of knowledge or finished systems, his interest was always directed toward the essence of a thing and the question of how genuine and certain knowledge could be obtained at all.

Plato (427–347 BC) formulated a dialectic to enable investigation of the connections between different concepts through reflection. A generic concept was broken down into all its different types until indivisible concepts were obtained. This method is called dieresis (division of ideas), and is the first known example of rules of definition. Today, a related method is applied to the structuring of complex facts.

Aristotle (384–322 BC) was the first to apply systematic analysis to the essence and methods of science, and subdivided philosophy into logic, physics, and ethics. In his formal logic he showed that thinking always uses three simple basic elements, which even today are still the most important elements of logic: concept, judgment, and conclusion. His main achievement in logic was developing the methods of deduction (inference from the general to the particular) and induction (inference from the particular to the general).

Archimedes (ca. 287–212 BC) was a mathematician and physicist. In his *The Method of Mechanical Theorems,* he described how, by means of mechanical ideas – what we would call models today – he found certain assumptions and solutions to mathematical problems, for which he was later able to provide exact proofs. The science of heuristics is named after his cry of "Eureka!" (I found it!). This method of problem-solving presents a counterpart to the procedures of logic, as it seeks solutions using such tools as analogies and hypotheses.

Modernity

For a long time after Aristotle, there were no significant new approaches of a philosophical or methodological nature: merely extensions or modifications. The modern natural sciences were not founded until the time of *Galileo Galilei* (1564–1642). He criticized Aristotle's assertion that the deductive method was scientific and his consequent exclusion of, for instance, the study of processes and their dynamics. Galileo's own investigations were based on induction, but he did not hold this alone to be sufficient either. It had to be accompanied by the experiment as a method and the objective of deriving and formulating laws on this basis.

René Descartes (1596–1650) is considered to be the father of modern philosophy. His goal was to develop a new, comprehensive, and exact science of nature. His search for a fixed foundation of human cognition has its basis in the method of doubt. Proceeding from his famous statement "Cogito, ergo sum" ("I think, therefore I am"), he attributed all human knowledge to the intellectual mind.

Descartes helped to establish mathematics as a general method. He held the opinion that – just as in his analytical geometry – everything in the world was synthetically constructed of the simplest rationally conceivable basic elements: numbers. Through analysis, intuition, and deduction all complex facts could be fathomed and understood by breaking them down into their basic components. Descartes's mathematical understanding of knowledge, combined with his firm belief in the rational obviousness of all existence, made him the forefather of rationalism. The entire history of the development of design was characterized by Cartesian thinking well into the 1970s.

Gottfried Wilhelm Leibniz (1646–1716) attempted to synthesize mathematical and logical processes in order to create a general science *(scientia generalis)* in which all truths can be depicted in their natural logical context. His catholic character, comparable to that of Aristotle, directed his interests to the entire spectrum of the sciences. Leibniz said that scientific thinking should always be placed in an interrelation between finding and proving, whereby finding was always understood to be researching, (i.e., finding out new things). For this he developed his own method, called the "art of inventing."

Immanuel Kant (1724–1804), the theorist of the modern concept of science, attempted to answer the question of what human cognition actually is. He criticized both rationalism (e.g., Leibniz) and empiricism (e.g., Locke) for basing their explanations for the possibility of knowledge on pure thought alone, or on pure perception, respectively. With his famous declaration: "Thoughts without content are empty, intuitions without concepts are blind," he attempted to develop a synthesis of both, and concluded that, while science may offer general and necessary principles, sensory experience must also be consulted.

Of particular importance in design is the Kantian concept of reason. Wilfried Fiebig (1986), a philosopher in Frankfurt, proceeded from this concept to conclude that the source of human ideas resides in sensory perception and rational conception, both of which enter into his concept of the unity of reason. Although this concept of reason dissolves the external separation (dualism) between perception and reason, in and of themselves, they remain dialectically present. Since the differences between these concepts can only be determined through their separation, a shared concept of reason is presumed in the unity of languages. In other words, reason is based on the appearance of language. The objective of design must therefore be to develop rational ("reasonable") solutions. This starting point was decisive for the development of a theory of product language, among other places at the Offenbach School of Design. Such a consensus no longer exists in design today.

Georg Wilhelm Friedrich Hegel (1770–1831) was the first to portray nature, history, and thought as processes; here he proceeded from a permanent movement, change, and development of the natural, historical, and spiritual world and attempted to prove the connections in this movement and development.

Friedrich Engels (1820–1895) went beyond Hegel's findings about natural philosophy and developed dialectic materialism. In particular, he protested against the separation of method from object. As he conceived it, the dialectical method is always the method of an object, the thing itself, for instance, nature, history, art, and justice. For Engels, understanding a thing as it really is meant knowing the conditions necessary for its emergence, its history, and its transition into something else.

For Engels, however, the three steps of thesis, antithesis, and synthesis were not merely a method, but simultaneously the history of ideas. Since he subscribed to the opinion that all in life is in flux, that everything supposedly static is merely a moment of eternal motion, he considered the concepts themselves to be dynamic rather than static.

In the twentieth century the individual sciences became even more specialized. Three branches of the humanities took on particular importance for the field of design: semiotics, phenomenology, and hermeneutics.

Semiotics and Design

The discipline of design not only generates material reality; it also fulfills communicative functions (Bürdek 1997b). Yet for a long time this aspect received little attention: designers always focused on the practical functions of products (i.e., their functional and technical performance) and the social functions of products (i.e., questions of operability and meeting user needs).

Since the beginning of the twenty-first century it has become clear – and increasingly accepted by those involved – that semiotics occupies a central role for design – both industrial and non-industrial. The same also applies to graphic design, as Meredith Davis (2012) demonstrates very clearly. In the design disciplines, therefore, particular attention must be devoted to semiotics. In architecture this phenomenon has been known at least since the onset of postmodernism, in other words since the end of the 1970s (Jencks 1978).

Even at the dawn of the twentieth century, there were products known as "talking furniture." In Nancy, the French designer Émile Gallé designed and produced furniture that supposedly spoke a lively language endowed with the "sentiment of the soul." His furniture sought to portray what he perceived as the soul of plants – artistic expression in delicately proportioned stands, wilting leaves, or fine woods. In day-to-day contact these were then supposed to exert a soothing and conciliatory influence on people, who were already plagued by technology and industry in this period (Bangert 1980).

Chairs provide a vivid example of how product designs must do more than satisfy ergonomic, constructive, manufacturing, economic, and ecological demands. Besides the question of what kind of sitting is concerned – for instance, sitting in the workplace, at home, in public areas, in school, in vehicles, short-term or long-term sitting, sitting by children or older people – design always has to deal with the connotations (that is, additional emotional or expressive meanings) the word sitting can also contain.

Using the example of a chair as a throne, Umberto Eco (1972) explained that in this case sitting down is only one function among many, and one that is often fulfilled quite poorly. What is more important is that the throne project majestic dignity, might, and inspire awe. Such patterns of interpretation can also be transferred to other chairs. An office chair, for instance, should meet ergonomic demands to the highest standard, while also demonstrating the user's position in the workplace hierarchy.

In fact furniture altogether is less utility object than medium, both in the past and all the more so in the present (Hackenschmidt and Engelhorn 2011). As Hackenschmidt and Engelhorn report, luggage was already functioning as a medium of cultural exchange in the sixteenth and seventeenth centuries. The objects they carried with them communicated the social status of travellers, and allowed the inhabitants of the far-off countries they visited to assess their position in society. Thus their social status was expressed semiotically not only in their dress, but also in the products they carried with them.

The opposite end of the spectrum today is the Monobloc plastic chair (Hofter, 1997). Available for less than three dollars throughout the world, it signalises a supposed equality among its owners. The idea of democratization expressed here is reflected in the prodigious volumes in which it is produced: the number in existence around the world is estimated to exceed one billion.

Such observations can be made for all products. Automobiles, for instance, are not only a means of transport, but also highly symbolic everyday or cult objects. His analysis of clothing occasioned Roland Barthes (1967) to state that fashion, too, has two meanings: practical utilization and rhetorical statement ("for cocktails, the little black dress"). The things of nature speak to us (if we have learned to understand their language), those that are artificially constructed must be given a voice, too (here the language and meaning are assigned to the things, for they cannot speak on their own). The objects (products) should say how they originated, which technologies were used to create

1   **The monobloc chair**

2   **Juan – A new monobloc chair**
Design: Reinhard Dienes (2011)
Fa. Senchuan/China

1

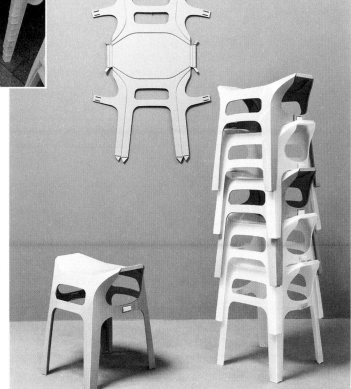

2

them, and from which cultural contexts they arose. They should also tell us something about the users and their ways of life, about real or supposed memberships in social groups, about their values. First, the designer must understand these languages; then, he must be able to teach the objects to speak. Once we understand this, we can recognize the respective shapes of lives in the shapes of objects (Bauer-Wabnegg 1997).

A Short History of Semiotics

Semiotics itself goes back to antiquity. This concept was used in ancient Greece in the field of medicine. There, it designated the branch in which the diagnosis and prognosis of diseases was performed through signs. In antiquity a urine sample to be analyzed was called a *signum* – a sign.

Plato presented a number of semiotic discourses, and the distinctions between the following words can be traced back to him:

sign *(semeion),*

meaning of the sign *(semainómenon),* and

object.

He was concerned with establishing the relationships between the sign, its meaning, and the thing it designated. This threefold relation was largely forgotten until Charles Sanders Peirce picked it up again in the nineteenth century.

Aristotle used various semiotic concepts, such as the science of signs, theory of signs, art of signs *(semeiotiké),* and sign *(sema or semeion).* He proceeded from Plato's discourses and developed a theory of phonetic and written signs, whose essence resided in the fact that with signs "something stands for something else" *(aliquid stat pro aliquo).*

In the nineteenth century semiotics underwent further development at the medical faculties of European universities. Following up on the ancient Greeks, a medical science of signs (Reimers 1983) was developed. It pursued a holistic approach, evaluating a past lifetime according to anamnestic signs (anamnesis = recall to memory, prehistory of an acute illness), observing the present condition according to diagnostic signs (diagnosis = discern), and put-

"Sign – Object – Interpreter" according to Peirce

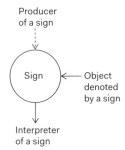

Producer
of a sign

Sign

Object
denoted
by a sign

Interpreter
of a sign

ting forward prognostic signs (prognosis = prediction) for the expected course of illness or recovery. All of these signs were then connected with each other. Explaining these connections consists in the recognition and interpretation of signs (i.e., semiotics).

In today's form of semiotics, as it is applied in design, two directions have had predominant influence: semiology, which emerged from linguistics, and semiotics in the current sense, whose origins can be found in American pragmatism.

Charles Sanders Peirce (1839–1914) Pierce is considered the actual father of semiotics. He was the founder of the school of pragmatism and was regarded as the last representative of universal scholarship: universality in his case was oriented toward the unity of knowledge, which he saw fulfilled in the logic of semiotics.

In 1867 Peirce began with the publication of his semiotic studies. He is credited with rediscovering the central concept of semiotics: the triadic relation. He emphasized the relative character of signs, that is, that they exist only as they relate to an object and an interpreter. This relation he called a three-way, or triadic relation. Peirce uses the concept of representation, meaning that something stands for something else, or is treated mentally as if it were the other thing. In this sense signs are representatives for something else.

Ferdinand de Saussure (1857–1913) Saussure lectured at the university in Geneva from 1906 until 1911. The work *Cours de linguistique générale* (1916) was compiled and published from his students' notes. Saussure is considered the founder of structuralist linguistics and structuralist thought in general. Thanks to his work, linguistics was able to establish itself as an independent discipline.

Saussure spoke of the referential character of language: people use language to refer to things that lie beyond language, namely, real existing objects and facts. Linguistic signs are not only physical sounds, but also psychological impressions. He called the whole complex the unity of idea and articulation. The idea of a chair thus has no natural connection to the sequence of its sounds. This connection is established only through collective agreement (i.e., convention).

Typology of functions according to Mukařovský

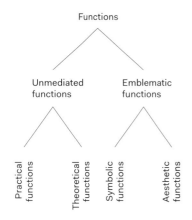

Functions

Unmediated functions

Emblematic functions

Practical functions

Theoretical functions

Symbolic functions

Aesthetic functions

Jan Mukařovský (1891–1975) This Czech linguist belonged to a literary circle in Prague in the 1930s that discussed the foundations of the theoretical concept of structuralism and reviewed the works of Ferdinand de Saussure at quite an early date. He analyzed the aesthetic functions of works of art, which in his opinion had to be classified as social phenomena. Mukařovský referred in his works to both the triadic concept of signs by Charles William Morris and to Saussure's key concepts of *langue* (the language system of a community) and *parole* (the speech act of the individual).

The central point of his semiotic approach in aesthetics is the replacement of the concept of the beautiful through the concept of function. Through deduction Mukařovský developed a typology of functions (1942) that made express reference to structuralism, in which he conceived of the hierarchy of the respective functions as a constantly dynamic process.

Charles William Morris (1901–1979) Morris picked up on the studies by Peirce and John Dewey (1910) to formulate a behavioristic approach to semiotics. He discerned the behavior of signs through the three categories of characteristic, evaluation, and prescription (or command). In his programmatic work, *Foundations of the Theory of Signs* (1938), he distinguished three semiotic dimensions:

the syntactic dimension, that is, the formal relations of the signs among each other and their relations to other signs,

the semantic dimension, that is, the relation of the signs to the objects or their meanings, and

the pragmatic dimension, that is, the relation between the signs and the users of signs, the interpreters.

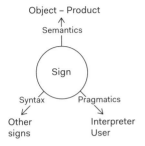

**"Semantics – Syntax – Pragmatics"
according to Morris**

Object – Product

Semantics

Sign

Syntax   Pragmatics

Other   Interpreter
signs   User

Max Bense (1910–1990) Through his work on semiotics, Bense probably exerted the most enduring influence on the creative disciplines in the second half of the twentieth century (Walther 2002). He was among the first to study the work of Peirce and Morris, and attempted to apply their conceptualizations to issues of aesthetics. Through his parallel teaching positions at the University of Stuttgart and the Ulm School of Design, he also initiated semiotic studies in the areas of information, product design, and visual communication at these institutions. Bense published a great number of works on semiotics (Bense 1954–1960/ 1967/1969/1971), which left their enduring imprint on discourses of design.

Jean Baudrillard (1929–2007) Baudrillard can be regarded as the actual founder of a semiotically grounded theory of design, because he applied semiotic-structuralist methods to the analysis of the everyday. He studied the language of objects (1991), by which he meant, for example, household objects, the automobile, and technical appliances. If the things with which humans surround themselves can speak, then they can report about the owners, about their values, desires, and hopes. Baudrillard's analysis of objects amounts to a political-economic exposé: commodities exist not in order to "be taken possession of and used, but to be produced and purchased. In other words, they structure themselves neither according to our needs, nor in the sense of a traditional order of the world, but exclusively for the purpose of an order of production and ideological standardization" (Baudrillard 1974).

Umberto Eco (born 1932) In numerous works Eco concerned himself with issues of the semiotics of literature, aesthetics, epistemology, semiotics, and the structuralist method. He utilizes the concept of the semiotic field, in which various different semiotic approaches are realized. For Eco, any semiotic study must presume that communication functions as the transmission of messages on the basis of codes.

Eco proceeds from Peircean considerations to investigate processes of communication. All cultural processes can be analyzed by means of semiotics. The codes are rules of transformation, through which certain signs are encrypted so that their meaning can be recognized when they are decoded. He continues to use the concepts of denotation and connotation that are so central to design.

With denotation Eco means the unmediated effect that an expression (a sign) triggers in the recipient of a message (in a particular culture). In the case of a chair, therefore, this is seating. With connotation, by contrast, he means everything that can occur to an individual (within a particular culture) as regards the meaning of a sign. Using the chair example, this may be a throne, a work of art, a judge's chair, or many other things. The connotation can thus be understood as the sum of associations evoked by a certain sign in a specific society.

In his *La Struttura Assente* (1972), Eco dedicated a detailed chapter to the topic of semiotics and architecture, which explicitly includes design and city planning. Using vivid examples, he demonstrates that the tenet of functionalism, of form following function, remains mystical if the code of the respective product has not been learned or imparted by society. How can an elevator be operated if no one can decipher the various buttons and arrows? From the perspective of communications technology, the form must denote the function so clearly that the operation of a product is not only possible, but also desirable, and thus leads to the movements which are best suited to fulfilling the functions. The form designates function only on the basis of a system of acquired expectations and habits (i.e., on the basis of codes).

Ugo Volli (born 1948) Volli argues that the field of semiotics is not preordained but only gradually came into existence (2002). He builds on the well-known axiom of Paul Watzlawick: "One cannot not communicate." People, objects (both natural and artificial), organizations, and so on are continuously generating "communication," disseminating information about themselves, which is interpreted by its recipients. In semiotic terms he designates this process "meaning" or "sense." We grasp the world around us (and especially things, objects, and products) only via the route of interpretation; they appear to us immediately concrete, and thus "meaningful."

To Volli the fundamental semiotic act consists not in the generation of signs, but in the capture of meaning. And here a bridge can very obviously be extended to design: Products must make sense, both practically and semantically.

Volli also points out that the phenomenon of meaning must be grasped as a "cultural unit"; anchored in the consciousness of production of communication, but also determined by the respective culture. To investigate this – also in relation to globalization – would certainly represent a fruitful topic for design research.

Semiotics in the Cultural Sciences

Not least through its growing media presence, design is attracting the attention of the cultural sciences at the beginning of the twenty-first century. In past decades the "cultural studies" and "cultural sciences" founded in the 1960s have failed to present meaningful research findings on the subject of design. That is certainly not unconnected with design's lack of cultural recognition: "It has only begun to penetrate the circle of recognized topics of cultural studies. Design lives in the shadows, probably on account of its complexity and its capillary connections to technology, society, economy, and culture" (Bonsiepe 2009). The studies by Helene and Matthias Karmasin (1997) and Karmasin (1998) are worth mentioning: "Design always also has something to do with social communication, and design has fundamentally important semiotic functions. It determines product semantics to a very great extent: it signalizes the message that the product assumes for the user, which can communicate his or her social message."

In Germany, not least on account of the dominant position of functional design (Bauhaus, Ulm School of Design, Good Design the influence of Braun, and so on), little in the way of semiotics has entered design practice. Berlin-based cultural historian Wolfgang Ruppert, however, was one very early initiator of discourses about the semiotic dimensions of products. His description of the five forms of production of meaning (Ruppert 1997) is a very useful model for explaining the complexity of product design:

The Purpose of Things This he understands as the usefulness of things: their instrumental character, and their use value. Without question, this was and still is the classical domain of designers, although the empirical basis on which they operate remains murky.

Meanings and Aesthetic Signs These relate to aspects such as aesthetic vocabulary, visual identifiability, representation, and ornamental value. Today this second level is certainly acknowledged as design competence, even if the vocabulary still appears rather underdeveloped.

Means of Commodity Production Here Ruppert includes the purchaser's desire to acquire, the coding as commodity, and also aesthetic presentation and attribution of meaning. This category includes experience and event design, which today enjoy great economic importance.

Innovation Alongside the sense of modernization, Ruppert here includes in particular the "semantics of progress" in the sense of forming new products in order to visualize their innovation potential. In an interview, Hartmut Esslinger (2011) very lucidly lays out how his successes for firms like Wega, Sony, and Apple were closely bound up with his immediate personal proximity to the manufacturing process: "... for the power is in the factories – and beyond that, however old they are designers need to know what factories can do today. Because the best designs and products always emerge through collaboration with the manufacturing side" This also makes it clear that designers certainly do not control the processes of progress on their own, but rather visualize and thus lend them their forms of expression.

Social Identities In the last stage of this nested semiotic model, Ruppert locates the context of the social lives of individuals and their freedom to shape them. The complexity of this issue is addressed in greater detail elsewhere (↗ p. 230).

The relevance of Ruppert's model lies on the one hand in overcoming traditional ways of thinking in design, which concern themselves exclusively with the usefulness or use value of the products. On the other hand, he succeeds in spanning an arc from aesthetic vocabulary (the question of what the products mean to us) right through to the contexts of social life (which are becoming ever more important for product design, given that today it primarily means lifestyle design).

Wolfgang Ruppert has published numerous studies on product culture, which represent precise semiotic analyses of everyday objects (1993a, 1993b, 1998). While his examples still originate from the mechanical and electrical worlds, Gert Selle's studies *Vom Thonetstuhl zum Mikrochip* (From the Thonet chair to the microchip; 2007) make the leap to contemporary digitalized product worlds.

In her compendium on *Design Kulturen* (Design cultures; 2013), the culture and media researcher Yana Milev identifies various current semiotic positions of relevance for design. It is notable that this is the first time that cultural studies has addressed the topic of design in such breadth. In that respect, the semiotics developed by Umberto Eco can certainly be understood as a transdiscipline with which the cultural sciences can explore the semiotic or semantic qualities of design. Milev describes man as a semiotic being, a design being: Human survival, she asserts, is tied to actions that leave signs and enable communication (Milev 2014). In diverse individual studies, cultural scientists confirm that the history of design is a history of the semiotic discourse, for what is design but the conscious shaping of signs? (Elize Bisanz). Moreover: "A design object is thus a multi-functional object; an industrially manufactured utility object, but equally, and more so, a representational object" (Milev, 2014, 318). The notable point here is that in terms of their design orientation the cultural sciences have arrived at the place design theory passed through decades ago.

Semiotics and Methodology

This in turn leads to the question of whether semiotics not only possesses interpretive (descriptive) qualities, in the sense of being able to say something about existing objects, products, and their role in communicative processes, but whether it cannot also be deployed as method and strategy for product development and product design. In her study of new value creation concepts, Sandra Hirsch (2014) argues that representations should be "understood as possibilities of new cultural meanings." To that extent links can certainly be grown from the new cultural studies (Milev 2014) and professional product development (industrial design). If new cultural meanings are to be created in and through products, then one must draw methodologically on semiotics, for this is where the required theoretical concepts have been and are being developed.

The term "design" originates from the Latin *designare,* meaning "to designate." Thus, through sequential differentiation, design transforms something undesignated into something designated. Accordingly design is designation through representation (van den Boom 1997).

Semiotics and Architecture

Semiotic studies on the subject of architecture were particularly popular. In the 1960s Robert Venturi pursued this approach explicitly in a fundamental study entitled *Complexity and Contradiction in Architecture* (Venturi 1966), in which he advocated meaningful buildings, which should clearly reject the International Style. In the circle of the "Stuttgart School" founded by May Bense, early works positing a connection between semiotics and architecture also emerged in the 1960s (Kiemle 1967). Georg R. Kiefer (1970) investigated architecture as a system of non-verbal communication and established a "semiotization of the environment," which conducts a conversation with humanity through signs.

In fact, these discourses were initiated more than two thousand yeas ago; Vitruvius's categories of *firmitas* (solidity), *utilitas* (usefulness), and *venustas* (beauty) (↗ p. 17) essentially already demonstrate that architecture also transports meaning – at that time under the label of "beauty."

It was not until the work of Charles Jencks (1978) that the analogies between architecture and language were introduced to a wider public: according to Jencks one can speak of architectural words, sentences, syntax, and semantics. His writings opened the doors for postmodern architecture – that is, an architecture of diversity – to attain importance worldwide; for this reason, Jencks can certainly be regarded as the most influential promoter of postmodernism.

Thereafter various architects concerned themselves with the textuality (meaning) of buildings. Peter Eisenman is one important representative of the semiotic debate in architecture (1991). "The giving of form is united with discourse to generate architecture as text," he declares (1995). Of course this metaphorical statement says only that beyond the material reality of architecture lies an immaterial level that explains it. Naturally "vocabulary" cannot be understood in any narrow sense here. Eisenman is also interested in differentiating architecture from "mere building." If the latter tends to be "meaningless," by implication the former must be "meaningful."

Architects like Zaha Hadid, Herzog & de Meuron, Jean Nouvel, Daniel Libeskind, Bernard Tschumi, and Peter Zumthor stress the semantic dimensions of their buildings. In a lecture held at Columbia University in 1989 ("Is Architecture a Text?"), Tomás Maldonado (2007) pointed out that at the end of the 1960s a start was made at understanding architecture as a visual system of signs. The architecture discourse, he said, emerged as a discourse about signs – thus as a semiotic one.

Certain authors went so far as to proclaim the birth of a new discipline of "architectural semiotics." The historical parallels are obvious, and product language and product semantics also draw on similar theoretical sources. In that sense these discourses are much more productive for design than permanent squinting at art. The latter largely promotes postmodernist nonsense that is blind to the reality of industrial products and good for nothing but bricolage.

The semiotization of architecture experienced its real boom at the transition from the twentieth to the twenty-first century. The formulation "architecture as text" means nothing other than that – alongside the functional conditions that architecture must fulfill, there is also another level of meaning. And that meaning of buildings needs to be interpreted and understood. Unfortunately such discourses are still quite rare in design. While architects have long since overcome the legacy of functional construction, the same cannot be said of most designers. Thus it is not only the "architect furniture" (Hesse/Lueg 2012) that defines the qualities of the architecture discourse. Now of course architecture has existed as a discipline for considerably longer than design, but the latter's shortcomings show up starkly in comparison.

Cities and regions are also becoming increasingly aware of the semiotics of built structures. The 2008 Olympic Games in Beijing were accompanied by spectacular construction projects conceived to crystallize the progress made by their masters. And according to the architect Wolf Prix of Coop Himmelb(l) au, the European Central Bank headquarters in Frankfurt am Main demonstrates that the European Union needs three-dimensional icons. In semiotic terms that is known as an "assigned meaning."

Semiotics at the Ulm School of Design

Interest in semiotics in Germany in the field of design can be traced back to the 1950s. Tomás Maldonado published a seminal article about semiotics in 1959, which was followed by an early *Terminology of Semiotics* in 1961. Gui Bonsiepe (1963) emphasized the importance of semiotics for design with the words: "The hypothesis that the world of objects and the world of signs are structured identically can indeed be quite fruitful. Moreover, the communicative aspects – and these are based on sign processes – of the relationship between the user and the utensil are probably the most important part of a theory of industrial design."

Under the motto of "Design as Sign," Hans Gugelot had already referred to the identity of sign and design in a lecture in 1962: "Any product with correct information content is a sign. That is why I stand by my decision to unify the concepts of design and sign... . For our perspective it is a matter of course to presume that man understands the language of things. To a certain extent, this can even be presupposed within a closed cultural circle."

The Ulm School of Design was the first institution – in part at the instigation of Max Bense – to attempt to exploit semiotics for design. In this connection particular mention must be made of Klaus Krippendorff's degree thesis (1961), in which he laid the groundwork for his later publication *Semantische Wende* (*The Semantic Turn;* 2006/2013). The phrase "programming product forms" used in the original subtitle was definitely a nod to the contemporary force of Max Bense's semiotics. Speaking of the 1960s, Krippendorff himself recalls: "Meaning had no currency at Ulm." Nonetheless, he is regarded as a significant pioneer of semiotics in design.

Semiotics and Communication

Early models of communication that were applied in design and based on telecommunications (Meyer-Eppler 1959; Maser 1971), proceeded from the assumption that these were what were known as transmitter/receiver models. The scientific foundations for this are found in cybernetics, which enjoyed particularly high esteem at the Ulm School of Design and in its methodology. That such technical models cannot be applied to interactions between biological, cognitive systems (Rusch 1994) did not actually become apparent until the paradigmatic works of radical constructivism. The works by Humberto Maturana and Francisco J. Varela, Heinz von Foerster, Ernst von Glaserfeld and Gerhard Roth, and especially the two comprehensive volumes by Siegfried J. Schmidt (1987, 1992), led to thoroughly new ways of regarding communication. This new concept designates a reciprocal process of exchange between actors, for whom the objective is "adaptation outputs," for only then can communication be truly successful. The basic thesis here is that perception (of signs or products) is always interpretation, that is, the attribution of meaning occurs in the human brain. In this case, it resorts to previous experiences or even conventions (Schmidt 1986).

A decisive feature of communication is that information is not transmitted (as in telecommunications), but constructed: "Here all kinds of situational, socio-cultural, and personal factors that have an influence on this process of construc-tion are taken into consider-ation. But all aspects of communication are de-scribed plausibly in the coherent model of the functioning of operationally closed autopoietic systems" (Schmidt 1987). A common criticism of the product lan-guage approach was that the products themselves do not actually speak at all. Certainly they do not, nor are they signals or messages (as presumed in the earlier models); nevertheless, during the process of communication (between the manufacturer, the vendor, and the user) they are ultimately assigned lan-guage (and thus meaning). The parties to such communication processes agree in a sense upon the meaning warranted by certain products (expensive, professional, technical, ecological, innovative, etc.).

The sociologist Niklas Luhmann (1984) once said in this context that "com-munication is contingent on communication." For the parties to such com-munication processes it is therefore necessary to produce what is known as connectibility, for only then can communication be successful. From this it follows that designers do not – as presumed in the traditional models – trans-mit messages to the world that are subsequently understood by potential re-cipients. Rather, in such communicative processes, the point is that inter-actions emerge (i.e., reciprocal relationships). From the analysis of product culture contexts, ways of life, and modes of behavior, it is necessary to offer communications that are understood, classified, and valued by potential us-ers. From this perspective, design must formulate and generate identification that can be effective on the most varied of levels. The products themselves function in such processes as vehicles of social interaction; they offer a wide variety of potential connections (Bürdek 2001a).

Different authors have used similar concepts to describe the communica-tive functions of objects or products. Jean Baudrillard (1968) spoke of the pri-mary and secondary functions of an object. Umberto Eco (1968) illuminated the "absent structure" of objects and subdivided these into the first and second functions. Of course, for him, this order is not a value judgment, as if one func-tion were more important than the other; on the contrary, the second func-tions (the connotations) are based on the first (the denotations, i.e., the objec-tive meanings). For Eco the entire world is constructed of signs, and the condition of a culture can be read from its signs.

Phenomenology and Design

Phenomenology, a method with a rich tradition in the humanities, has found only cautious application in design. It is understood to be the system of phenomena that can be described by forgoing theoretical analysis (especially reduction). The first phenomenological approaches emerged in the eighteenth century. Kant, for instance, formulated a *phaenomenologia generalis,* a science held to be one of the precursors of metaphysics, but not until the nineteenth century was this philosophical orientation elaborated more intensively.

Edmund Husserl (1859–1938) It was Husserl who shaped phenomenology into its current form. He is regarded as the founder of a phenomenological philosophy, which was made public in its early form in his *Logical Investigations* (1900–1901). His objective was to advance "to the things themselves" (i.e., to the original logical forms of thought).

The history of phenomenology is closely intertwined with that of hermeneutics (↗ p. 102 ff). With his *Ideas Pertaining to a Pure Phenomenology and to a Phenomenological Philosophy* (1913), Husserl established himself as the representative of a transcendental subjectivism. In this theory, every object is studied from the perspective of its manifestation, in which the object may be:

a phenomenon in the external world of the senses,

a visual quality in the sphere of experience, or

the symbolic manifestation of intellectual structures or

processes.

Martin Gessmann (2014) reminds us of the importance of phenomenology when he points out that discussion of things (today one would say products) starts from their manifestations. In other words from the forms out of which order arises, rather than Platonically from pure thoughts or ideas. Husserl's methodology begins with the manifestation of things, from which to generate founded knowledge. Martin Heidegger later traced the thoughts – "to the things themselves" – in an approach that still retains its relevance for design theory.

Husserl introduced the concept of lifeworld to emphasize that the analysis of objects must always reflect a particular world (and time). Accordingly, a phenomenological method is a procedure that attempts to understand the lifeworld of man directly and as a whole, taking everyday life and its environment into account. Only by delving into these lifeworlds is it possible to grasp the meanings of everyday objects. These are then subjected to hermeneutic interpretation, an approach from the humanities. Moreover, any phenomenological statement can claim validity only within the context of a certain spatially and temporally restricted historical horizon. When applied to design, therefore, phenomenology aspires to nothing less than a comprehensive investigation and characterization of the entire horizon of a product.

This is very closely connected with ideas from communication theory, to which Jürgen Habermas (1981) refers: "I therefore propose to use the concept of communicative action as a key to theory-formation, in order that we gain a better grasp of the obstinate structures of the lifeworld."

Examples of Phenomenological Studies

The work of philosopher Martin Heidegger (1889–1976) exhibits strong connections to phenomenology, for example, in his works on art (1968). Heidegger succeeded Husserl at the University of Freiburg and published phenomenological studies on concrete objects. Three of his essays count among the classics of the field: "Das Ding" (What is a Thing?), "Die Frage nach der Technik" (The Question Concerning Technology), and "Bauen Wohnen Denken" (Building Dwelling Thinking) (1967), all of which are certainly within the context of designing. The Swiss architect Peter Zumthor, for instance, refers explicitly to these philosophical positions (↗ p. 215 ff).

Not until the 1980s did the phenomenological approach re-enter the discourse. Two phenomenological studies were dedicated to the Walkman, by now a legendary product. Invented in Japan and brought onto the market by Sony in 1980, it was the origin of a categorically new and soon omnipresent product group – the playback of music possible under all circumstances. Shuhei Hosokawa (1987) directed his essay not to the original product, but to its effects on the urban environment: "the Walkman as an urban strategy, as an urban sound/music device." Here he applies Baudrillard's categories (1972) of primary (practical) and secondary (non-material) functions. Hosokawa is less concerned with the object in and of itself than with the object in use: what it means for the user, how it is perceived by the world around it, and what image of urbanity is behind it. He displays these lifeworlds in their entirety.

A significantly more comprehensive phenomenological study on the Walkman was published by Rainer Schönhammer (1988). Proceeding from the tradition of applied phenomenological research (Waldenfels 1985, 1992), Schönhammer describes how the Walkman decisively influences the lifeworld of its users today. He also calls his study a snapshot of the cultural history of sensory experience: "The possibility of using the device to secure a kind of musical shelter in exposed situations creates a corresponding valence of the object: the Walkman becomes a symbol of a life beyond the separation between subject and world, a symbol for the permanent possibility of experiencing fusion" (Schönhammer 1988). In this way, "the separation from what is happening acoustically in the space surrounding the headphones in itself will give occasion to an experience of alienation. The separation can be used to subject oneself to a musical event of particular forcefulness. Shutting out the acoustic environment can be both a (secondary) objective of its use and an undesired condition, which the user seeks to escape by adjusting the volume accordingly. The provocation of others is taken into consideration in a variety of ways" (ibid.).

In his study on the remote control, Schönhammer (1997) pursued the question of how these "magic implements for the household" have become established and propagated. The effect that they exert from afar, namely enabling the user to operate products without touching them, changes the way we handle these products on the most elementary level. Be it for television, stereo, CD player, video, or garage door, the remote control has become an "intervening technology of culture" with which we may think we determine our media behavior autonomously, but which ultimately only further cements our dependency on electronic media.

At the end of the 1990s, two design-oriented publications set out to build on the tradition of philosophers like Husserl and Heidegger and brought the tradition of phenomenology to bear in the present. Jens Soentgen made his reputation as a modern phenomenologist by dedicating himself to *Materials, Things, and Fractal Creations* (1997), thereby consciously establishing references to current design. Soentgen makes clear that the staunchly semiotic orientation of product language can indeed be expanded by a phenomenological dimension, for "semiotics is a theoretical option which may have many advantages, but also [has] the disadvantage that it must always conceive of everything as signs and ignores anything that cannot be reinterpreted as a sign" (Soentgen 1997). He also points out the critical difference between these two human-science methods: "describing phenomenologically means describing something as it appears without considering previous knowledge, without considering hypotheses, without any consideration for anything which does not belong directly to the perceptible sensory existence of the thing itself. Signs, on the other hand, are always mediated, be it through experience or through convention; semiotics thus concerns itself with the mediated or with that which can be thought of as mediated, and phenomenology with the unmediated, the direct" (Soentgen 1997b).

In another collection of essays, Soentgen (1998) vividly discussed a variety of phenomena that determine our everyday life, including "Kitsch," "Marble, Stone and Isopropyl Alcohol," "Patina," and "Shining Chrome." All of these also serve as instructive and illuminating examples of how a humanities orientation can be applied to design.

Volker Fischer (2001) subtitled an essay "A Phenomenology of Electronic 'Devices'" as a means of designating all of those useful and useless digital helpers (like mobile CD players, minidisk recorders, cell phones, Walkmans, cameras, Game Boys, Tamagotchis, and Lovegeties) (↗ p. 237). Fischer not only discussed these gadgets as individual examples of product design, but put them forward as the basis for exemplifying all of the lifeworlds that have an enduring influence, especially on children and teenagers in the way they deal with contemporary "digital devices." Thus the Tamagotchis of the late 1990s and the Lovegeties of the early 2000s represented early examples of electronic devices where people's attention was diverted from one another to digital products. Today this role has been seized by the smartphone, which can more or less be described as the user's second personality. That the changes in users' behavior have significantly greater consequences here than product design (which in many of these cases can be considered fairly banal) is only one of the insights we owe to phenomenological analyses.

Hermeneutics and Design

Hermeneutics in the strict sense is the art of interpreting, explaining, and translating texts. Interpretation is the key to understanding. This can be applied to nearly all contexts of life, including actions and gestures, works of science, literature and art, and historical events. As a theory, hermeneutics explains reflections on the conditions and norms of understanding and expresses them in language.

A Short History of Hermeneutics

Hermeneutics has two ancient historical roots: on the one hand, Greek philosophy – Plato, for instance, used the concept of *techné hermeneutiké,* which means the art of interpreting and explaining texts – and on the other hand, the exegesis of the Bible in Judaism.

Modern hermeneutics emerged in the nineteenth century, at the time when scientists were changing their Cartesian conception of the world as a machine. This was also the period during which the Englishman John Stuart Mill distinguished the natural sciences from humanities: the latter he designated the "moral sciences."

This subdivision was scrutinized by Charles Percy Snow (1959) in his book *The Two Cultures.* He saw the separation of literary from natural science research as a consequence of the industrialization of Europe. Today's discussions about the impact of technology, especially the problems in dealing with microelectronics (Weil and Dorsen 1997; Bürdek 2001), are examples of how the progress of natural science is challenged by studying advances in terms of the humanities (i.e., by inquiring as to their meaning).

Friedrich Daniel Ernst Schleiermacher (1768–1834) Schleiermacher is considered the first representative of modern hermeneutics. Although he did not write any independent works on hermeneutics, his Bible interpretations, which he put forward in lectures and talks, are classic hermeneutic works. Schleiermacher developed general rules of exposition that can also be applied to non-theological objects of interpretation. He proceeded from the universality of language: language and thinking constitute an inseparable unity. Just as in the Kantian concept of reason – the unity of sensory perception and intellectual conception – here, too, we find an important prerequisite for the scientific interpretation of design.

Johann Gustav Droysen (1808–1884) Droysen founded historiography as a hermeneutic science. He defined the essential methods in the humanities as recognizing, explaining, and understanding. The three basic theoretical questions of the historical sciences are attributed to Droysen:

the question of their object,

the question of their methods, and

the question of their objectives.

Wilhelm Dilthey (1833–1911) Dilthey is considered the actual founder of the humanities and the father of the hermeneutic, scientific philosophy of life. Using the example of psychology, he demonstrated the difference between explanatory (natural) and descriptive humanities. This subdivision is based on his statement (which remains pertinent even today): "We explain nature, but we understand the workings of the mind."

At this juncture an analogy to design theory can be established as products also always have this dual nature, consisting of a material reality and a non-material reality (i.e., the meanings they convey).

Otto Friedrich Bollnow (1903–1991) Bollnow was strongly influenced by Dilthey's life philosophy; he has often been designated the hermeneutist of "small understanding" or of "small forms." His work *Verstehen* (*Understanding*, 1949) attained particular importance. It picks up on a thought of Schleiermacher's that the idea is to "understand a writer better than he understood himself." This sentence neatly summarizes the actual objective of hermeneutics, namely to understand by reconstructing how an idea was produced (Gadamer 1960).

Hans-Georg Gadamer (1900–2002) Gadamer was probably the most important hermeneutist in the twentieth century; among his teachers was Martin Heidegger. His primary work, *Truth and Method* (1960), deals with the central question of truth's inaccessibility to any consciously scientific method. What was important for Gadamer was that the object being interpreted and the person who interprets it are involved in a kind of exchange with one another. Interpretation thus always also means influencing what is understood. Hermeneutics is, in and of itself, not a mechanical procedure, but rather an art.

Gadamer (1988) also grappled with the Snovian problematic of two cultures, according to which human knowledge is grasped in two kinds of languages: instrumental language (formulas, calculations, mathematical symbols, scientific experiments) and the language of philosophy.

Historical developments are portrayed in language. Human experience is set out in language; language is the means of understanding the world. Hence, Gadamer firmly embraced the theory that language, located at the center of philosophy, should be regarded as the core problem of the humanities, and the same, obviously, also holds true for design.

Martin Gessmann (born 1962) Coming from the Heidelberg School, Gessmann continues the tradition of Gadamerian hermeneutics (in particular the method of text hermeneutics) and relates it very relevantly to design: "Devices as texts that reveal their own worlds."

As a philosopher of culture and technology, he dedicates himself in depth to the question of "what people really need" (Gessmann 2010). For "an up-to-date philosophy of technology" there needs to be "an expansion of the analysis of technology in space into an understanding of technology in time" (ibid.).

His ideas refer explicitly to questions from design, which he describes as an ingredient we need. In the twentieth century this also (especially) means the aestheticization of lifeworlds, as well as the performance of the products. Changes in the form of products are played out against ideas about usage, superseding the dictum "form follows function." Taking apart examples such as cars, video phones, ticket machines, cell phones, refrigerators, and mountain bikes, he compares their congruities and incongruities with the expectations of potential users. In many cases it becomes clear that the anatomy of the device is incompatible with the biology of our brains. As such, Gessmann puts his finger on a glaring shortcoming of the culture (not only in design).

In *Zur Zukunft der Hermeneutik* (The future of hermeneutics; 2012), Gessmann shows that this classical method is acquiring new relevance today. The point is to tie the texts back to the lifeworlds again. In the tradition of twenti-

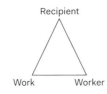

Hermeneutic triangles

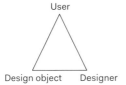

eth-century philosophy, he is seeking to accomplish an "enlightenment of dialectics."

Intersections with "material culture" become apparent here, as Hans Peter Hahn (2005) notes: "Material culture is a foundation of the social lifeworld; it plays an important role in human identity and in the constitution of societies as a whole." This would appear to me the most relevant field of research for a design discipline to investigate and harness for practice. The pros and cons are obvious.

Some Basic Hermeneutic Concepts

Hermeneutics has developed a number of concepts that prove useful in design.

Fusions of horizons

The Hermeneutic Triangle This consists of a work, a worker (the producer of the work), and a recipient, describing in other words the relationship between the designer, the design object, and the user.

Previous Understanding and the Fusion of Horizons
These terms are important basic concepts in hermeneutics. The first is understood to mean that each recipient already has knowledge about, and a consciousness of, the object to be interpreted, for only then is actual interpretation possible.

Fusion of horizons means that "wanting to understand" proceeds from the assumption that the recipient's previous knowledge can be unified with the horizon (and thus intentions) of the artist (or designer) and vice versa (i.e., that they meld together).

The Hermeneutic Circle The hermeneutic circle serves as the basic pattern of intersubjective understanding. The process of understanding is not linear, but more akin to circling in, where understanding the whole presupposes understanding the parts and vice versa. One of the uses of this phenomenon, also known as a "philosophical circle," is in Hegel's idealism: In order to recognize something, I must know what recognition means, which means I must have recognized something already.

Interpretation of a Work According to Rudi Keller (1986), the process of interpretation consists of the following steps:

perceiving a sign,

interpreting its reference, and

understanding its sense.

Interpretation thus basically means explanation, exposition, and signification. It is usually understood to mean the interpretation of works of art. Interpretation is thus not emotional, superficial talk, but instead, as a method of the human sciences, has a trans-subjective character: just as with the "unity of reason" (↗ p. 82), the concern here is the dialectic of rational and subjective aspects.

Sense and Reference The concept of reference (or denotation) used here is very similar to the concept of semantics used in semiotics. It is, however, important to distinguish reference from the concept of sense (or meaning). Keller (1986) used the example of language to explain the difference: Either one knows the reference of a word or one does not know it. One knows it whenever one knows how an expression is used (in accordance with an agreement or convention). "Understanding the sense" thus means grasping the intention, which is analogous to being able to classify a move as part of strategy in a game of chess. This example makes it clear that it is not until interpretation – in this case through familiarization with the rules – that the sense (of a chess move) can be concluded from the reference (of a chess piece).

On Applying Hermeneutics

Linguistic and textual critique concludes with the steps of perception, interpretation, and understanding the sense. However, if one wishes to transcend the descriptive level, a further step must follow: application. Gadamer (1960) recalled that in the tradition of the eighteenth century the hermeneutic process was already organized as follows:

subtilitas intelligendi (understanding),

subtilitas explicandi (exposition),

subtilitas applicandi (application).

These three elements must interact with each other to make up comprehension.

Critique of Hermeneutics

Critical Theory and the social sciences of the Frankfurt School had already voiced significant reservations about traditional hermeneutics in the 1970s. Jürgen Habermas (1968), in particular, diagnosed its missing critical distance; furthermore, he believed that recognition is always driven by interests. In his *"Universal Pragmatics,"* he described the principles of universal conditions of human understanding, but not until his *Theory of Communicative Action* (1981) did Habermas develop a system that built on language to make interpersonal understanding possible at all. With recourse to the "linguistic turn," it raises an interesting parallel to the development of design theory, because this became the foundation of both product language and product semantics.

On Empirical Hermeneutics

The Frankfurt School produced an important further development in hermeneutics. Thomas Leithäuser and Birgit Volmerg (1979) outlined first reflections on an "empirical hermeneutics." They said that it was necessary to lead a meta-hermeneutic discourse in order to avoid the subjective misinterpretations that often occur in hermeneutic circles. The psychoanalytical approach behind this idea is based on empirical investigations of everyday consciousness. Methodologically, empirical hermeneutics has its roots in linguistic philosophy ("the linguistic turn"), and thus also demonstrates an interesting affinity to the communicative discourses in design.

The methodologically decisive step of empirical hermeneutics thus is to take the given, real sociocultural conditions as the point of departure in any attempts to interpret, and to reflect on these permanently to prevent speculative explanations. This opens up important potential junctures for the practice of design.

Developments in Design Methodology

The roots of design methodology can be traced back to the 1960s, when it was the subject of particularly intensive work at the Ulm School of Design. The emergence of methodology as a field was a consequence of the great number, and completely new nature, of tasks assigned to industrial designers at this time. Christopher Alexander (1964), one of the fathers of design methodology, listed four reasons why the design process needed its own methodology:

design problems had become too complex to treat them purely intuitively,

the amount of data required to solve design problems had increased so rapidly that one designer could not collect, let alone process, them all,

the number of design problems had increased rapidly, and

totally new design problems were emerging at a faster rate than previously, so ever fewer design problems could be resolved by referring back to long-established practice.

Often it was incorrectly presumed that the objective of methodological research was to develop a uniform and stringent method for designing. This view overlooked the fact that different tasks require different kinds of methods, and that the first step in any design process is to decide which method should be used for which problems. The methodological effort involved in redesigning a simple household utensil is significantly lower than in developing complex public transport systems. Design methodology was guided by the principle that it was important to understand what the task was before beginning with any changes or new designs. In retrospect, this early phase can be designated as the analytical paradigm of architecture and of design as well (Tzonis 1990).

The System Research of the First Generation

Important works on design methodology emerged in the 1960s, initially from the United Kingdom and North America. They were strongly influenced by space research, where complex problems had to be solved. Horst Rittel (1973) called these early approaches "system research of the first generation," whose basic assumption was that it must be possible to dissect the design process into distinct steps:

1. Understand and define the mission (formulation of the task). This must be done very conscientiously and is the necessary prerequisite for everything that follows.

2. Collect data. In this phase one informs oneself about the current condition, the technical possibilities, and the like.

3. Analyze the data obtained. Draw conclusions from the information by comparing it with the mission (the target condition).

4. Develop alternative solutions. Frustration is frequent in this phase, but so are occasional creative leaps. In any case this phase should end with the development of at least one solution and the demonstration of its feasibility.

5. Assess the pros and cons of the alternatives and decide on one or more solutions. This phase may be accompanied by all kinds of complicated processes, such as simulations, which should provide the system researcher with an idea of the quality of solutions.

6. Test and implement the solutions. After testing, present the solutions to the decision makers. On the basis of this presentation they will choose between the alternatives offered and order the implementation of their choice.

Because the works of Horst Rittel were practically unavailable for such a long time, I would point to two publications (Rittel and Reuter 1992 and Rittel 2013) that remain germane in the context of renewed interest in design methodology. Rittel puts forward a strictly scientific and mathematical methodology and cooks to apply it to product design. Under the aspect of rationalism in design, which was especially strong at the Ulm School of Design in the 1960s, that would certainly appear serviceable. Many authors developed similar strictly rational models, replete with various detailed procedures. For instance, Morris Asimov (1962) developed what he called a morphology of design; Bruce Archer published voluminous checklists (1963–1964), which sought to determine every step in the process of design, but were so highly formalized that they could hardly be used. John R. M. Alger and Carl V. Hays (1964) directed their intensive efforts to a procedure for evaluating design alternatives, and Christopher J. Jones (1969) made essential contributions to methodology on

Decomposition and composition
after Christopher Alexander, 1964

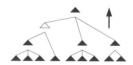

Program, consisting of sets

Realization, consisting of diagrams

the international level. I published detailed overviews of these at the conclusion of my studies in Ulm (Bürdek 1971a, b). In the 1980s Nigel Cross (1984, 1989) continued in this tradition, which was sometimes overdone, especially in the area of industrial design engineering at the Delft University of Technology (Roozenburg and Eekels 1995).

Christopher Alexander's Method The work of Christopher Alexander (1964) played a special role in the development of design methodology, as he focused specifically on the problems of form and context. Alexander consistently advocated introducing rationalism to design, as derived from the formal sciences of mathematics and logic. Alexander's primary concern was to break down complex design problems into their components as a means of finding concrete solutions.

If the form is the solution of the design problem, and the context defines the form (as it comprises the requirements that the form must fulfill), then discussion about design is not about form alone, but about the unity of form and context (↗ p. 114).

Alexander developed a method for structuring a design problem (defining the context) and then using the resulting hierarchical composition to develop the form.

To put it in its context in the history of science, Alexander's method integrates the Cartesian dissection of a problem with the deductive method. In the 1970s this strict methodological approach, involving first the decomposition and then the composition of design processes, was adapted and implemented in data processing systems. However, the euphoria for processing problem structures by means of computers evaporated quickly, not least because of the significant cost at the time. What remains is Alexander's basic approach of using deduction to dissect complex problems into sub-problems and making the search for alternative solutions to these subsidiary issues the first step in the design process.

This method proved quite effective in the practice of industrial design, but its limits became clear in the 1990s when the relationship between form and context experienced a crucial shift. As functionalism was replaced by postmodernism, the increased focus on the communicative function of design, including the new non-material subjects it presented (like interaction and interface design), required completely new approaches and methods (↗ p. 248). For this reason Mihai Nadin (2002) made a radical break with "Cartesian reductionism," which prohibits the application of non-deterministic (i.e., dynamic) models of change. Using even those networking potentials available today, as insufficient as they may be, would require throwing Cartesian thinking overboard.

On the Methodology of the Ulm School of Design A first retrospective on the phase where design was transformed from an art to a science was completed by Tomás Maldonado and Gui Bonsiepe in 1964. At this time the Ulm School of Design had distanced itself quite clearly from design as taught at the German schools in the arts and crafts (Werkkunst) tradition, most of which offered little more than a slightly modified version of the basics of Bauhaus, and all of which had a hard time making a successful transition from handicrafts design to industrial design. Because the Ulm School of Design articulated a strong interest in the relationship between science and design, numerous scientific disciplines and methods were studied in terms of their applicability to the design process.

Extensive discussion was dedicated to methods and to methodology itself. The latter consists in a systematic classification of all methods involved in the design of products. However, it would be incorrect to conclude that there is any such thing as a single generally valid methodology of product design. On the contrary, there is merely a collection of methods, among which a number of mathematical ones have achieved special standing (Maldonado and Bonsiepe 1964).

This mathematical approach shows particularly clearly that the intention of the "Ulm methodology" was to apply a methodology to the actual design process, that is, to the aesthetic character of the products. In the 1960s the aspect of rationalization was promoted intensively by the new technological capabilities of industry, while the language of form rapidly took on the standing of a new style principle: "Ulm functionalism."

Trans-Classical Science Probably the most important contribution to explaining and reorienting the scientific theory of design came from Siegfried Maser (1972), who distinguished the following kinds of science:

real sciences,

formal sciences, and

humanities or human sciences.

Maser applied the criteria of objective, progress, principle, path, consequence, and critique to determine which sciences might serve as the basis of an autonomous body of design theory. Because each of these criteria contains components of the classical sciences, he conceived of design theory as a trans-classical science along the lines of control sciences such as cybernetics. In this case, practice is the sphere of action and theory the sphere of argumentation. The role of theory is to provide reasons for action or to question, justify, or criticize it.

Changes in real conditions are at the center of a trans-classical or control approach (Maser 1972): "Using the terminology of cybernetics, this can also be formulated as follows:

1. Existing (ontic) conditions initially should be described as precisely and comprehensively as language allows (classical!).

2. From this knowledge a target condition should be determined, accompanied by at least one plan for converting the existing condition into the target condition.

3. The actual change to reality is based on the plan provided."

These steps represent the most basic form of the design process.

Models of the Design Process In the *Introduction to Design Methodology* (Bürdek 1975), I attributed the lack of elementary tools of methodology to a practice-oriented model of the design process. A number of simple methods and techniques were listed there.

The model emphasizes the design process as an information processing system and is characterized by numerous feedback loops, which illustrate how far the design process is removed from linear problem solving. Allowances are made for a design practice in which such factors as objections, missing or updated data, technological advances

A model of the design process

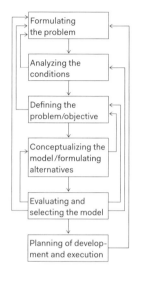

different sources does not serve to make the process more transparent, but rather less so.

Introduction to Design Methodology also introduced a basic canon of methods that had proven effective in practice and suggested that they be taught as part of design training. These included: preparing analyses (market, function, and information analyses), compiling a list of requirements and specifications, creativity and problem-solving methods, methods of rendering (two-dimensional and three-dimensional), evaluation procedures, and test procedures.

As I compiled this canon it became clear that the repertoire of methods to be applied depends on the complexity of the problems posed (on a scale ranging from a coffee cup to public transportation); this point was overlooked all too easily in discussions about whether or not methodology made sense. Part of training in design methods entails explaining to the pupil which repertoire should be implemented in which case, and this very aspect requires maintaining a critical distance from methodology.

The Paradigm Shift in Methodology

The reorientation in methodology that began in the late 1970s amounted to nothing less than a paradigm shift. This concept was propagated by Thomas S. Kuhn (1967), who understood a paradigm to be those components of a scientific discipline that are held to be generally valid by the majority of researchers in the given discipline. The concept of a paradigm shift expresses the view that science does not progress at a steady pace, gradually accumulating knowledge, but rather experiences occasional revolutionary breaks, which entail more or less radical changes in the dominant ways of thinking (Seiffert 1983).

The work of Paul Feyerabend (1976) was particularly influential for methodology. He objected to the idea that only one fixed method (e.g., the Cartesian) should be accepted as generally valid: "A unified opinion may be the right thing for a church, for the intimidated or greedy victims of a (traditional or new) myth, or for the weak and complaisant subjects of a tyrant." Objective knowledge required many different ideas, he asserted, adding that only a method that encourages diversity can be reconciled with a humanistic standpoint.

This conception did not actually become important in design until the early 1980s, when postmodernism fostered new design tendencies. A paradigm shift occurred in design methodology as well. Until well into the 1970s, most of the methods applied had been deductively oriented, with work proceeding from a general problem and oriented toward a special solution (from the outside in). In what became known as new German design, an inductive approach was increasingly applied, asking what effect (meaning) a design might have – but never who its potential users might be.

Christopher Alexander's Pattern Language In methodology itself, it was a major publication by Christopher Alexander that marked what was probably the decisive paradigm shift. In 1977, together with his colleagues at the Center for Environmental Structure in Berkeley, California, he published what is probably the most important work on issues of planning and architecture: *A Pattern Language*. This book and its successor, *The Timeless Way of Building* (1979), represent a decisive step in the development of methodology.

The design method known as Pattern Language elucidates and reveals the social and functional issues of design discourse and how they can be implemented in the three-dimensional world. Its central section comprised a plan to provide the residents of cities and houses with the means necessary to shape their environment themselves. The core of this plan was that the residents understand that everything surrounding them – structures, buildings, and objects – possesses its own language. In no fewer than 253 individual examples he describes the individual words (pattern) of this language, which can be used to create an infinite number of combinations (e.g., essays and speeches). Such patterns then constitute regions and cities, neighborhoods, buildings, spaces and niches, all the way down to details like the atmosphere of the dining room, the bedrooms, seating, colors, and lighting. Each individual pattern is connected to the others; none is an isolated unit. All are hypotheses and thus provisional; they can be developed further on the basis of new experiences and observations.

On the Ambiguity of Form and Context If form represents the solution for the problem of design and context defines the form, then discussions about design are not only about form, but about the distinction between ... opened a discourse which became relevant again in the 1990s.

The transparent factory in Dresden, Volkswagen AG (2011)

Up until the 1980s context was generally understood to mean only those practical demands (such as ergonomic conditions, construction specifications, and manufacturing options) that designers had to take into consideration in their designs. In reality, however, the design is often dominated by an entirely different set of conditions. Today, the contexts are the actual topic of designs: first the relevant lifestyle must be formulated and designed as a backdrop that determines which products can endure. A telling example is provided by the automobile manufacturer Volkswagen AG, whose Autostadt Wolfsburg (Wolfsburg Car City, opened 2009) and Gläserne Manufaktur (Transparent Factory, opened 2002) in Dresden are examples of how context can become more important than the products themselves. This showcasing of "the car" is supposed to culminate in an all-embracing experience and thus ultimately reinforce the purchasers' brand loyalty. The interior of the Mercedes-Benz Museum in Stuttgart (design: UNStudio; opened 2006) is modeled on the double helix of the DNA molecule. The idea is to visualize the thought driving the innovation of the Mercedes-Benz brand: continual reinvention. The museum itself reaches far beyond the design and technology of individual vehicles, concentrating on an all-round visitor experience.

Design problems are therefore no longer questions of form alone; instead, it is becoming increasingly important to design contexts, to set the stage for contexts, or at least to provide contexts as models of interpretation for a design. The question today is not: "How are these things made?" but "What do these things mean for us?"

New Design Methods

Although the transition from the natural science paradigm to the humanities paradigm started rather hesitantly in the design of the 1980s, the advancing process of digitalization in the 1990s necessitated a fundamental reorientation. New methods were also needed for design practice, as design concepts for hardware and software required empirical testing.

Thus it came as no surprise that Christopher Alexander's Pattern Language took on new relevance in the context of software development; after all, that is where the linearity of design processes (problem – analysis – solution) was abandoned and the focus shifted to the stratified nature of users' needs and interests. Patterns increasingly influenced the development processes (Borchers 2001).

These patterns reveal a crucial problem for mass culture and society: how to deal with electronics. Donald A. Norman (1989) stated that a significant portion of the design process should be concerned with how the objects to be designed will be employed and operated. In the design of digital products (hardware and software), the emphasis shifts away from the external form toward the user interface.

Personas Like Donald A. Norman, Alan Cooper (1999) criticizes the utilization of electronics and the effects on the user. Rather than software engineers, whose understanding of the product is largely technical, he argues for interaction designers with an understanding of potential users and their behavior to program electronic devices. He calls this "behavioral design."

Alongside the application of scenarios (↗ p. 118 ff), where the everyday conditions of real users play an important role in software development, Cooper describes the new method of "personas." He regards a precise description of the users and their wishes and ideas about what they want to get out of a product (whether hardware or software) as one of the most important foundations of development. Of course personas are not real people, but hypothetical archetypes whose wishes and objectives are to be prioritized. Cooper consciously avoids the term "user," and speaks of concentrating on individuals. In the development process it is necessary to consider as many different people and wishes as possible.

Cooper also identifies a specific problem in software development: That the ideas of staff working in the companies involved are often quite different to those of purchasers. IT managers wish to satisfy the needs of product users, whereas marketing managers are convinced that the product with the most functions will sell best. Cooper regards the exact description of personas and development objectives and the application of scenarios as the most important methods in the design of hardware, software, and combinations of the two.

Mind Mapping Probably the most radical departure from the problem-solving methods – be they linear or characterized by diverse feedback mechanisms – is what are known as mind mapping models. These models have been marketed under the catchword of "visualizing knowledge" since the mid-1990s in the form of interactive software. Developed by Tony Buzan in the 1970s (Buzan 1991, 2002), mind mapping methods are designed to assist in structuring problems, product development, and process planning. These models are conceived in the tradition of the *Ars Memoria,* techniques of remembering that date back to antiquity.

When linear thinking is abandoned, intuitive leaps and innovative ideas and products often result. The simple reason for this is that problems (in design, too) are becoming so complex that traditional methods (like trees, quasi-groups) can no longer be used to outline them, let alone to solve them.

The mind mapping programs associated with the field of knowledge management allow problems to be presented using a multimedia approach (texts, pictures, films, and music) that can suggest to the users completely new ways of structuring problems. The interactive nature of this method provides for extremely versatile problem descriptions and thus holds great potential for innovation. Mind maps are available in different versions, as freeware (Free-Mind, Freeplane, MindMup, VUE) or to purchase (Mind Map, Mind42, Mind-Genius, Mindjet, MindView).

The Scenario Technique The concept of scenario was derived from the Greek term "scene," which designates the smallest unit of a play (drama, film, or opera). Today, it can mean a draft (of a film, for example), or, in the field of project and product planning, the hypothetical sequence of events constructed to take into account causal connections. In product development such scenarios are implemented as important methods in two different areas.

Scenarios as Prognostic Instruments In the 1960s Hermann Kahn, an American researching developments of the future, invented a procedure for depicting possible future developments in the sciences, in politics, and in society as a whole, to facilitate the derivation of alternative action plans. This approach armed users with the tools necessary to assess possibilities in the given spheres of action (from the best case to the worst). Kahn himself introduced these methods in a number of books (Kahn 1977, 1980), but many of his prognoses appear improbable today.

The method of scenarios was also adopted by other authors and has proven its worth as a relevant instrument. Alvin Toffler applied it in three important works (Toffler 1970, 1980, 1990), whereby his supposedly sensational prognoses apparently also opened the floodgates for the speculative works that followed.

Subsequent publications based on this approach were even less scientifically grounded than Kahn's. Increasingly, authors dedicated themselves to known trends, which they propagated as a kind of scenario. Particularly successful in this endeavor was John Naisbitt (1984, 1995, 1999). A scenario portrayal oriented toward product development was published by the Japanese scientist Michio Kaku (1998); it is especially concerned with future generations of computers, biotechnology, and medical technology. He writes: "In order to fulfill the promise of the information highway, several problems have to be solved and several milestones have to be reached between now and 2020: (1) resolving bandwidth bottlenecks, (2) designing better interfaces; (3) creating personalized agents and filters." That was pretty close to the mark, given that the identified problems have already largely been solved.

At the same time it must be noted that the problems of that phase were largely scientific and technical in nature. The future belonged to the grand project of modernity, which was pursued in particular by the European intellectual left. But their fantasies of technological salvation were derailed at the latest by the early 1970s with the Club of Rome study (Meadows, 1972).

In the twenty-first century user behavior worldwide (individual and collective) has been changed dramatically by the internet and the "devices" invented for it – such as smartphones, tablets, apps, and social networks. Socioeconomic circumstances played only a marginal role in the scenarios of the 1980s and 1990s, but have in fact proven to be significant. Manfred Faßler describes this brilliantly in his analysis of habitats (2011): "The networks of artefacts, things, people, signs, norms, organizations, texts, and so on that B. Latour speaks of, take over the regime. These are not hybrids or chimeras. The circumstances of life are recomposition – biologically, materially, informationally. The overall fitness of the biological, social, and informational conditions of life is recreated and reassessed."

Even if the circumstances of society are changing dramatically, the scenario technique has become established in design practice and has consistently proven its worth. In the 1980s, for example, Daimler AG founded an interdisciplinary study group in Berlin (now based in Sindelfingen, Beijing, and Sunnyvale, California) under the direction of Eckard P. Minx (Minx, 2001). The researchers all possess dual training: they are experts in their discipline and interdisciplinary team partners in projects.

They include psychologists, economists, communications experts, economists, physicists, and philosophers. Their remit is to conduct strategic early warning at the boundaries of the corporate system, in particular preparing the social and technological scenarios of the kind that are crucial for an automobile manufacturer (www.technicity.daimler.com). The consistent scenarios developed by the study group provide a baseline that organizations or companies can use to plan feasible action alternatives. Among the works documenting how much these alternatives differ from the speculative prognoses mentioned above are two scenarios on the topic of *City, Mobility and Communication in the Year 2020* (Minx et al. 1994).

Interestingly, designers are not part of this team, whose task is to visualize future scenarios and conceivable vehicle concepts on the basis of interdisciplinary research. There is also an advanced design department working on ideas for the more distant future – including the "concept cars" that all vehicle manufacturers develop to demonstrate designs for cutting-edge and speculative technological and societal scenarios.

Another example of historical import is the Philips Design headquarters in Eindhoven under Stefano Marzano. In the 1990s, in collaboration with the Domus Academy in Milan, it conducted a broad-based study on the future of digital media, which vividly formulated scenarios and visualized them using design concepts (Manzini and Susani 1995). The study was important for the company's internal dialog regarding questions of future product development, but even more so for the competition, as it clearly signaled Philips' ambition to lead the avant-garde of the industry through design.

Scenarios in Software Development Scenarios are applied in a similar manner in the field of software development, primarily in the design of interaction and interfaces. Here they are used to save time (and thus costs) in the design, development, and programming of new applications, where hardly any feedback is received as to their potential acceptance by users. Scenarios for software development include short operating procedures, simulated with prototypes of a new hardware or software product. These allow relatively fast and economical empirical testing of user acceptance, comprehensibility of operating routines, and even the aesthetic characteristics of user interfaces.

Virtual prototypes for hardware simulation were introduced at the beginning of the 1990s (Bürdek and Schupbach 1992) and have proven to be a useful tool. By means of what are known as "author systems," they generate interactive visual renderings of products, which can be operated by the potential users (VDI 4500).

Mood Charts Working with visualization methods is gradually becoming a necessity in product development and design. Verbal descriptions of objectives, concepts, and solutions are no longer sufficient, especially for designs developed for the global market. The semantic differences between concepts result in misunderstandings, even among designers, technicians, and marketing directors collaborating in the same development team. Obviously, the problem is even more complex and more misleading in national and global contexts.

In keeping with the view that context determines form, starting in the 1980s collage principles from the artistic sphere were applied to design. At the beginning of the twentieth century Georges Braque and Pablo Picasso began creating *papiers collés* – montages of pictorial elements and texts comprised of paper, fabrics, wood, and other materials. Such montages were produced in the futurist, Dadaist, and surrealist schools; text montages were created in the field of literature, and the same creative principle was used in the music of the 1960s.

In design, such collages (charts) are produced in order to visualize and portray the lifeworlds of users (their mood), the market fields in which companies are active, or entire product fields (contexts) (Küthe and Thun 1995). Detailed studies of the relevant lifeworlds are completed and visual horizons developed based on them. The most consistent visual horizon that can be achieved then serves as the context for the work of design. A visual horizon can also be used to test design variants in a later phase. Its coherence with given product environments therefore does not have to be described laboriously in words, but can be checked by comparing images. Here the limits of this method become clear, however: while it facilitates communication about the objectives and results of a design, it neither encourages innovation nor generates new product-cultural models. Technological innovations often have far-reaching effects on our modes of behavior (take the example of cell phones), and the development of new models is a highly complex socio-psychological process that cannot be portrayed on the level of pictures alone. Nevertheless, there is no dispute about the application of mood charts in product development, as they have proven quite useful for internal communication between the various disciplines involved in developing a product.

Empirical Methods At the close of the 1980s (as postmodernism began to decline), it became clear that the practice of design could not rely on creative or clever designs. One consequence of the increasing costs of product development (for instance, today it is not possible to launch a completely new automobile model for less than one billion euros) is that companies wanted (and had) to be certain long before launching new products that these would find acceptance among potential customers. The processes developed for this purpose are finding increasing application for both products (hardware) and software (interfaces).

Target Group Determination through Milieus No methodological expense is spared to determine the potential user groups of new products. Traditional socio-demographic characteristics (age, education, gender, income, and place of residence) have become largely irrelevant, so now the point is to determine and categorize the habits of the target groups (which indeed crosscut classical characteristics). In his work of cultural sociology, *Erlebniswelten* (Worlds of Experience), Gerhard Schulze (1992) combined such lifeworlds into what he called "milieus" (↗ p. 230).

Sinus Sociovision has performed broad-based social science research on our contemporary lifeworld since the early 1980s. Since then the *Sinus Milieus* have been published at regular intervals, presenting not only the fundamental value orientations of our society, but also our attitudes toward work, family, leisure time, money, and consumption. These more general observations are bolstered by qualitative assertions, making reliable data available to staff in product development, marketing, and design as to which values are shared by the respective milieus (i.e., the potential target groups for new products). Of particular interest here are the qualitative changes over the course of time. Milieu research has become increasingly international: today milieu data are available for numerous countries in Europe, but also for the United States (since 1997) and Russia (since 1999).

The great relevance of these methods for design in particular led Sinus to develop "videre" (virtual design research) and apply it in practice. This is a package of methods for exploring and assessing lifeworlds. Products that do not yet exist in reality can be tested on and with potential users using visualization technologies ("virtual prototyping"). In connection with milieus their validity can thus be verified long before manufacturing or product launch.

Product Clinics The objective of this method is to present new products to a series of test subjects (potential buyers) and to question them from various perspectives. This can be done using sketches or renderings, preliminary or final models, or real or virtual prototypes. The questions asked must be designed scientifically so that the results can be verified and compared. Product clinics can produce reliable results using even relatively small random samples (of five to eight subjects), as long as they are carefully pre-selected. The financial benefits of such an economical method are obvious.

Different batteries of questions can be developed for specific clinics to provide the information required at the given development stage of the project. Such questions may concern the market prospects of a product, what distinguishes it from competing products, or how well it fits into the subject's sphere

Improvisationsmaschine
Annika Frye, HfG Offenbach (2012)

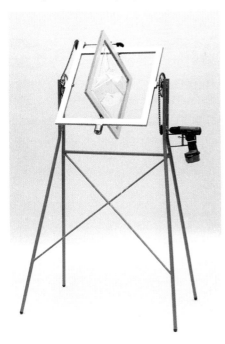

of life. Indirect associations evoked by a design, expected image transfers, and any analogies to other products that occur to the subject are all integrated into the evaluation of a design. Subjective reactions, impressions of material and surface qualities, smells, and other impressions rendered by test subjects are of great importance for the further development of the product (Heß 1997). The automobile sector relies particularly heavily on product clinics, not least because of the enormous cost of development and the risks associated with market launch.

One relevant aspect of product clinics is that designs must be judged in their respective (future) contexts. These should be generated as a part of the design process in order to obtain adequate statements from the test subjects.

Usability Another set of comprehensive test procedures developed to test software concepts before their market launch is subsumed under the concept of usability. Here, too, even with relatively small groups of test subjects, fast and reliable findings can be obtained about the reactions to the interfaces through which users interact with and navigate through software, about the understandability of the specific solutions, and about the software's potential for intuitive operation (look and feel). The EN ISO standard 9241-11 sets the benchmark for the most important aspects of usability on an international level.

Two new topics that escape strictly scientific evaluation methods have taken on new importance. First is the issue of the usefulness of applications, that is, how much learning and training are needed to use the software, and how high the effective benefit of its use is in comparison. The second addresses the "joy of use," the emotional side of interface design: today software also has to be fun.

Annika Frye (www.designimprovisation.com) investigates completely new design methods in her dissertation at the Offenbach School of Design. She describes the improvizations applied in (series and one-off) design processes and develops experimental production machines with which new semantic product forms can be generated.

Recourse to empirical methods has increased the relevance and promise of design for industrial applications. Decisions about new concepts no longer come from "gut feelings," but can be grounded in the natural and human sciences. As a consequence, today design can hold its own against other scientific disciplines.

Design and Theory

129   The Information Aesthetics Approach

130   The Influence of Critical Theory

131   On the Road to Disciplinary Design Theory

135   Aspects of a Disciplinary Design Theory

148   On the Communicative Function of Design

154   The Formal Aesthetic Functions

164   The Marking Functions

169   The Symbolic Functions

177   From Product Language to Product Semantics

Parallel to the development of design methodology, various attempts were made in the 1970s to develop and formulate a theory of design with binding force for the discipline. While design methodology always had the declared goal of explaining the process of design itself and providing the necessary tools to optimize that process, the objective of design theory is more vague. Certainly one important task would be to use hypotheses or experiences to obtain the knowledge on which to base the discipline's general framework – knowledge that addresses the questions of what design can do, what it should do, and what it wants to do.

Two different types of approach to theory can be taken: deductive or inductive, from the outside-in or from the inside-out. A deductive perspective looks to all the other subjects taught at universities, selecting those that appear relevant in a process akin to quarrying. This method was practiced at HfG Ulm (↗ p. 37f). The inductive alternative means analyzing design processes to ascertain which academic disciplines could be relevant.

In the 1970s the Offenbach School of Design came down firmly for the latter, at a time when most design programs (worldwide) went for the former (their curricula accordingly read like a distillation of the lecture plan of an entire university). Thilo Schwer, who meticulously traces the genesis of the theory of product language at the Offenbach School of Design (Schwer 2014), reminds us that the concept of design was formulated as narrowly as possible there: the depth rather than scope of the problem was uppermost in the 1970s.

It is incontrovertible that medicine makes a great contribution to the good of humanity. But progress in the discipline also means generating knowledge at increasing detail and precision, to be used to develop more effective methods of treatment.

In design it is often the exact opposite. Ever larger projects are initiated, hoping to help make the world a better place. Unfortunately the promise generally remains unfulfilled, because the devil lies (scientifically) in the detail. In this connection Martin Gessmann (2014) recalls a sentence of Martin Heidegger's: "He who thinks great thoughts is bound to make enormous mistakes"; a statement that can certainly be applied to design.

It is these two approaches that determine theory development in design. This is also confirmed by Michael Erlhoff's *Theorie des Designs* (Theory of design; 2013), which represents more or less a guided tour of the history of ideas: from Kant through Hegel, Freud, the Dadaist Schwitters, Adorno, Bloch, Eco, Foucault, and Luhmann to Sloterdijk, among many others. However, such an approach has no consequences for the practice of design (at least, of product design) (Bauer 2014).

Another problem is that in the sciences it is absolutely normal and productive to be continuously working on and adapting your research questions. In design, on the other hand, it would seem as though we just invent the wheel over and over again. As a consequence much of what we do remains simply amateurish and there is little or no real progress in the discipline. Not least for this reason, design lacks recognition in academia (see www.mapofscience. com) and is regarded in some quarters as arbitrary or even trivial.

Leaving aside all the enthusiastic inter-, meta-, multi-, and transdisciplinary proclamations, a different approach must be mentioned, which is actually more common – and definitely successful – in academia. I am referring to co-evolution. This concept from evolutionary biology describes the interrelationship and/or mutual adaptation of two or more closely interacting species. The sociologist Manfred Faßler applies the same term to social questions, calling his research program "co-evolutionary anthropology." Applied to the organization of life (and thus also to design), it implies that various disciplines, such as engineering and computer science, act jointly to generate new forms of life and interaction. Then new products can emerge to serve the new forms of self-organization. For Faßler it is not the forms, but the formative praxes that increasingly determine our lives and habits. And that is one place where new thinking in design could begin. The Offenbach software designer Wolfgang Henseler argues in this connection that design must not restrict itself to solving formal and aesthetic problems, but must also keep in mind the conditions and consequences of the designing of a product (Weinberg, 2014).

Due to the multiplicity of interactions involved in design, creating a theory of design with aesthetics at its core would certainly not have been sufficient. Methodologists focused instead on technological, socioeconomic, ecological, and even political categories as they attempted to ground the discipline and provide it with academic legitimacy.

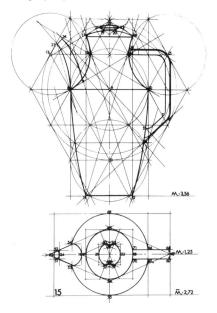

The Information Aesthetics Approach

At the Ulm School of Design, ideas from information theory were applied to design practice. The works of Max Bense and Abraham A. Moles (1965) exerted a particular fascination, as they appeared to show possibilities for making aesthetics measurable.

Rolf Garnich (1968) subtitled his dissertation published during this period "A General Mathematical Method for the Objective Description of Aesthetic Conditions in the Analytical Process and for Generative Design in the Synthetic Process of Design Objects." Today, this work's attempt to pin down the aesthetic dimension of coffee pots seems rather exotic.

In architecture, too, the information theory approach enjoyed great resonance. Looking at aesthetic problems from this perspective was the object of a far-reaching work by Manfred Kiemle (1967). It remained up to Siegfried Maser (1970) from the Bense School in Stuttgart to publish what was probably the conclusive work on this topic, *Numerische Ästhetik* (Numerical aesthetics).

Nevertheless it took a long time for methodologists to dismiss the idea of applying information theory to design. The idea that aesthetic matters could be judged with Cartesian rigor simply proved too seductive. A full ten years after this movement peaked, the former design college instructor Herbert Ohl (1977), who had since been appointed Technical Director of the Rat für Formgebung (Council for Design) stated triumphantly that, "design has become measurable" (1977). By then, however, the critique of functionalism and the discussion about ecology had advanced to the point where such a statement could be regarded as little more than a relic from design's frivolous youth.

The Influence of Critical Theory

In the wake of the student movement and socially critical works from the Frankfurt School, design, too, came under attack at the end of the 1960s. As the profession was not yet firmly established, it was an easy target for pithy slogans: "There are professions which do more damage than that of the designer. But not very many. Actually, only one profession is even more questionable: that of the advertiser. Convincing people to buy superfluous things with money they do not have, only to impress others, is probably the shabbiest way to make a living these days" (Papanek 1972).

Designers, too, read the works of Theodor W. Adorno, Max Horkheimer, and Herbert Marcuse, and went on to publish contributions on the social function of their discipline. The diploma theses at the Ulm School of Design by Michael Klar in 1968 and Thomas Kuby in 1969 were the first to emerge out of the far-reaching critique of the aesthetics of commodities (Haug 1971).

A major event for design was the founding of the IDZ Berlin (Internationales Design Zentrum), which opened with the publication of *design? Umwelt wird in Frage gestellt* (design? Questioning the environment) (Berlin 1970). Containing over forty papers by various authors, this volume discussed the role of design in society as a whole and thus the context for its critique. Here Haug characterized design as follows: "In a capitalist environment, design takes on a function comparable to that of the Red Cross in times of war. It attends to a few – never the worst – wounds inflicted by capitalism. It works cosmetically in a few places and keeps up spirits, thus lengthening capitalism as the Red Cross lengthens war" (Haug 1970).

Thanks to positions like those advocated by Haug (1970, 1971, 1972, 1986), design eventually succumbed to paralysis. Design nihilism was the consequence, especially at the design schools, and has perpetuated the deep rift that remains between design theory and practice in the minds of many to this day (Bürdek 2002). This point of departure also precluded any emancipative approach. The only alternative remaining was the illusion that producing analyses of society would help the working class prepare for class struggle.

On the Road to Disciplinary Design Theory

Integrating discussions about design theory into the general social discourse, however, encouraged new approaches as well. These were developed in particular at the Ulm Institute for Environmental Planning. Under the title *The Dialectics of Design,* Jochen Gros (1971) published a number of theses advocating a reorientation away from the traditional principle of purity of form (functionalism) toward a principle of primacy of form (expanded functionalism). His integration of psychological aspects into the concept of design had a profound impact on the way design was regarded.

Nevertheless, the idea that design theory should acquire and advance the specific technical knowledge required for the discipline took shape only gradually. While the superstructure, that is, the conditions of society, must be investigated in an interdisciplinary manner, design theory must contribute something specific, perhaps a precise technical language with which to describe the knowledge of the discipline. Specialized disciplinary expertise is essential to interdisciplinary collaboration.

Siegfried Maser played an important role in this, creating for the first time the necessary prerequisites for scientific theory (1972, 1976) (↗ p. 111 f). To illustrate his approach to science theory he coined the concepts of "knowers" and "doers." Knowers of a field are those capable of putting together as much knowledge as possible to work toward a concrete solution to a problem. Thus, a knower must have as much knowledge as possible about as many areas as possible. The doer, on the other hand, is a specialist in the classic sense. He knows his own discipline (physics, chemistry, technology, marketing, or design) as completely as possible and is consulted to solve actual problems during the development process.

This distinction can become essential in design practice. While the designer is the doer responsible for all creative, communicative aspects of products, he is a knower in questions of ergonomics, manufacturing, and calculation, areas in which there are numerous other specialists.

The doer–knower idea was developed further from the mid-1970s, especially at the Offenbach School of Design. In the 1980s several publications appeared on the subject (Fischer and Mikosch 1984; Gros 1983, 1987), which long remained isolated in the field of design, but nevertheless received a lively reception among those involved in product development (design, economics, ecology, technology), especially in the business sphere.

Nevertheless, designers and design institutions still like to – or at least claim to – regard themselves as "do-gooders," and miss no opportunity to demonstrate this at international congresses like those of the ICSID (International Council of Societies of Industrial Design). Cape Town, as World Design Capital in 2014, tried to address urgent social, economic, infrastructure, planning, and education problems with the help of design (Bartels 2014). Looking more closely at the practice often reveals yawning gaps between claims and reality, however in the great majority of cases, designers work only on objects – and not on the whole world.

As the concept of core competency became accepted in the management schools of the 1990s (Prahalad and Hamel 1992; Boos and Jarmai 1994), design theory, too, hesitantly sought a new orientation. The hymn of interdisciplinary, transdisciplinary, and multidisciplinary design was still sung with enthusiasm, but increasingly it became accepted that its words were little more than rhetoric. For instance, the English definition of the prefix "inter-" is "between or among; mutually or together." This "between" is thus a space, emptiness, something that definitely should not be determined by design: "The point is rather to bring specific qualifications into such projects – in this case, emphasizing the procedural alone is truly not sufficient" (Bürdek 1997b).

In the second half of the 1990s a broad discourse began debating whether design had become established enough as a discipline to permit doctoral students to write dissertations on topics in the field of design. A discussion ensued about the "scholarliness" of design.

While exact figures are unavailable, there are estimated to be between 150 and 450 doctoral programs worldwide; Germany alone has about twenty.

At international conferences, scholars of design took stock of the state of the art, while at the same time encouraging the areas of research and development to create global networks. Voluminous proceedings reflected a quite representative picture of current design theory and research. Important conferences were held during the late 1990s and early 2000s:

Doctoral Education in Design, Ohio State University, Columbus, Ohio, 1998

Design plus Research, Politecnico di Milano, Italy, 2000

Doctoral Education in Design: Foundations for the Future, La Clusaz, France, 2000

International Symposium on Design Science, Fifth Asian Design Conference, Seoul, South Korea, 2001

Integration of Knowledge, Kansei, and Industrial Power. Sixth Asian Design Conference and *Third Doctoral Education in Design,* Tsukuba, Japan 2003

In the meantime almost all design research conferences have established a section for doctoral presentations, in order to offer the numerous PhD candidates an opportunity to report on their research work. At the conference of the Design Research Society in June 2014 in Umeå (Sweden) there were about 370 participants, illustrating the boom in this field.

In Seoul, the English design methodologist Nigel Cross (2001) drew an interesting conclusion that aptly characterizes the development of design. He claimed that, in hindsight, paradigmatic changes can be detected in forty-year cycles:

In the 1920s scientific findings were integrated into design training for the first time (Bauhaus).

The 1960s were the heyday of design methodology (England, Ulm School of Design, United States), and can be called the era of scientific design.

In the 2000s the emphasis has been on enhancing design's profile as an independent discipline.

Cross's speech initiated an international debate, not least about design's standing in academia as compared with other (scientific) disciplines. It was thought that attaining the same status as other disciplines would liberate design from the taint of charlatanism and ensure its acceptance by the scientific community. The only way it can establish itself there is to become a self-reliant discipline that develops independent knowledge and is capable of communicating with other disciplines. The requisite body of knowledge is just starting to emerge: "Design as a discipline, rather than design as a science. This discipline seeks to develop domain-independent approaches to theory and research in design. The underlying axiom of this discipline is that there are forms of knowledge peculiar to the awareness and ability of a designer, independent of the different professional domains of design practice" (Cross 2001).

In future it will become increasingly important to develop and communicate design knowledge both vertically (within the discipline) and horizontally (between disciplines). At the first Doctoral Design Conference in Columbus, Ohio in 1998, Alain Findeli (University of Montreal, Canada) pointed out that design knowledge is already being transferred to other disciplines such as engineering sciences, marketing, communication sciences, and education. The next logical step is then to lay down precisely what constitutes design knowledge.

At the Second Design Research Symposium held by the Swiss Design Network at HGK Zürich sociologist Franz Schultheis presented a number of important ideas. Under the title "Disciplining Design" (2005) he pointed out that every new scientific discipline passes through a long and arduous process of establishment, acceptance, and institutionalization, in short: "disciplining." To draw upon a comparison, we can trace the history of medicine back over millennia to prehistoric times, but not until the nineteenth century did the application of scientific methods liberate healing from the quackery of laying-on of hands, bloodletting, and humoral pathology. In the twentieth century medicine became a recognized science, and today it possesses an enormous variety of specialisms. But it was not until the development of medical diagnostics (by technical, biological, or chemical means) that it was able to establish itself as a highly respected discipline. Today it is a high-tech science par excellence (Bürdek 2011).

In medicine we also see what interdisciplinarity really means. The bundling of competence benefits patients most of all, because practicing physicians can tap the knowledge of a major center and consult with specialists directly. Diagnosis and therapy thus no longer stop at the hospital gates. One enlightening example is a medical center that brings together all the disciplines involved in treating conditions of the head: eyes, ears, nose, throat, jaw, and face. Especially when operating at the boundaries of the disciplines, interdisciplinary cooperation ensures optimal results (Klinikum-Stuttgart 2012).

It should be obvious how far the world of design still remains from such achievements. However enthusiastically propagated, the collaboration of product designers, graphic designers, and artists hardly lives up to the label of interdisciplinarity. Hans Ulrich Reck (1996) says it how it is: "Design is never going to reach a point where the consistent application of scientific findings will on its own produce perfect design. Too many factors remain unresearched. And even if all the design factors are rationally explained, the enormous volume of information could at the moment only be handled intuitively. Nonetheless, industrial design today is only at the point medicine reached five hundred years ago. We must finally leave the era of quacks and barbers behind us and learn to build our work on solid and comprehensible arguments."

Aspects of a Disciplinary Design Theory

The discourse about the need to develop design theory puts forward various views about how this theory should be constructed: as an interdisciplinary, a multidisciplinary, or even as a transdisciplinary theory. Rarely does anyone mention that a design theory could also be disciplinary. Perhaps the apologists of design theory have so little faith in their own contributions (where they are expected to be authorities) that they must always lean on other disciplines (where they need only be knowledgeable). Moreover, interdisciplinarity (i.e., collaboration between various disciplines) is all the rage these days, not least because of the increasing complexity of problem-solving in which design plays a role.

Design has always had a hard time developing a specific basis from which to reach out to other disciplines. There is no conceivable reason for this, as the much lauded interdisciplinarity cannot come into its own unless individual disciplines work together. Lutz Göbel's observation (1992) that companies increasingly need neither specialists (who know a lot about a little), nor generalists (who know a little about a lot), but rather integralists (people who have a good overview of various disciplines with deeper knowledge in at least one area) is relevant for design as well. Integralists must be especially capable of thinking about and acting on issues in their entirety.

As doctoral design programs were developed and design became increasingly established in the upper echelons of private industry (keyword: design management), it became necessary to identify expertise in the field and to provide for a massive increase in personnel. Carnegie Mellon University succeeded in putting through an initiative to orient its doctoral program so that the graduates carried the title of "stewards of the disciplines" (see next page) (Golde and Walker 2001).

"'Steward of a discipline'

We believe that the purpose of Ph. D. training should be the creation of ‚stewards of the discipline'. The degree should signal a high level of accomplishment in three facets of the discipline: Generation, Conservation and Transformation. The Ph. D. holder should be capable of generating new knowledge and defending knowledge claims against challenges and criticism; of conserving the most important ideas and findings that are a legacy of past and current work; and of transforming knowledge that has been generated and conserved into powerful pedagogies of engagement, understanding and application. Moreover, a steward should understand how the discipline fits into the intellectual landscape, have a respectful understanding of the questions and paradigms of other disciplines, and understand how their discipline can speak to important questions.

The formulation of stewardship is discipline-specific. What it means to be a steward of chemistry may in some measure be different than in English or mathematics. Similarly, the process for creating stewards may differ by discipline. We are committed to locating this initiative in the context of each discipline, recognizing that there will be discipline-specific lessons as well as cross-disciplinary insights to be gained."

All of this appears to be fairly new for design, although in the early 1970s, for instance, at the Offenbach School of Design, work with the concept of "sensual functions" was to launch a disciplinary discourse on design (Gros 1976). The double coding of the word "sensual," meaning "perceptible (by the senses)" and, at the same time, "sensuous" (thus similar to the Kantian concept of the "unity of reason") was, however, either not understood correctly or even deliberately misunderstood. It was too tempting to follow the direct path from "sensuality" to sensual-erotic design, which certainly had its charm after the long predominant rigidity of morose German functionalism, but the mere fact that these concepts cannot be readily translated into all other languages condemned it to failure.

Therefore at the beginning of the 1980s the concept of sensual functions was replaced by that of product language. The new reflection on semiotics which took place at this time – perhaps inspired by Charles Jencks's *The Language of Post-Modern Architecture* (1977) – constituted an interesting parallel.

A few years earlier Gert Selle introduced the term of "product language" into the design discourse (1973), interestingly citing the work of an economist – Theodor Ellinger (1966) – who has remained largely unknown in design circles.

Ellinger wrote: "One can speak of a product language to the extent that design objects are not only functional, but also informational" (see also Bürdek 2012). In that sense the term is surely right and proper.

If design one day becomes anchored as an independent academic discipline, the sociologist Franz Schultheis wrote in 2005, enduring struggles over the legitimate definition of "design" in teaching and research must be expected. While there may still be objections, that struggle appears today – ten years later – to have been decided. In the international design discourse, too, there is broad consensus that the topics of product language and product semantics belong to the core competencies of design.

Dagmar Steffen, who was involved in developing product language (2000), notes in her Wuppertal dissertation (2011), that even theoreticians who are critical of these approaches no longer question the position artifacts currently enjoy as signifiers and communication media (semiotics). She quotes Wolfgang Jonas (1994): "'Product semantics' would currently appear to be a widely accepted and still rather vibrant theory model in design... . It is undeniable that products (whether designed or not designed, with 'functional' or 'product language' design) increasingly and often overwhelmingly possess communicative functions... . In particular, things become means of language and understanding in the social environment. They convey statements about their users, their status, and their understanding of their roles."

Today that is accepted in both research and practice. In her investigation of "industrial design as a means of socioeconomic value creation" (according to the subtitle), Sandra Hirsch (2014) names product language as a significant factor in the development of industrial products. Design-driven innovation "describes the development of pioneering prospective meanings whose possibilities are communicated via a corresponding product language."

In his review of the early years at Apple, Hartmut Esslinger (2014) uses the term design language, which he describes as a "visual system" (↗ p. 150). He sees it as a core strategic element for the corporation: "The complexity of the technology of a product also defines the extent of its design language." The point here is to refine the product language in a company-specific strategy. Under Dieter Rams, for example, Braun consistently improved its strategy for designing individual products (user-oriented using minimal means) and by that route secured a unique market position.

The above shows clearly that, on the one hand, a scientific design theory must be founded in the humanities. On the other hand, the disciplinary nature of such a theory must be emphasized. Design, too, must define its specific competence, its own body of knowledge – and thus its own theory.

Responding to the question of how a science is actually characterized, Siegfried Maser (1972) listed three important categories: goal, object, and method. Although in the past design had not claimed to be a science in and of itself, these categories are certainly suitable as guides in sketching a disciplinary design theory.

The Goal The goal is to develop a technical language; that is, concepts and propositions are to be formulated so that they have general validity for the entire discipline.

The Object The object is what is special to a discipline. In design this means questions of form and context or form and meaning, which can be described by the concept of communicative function.

The Method The method is located in the sphere of the humanities, as neither the methods of natural science nor those of other formal sciences allow the essence of communication to be described in terms specific to design.

Language – or communicative action – was once designated by Jürgen Habermas (1985) as the "key to constructing theory," which better allowed us to deal with the capricious structures of the lifeworld. Reality is imparted and explained through language, and this also holds true for design. A further analogy is significant here: language is not uniform; there are different languages and within them more dialects and sociolects exist. Language is a many-layered entity that can describe complicated and complex facts. At the same time, each language has rules of usage. Moreover, over the course of its development, each language becomes increasingly differentiated, providing even more possibilities to describe phenomena and thus contributing to their distinction. This is just as true for the language of products. Communication develops through a continuous process of exchange, which is based in turn on perpetually new "agreements" (conventions). The products do not speak in and of themselves, but they come to speak through language.

In her dissertation at the Offenbach School of Design, Sandra Groll expands the communication theory approach in design into a societal one: "It might appear disconcerting to examine the design of lifeworld objects through the concept of communication rather than use. This quickly generates a sense of comprehending design in its social function as a pure means of distinction, with which individual identities visualize their social aspects" (Groll 2014). What this means is that products in social communication contexts also communicate back, in the sense of providing information about their users. The so-called "Apple Community" is a case in point.

The following examples will illustrate how the disciplinary approach to design theory has proven to be valid globally – and particularly successful, even in practice.

The Information Function of the Product

Wilhelm Vershofen's statement (1939) that products have both basic and supplementary uses set the general course for the science of business administration from a very early date. This orientation also proved sound for design. The industrial engineer Theodor Ellinger (1966) proceeded in this direction to develop the concept of product information, which was defined as a product's ability to communicate information about itself actively in the market: "The product can possess a multi-layered, perhaps even symbolic language, which is far more comprehensive than normal verbal language." To describe this, Ellinger also introduces the concept of product language, which he describes as follows: "Product language includes very heterogeneous forms of expression such as dimension, form, structure of the physical surface, movement, quality of material, means of fulfilling function, colors, and the graphic design of the surface, sounds and tones, taste, smell, temperature, packaging, and resistance to external influences. All of this information has a strong effect – positive or negative – on the potential buyer."

This was indeed quite a broad description, when one considers that aspects such as sound design (Langenmaier 1993), the olfactory characteristics of products, or even "haptic design" (Strassmann 2003) have become serious topics only in recent years. The automobile industry, in particular, invests significant sums to research and develop these areas, as they represent important characteristics for the branding of the company. The door of a Daimler vehicle must close quite differently from one from BMW, and even the motors must be clearly distinct acoustically. As a result, "semantic added value" is granted the utmost attention, especially in the automotive industry. Thus, Daimler runs a research center in Berlin that concerns itself exclusively with the emotional sensations of the vehicle's occupants: their sensory perception while clicking switches, the textures of the materials used in the interior, the influence of telematic (location) systems – the emotional worlds of the users are investigated empirically (HTR 2003), and the findings obtained from this study flow into the next new model.

In general, Ellinger's thoughts appear quite up-to-date, for instance on the triangular relationship between the poles of manufacturer, product sold, and potential buyer, or the differentiation of product information into existential, origination, and quality information, because they do in fact describe much of what is also dealt with in the debates about branding. Collectively, these debates are about corporate identity, which is also generated and imparted through design.

Design as an Everyday Language

Drawing explicitly on Ellinger's ideas about product language (↗ p. 136), Gert Selle argued in 1973 that design had become an everyday language. He was referring, in particular, to the societal function that increasingly falls to products. Signals are emitted through products, signals about the users (e.g., their status), and also about the producers of these objects. He regarded product-language codification as an important future task of design and advocated that it be researched scientifically: "For language is a means of interpreting reality, and product language provides the consumer with opportunities to identify with the product and its linguistically proposed level of reality, which often appears irrational and dreamlike." However, for Selle, it is also quite apparent that such a product language approach is not affirmative, but to be pursued critically; the point is to reveal the knowledge interests located behind the "design of certain product languages" and to communicate them, too. In this light, he subsumed design under the phenomenon of mass communication, which was quite a farsighted position at the time.

Ultimately it has taken about forty years for this approach to engender a broader academic consensus. Claudia Mareis (2014) writes: "The Offenbach approach marked a paradigm shift within the design theory of the post-war era and stands for the displacement of interest from the functionality of design artefacts to their dimension of meaning and symbolism." And now the cultural sciences in particular have recognized that design and the associated product languages are a field for relevant research (Bürdek, 2014).

The Meaning of Things

In the 1970s two economists in the United States performed empirical studies about the home, analyzing the relations between residents and their objects in particular. This study (Csikszentmihalyi and Rochberg-Halton 1989) was practically ignored in the field of design, although its authors picked up not only on the studies of the psychosocial meanings of things carried out by the French anthropologists (Claude Lévi-Strauss) and structuralists (Roland Barthes), but also by semiotics and social ecology. In contrast to socialization (the process of an individual taking his or her place in society), they coined the concept of "cultivation," which designates the process of a person confronting things (products) and appropriating them: "The self is enriched and expanded through the symbolic acceptance of material reality, indeed, it has no identity at all until this happens. The subsequent feedback of the external signs is imperative both for the development of the self and for the constitution of society" (Lang 1989).

Csikszentmihalyi and Rochberg-Halton designate things as units of information that are perceived and represented in a person's consciousness. From the semiotic perspective, these are signs, whose triadic relation has already been discussed in greater detail (↗ p. 86). They also state that the objects surrounding us are not merely tools, but in fact constitute the frame of reference for our experiences, thus making an essential contribution to the way we structure ourselves. The communication science concept of "connectivity" is also suitable in this context: experiences (conventions) also shape the way we deal with products. The helplessness that often befalls us at ticket machines for public transport systems in strange cities, for instance, has to do with lack of experience, which makes us even more confused. It is hardly necessary to emphasize again that cultural differences are relevant in such cases. The field of "cultural studies" attempts to compensate for these very shortcomings, but has yet to be extended effectively to design.

With reference to the home, it is apparent that the things with which people surround themselves may at least potentially reflect their inner lives. The home becomes the mirror of the personality. In the 1980s, at the latest, the home became a status symbol, replacing the automobile for large sectors of the population. The interior takes on the role of contributing to the stabilization of the social order through hierarchical differentiation. Furniture designs illustrate this vividly: be they IKEA, Bauhaus classics, Italian *bel design,* new German design, or the avant-garde of the present, objects are loaded with so much semantic baggage that for the most part their only remaining function is to serve as orientation aids in the context of the larger society.

The Munich School of Eugen Leitherer

While teaching at the University of Munich, Eugen Leitherer investigated industrial design as a scientific object (1991). Methodologically speaking, he performed this study on the level of sensory perception. On the definition of design he writes, "Industrial design thus shapes particularly perceptible qualities of products which can be subjected to evaluation," an observation that is certainly specific and perhaps even disciplinary, but also draws attention to critical issues: "Giving form to industrial products as designers do – that is, concretely determining their groups of qualities and especially their external appearance, their aesthetic-cultural quality – is an extremely risky matter."

In order to specify what is disciplinary in design, Leitherer refers to the developments of linguistic philosophy (Ferdinand de Saussure, Karl Bühler, and others) and utilizes the concept of product language in the classic semiotic sense:

on the syntactic level, as the language of the signals or their relations among each other,

on the semantic level, as the meaning of the signs for their recipients, and

on the pragmatic level, as the language of the sign users and their intentions.

"Design's task is to group these elements such that they 'express,' impart messages, or more precisely: 'talk'." Leitherer attempted to produce at least an initial sketch of the basics for a "linguistic work of product language" that built on the foundations of Gestalt theory.

Also worth mentioning here are the dissertations of his students Hans Jürgen Escherle (1986), and especially Sibylle Kicherer (1987), who commented extensively on the product language approach, but also presented important arguments about how product design could become effective in the company strategies of corporate design or design management. She described the communication between product, user, and company as the disciplinary core of design.

The Cologne School of Udo Koppelmann

Udo Koppelmann, who teaches business management at the University of Cologne, has been concerned with the interactions between design and economics since the 1970s. He builds on Vershofen's concepts of the basic and supplementary uses of products and elaborates the more up-to-date distinction between "services in kind" and "expected services" (Koppelmann 1978).

In a fundamental discourse, Koppelmann's approaches were compared with the product language approach in terms of terminology, semantics, and content (Bürdek and Gros, 1978). Here the parallels are quite clear between services in kind and expected services on the one hand, and between practical and semiotic (product language) functions on the other. Koppelmann focused his remarks on the "means of design," which he differentiated into elementary means like fabrics, materials, shapes, colors, and signs, and complex means like principles of function and construction, historical principles of problem solving, and product parts. Building on this theoretical foundation, numerous dissertations originated in the "Koppelmann School" over a period of around twenty years, all of which concerned issues of design and thus must be counted as part of the disciplinary body of knowledge of design. Worth mentioning here are the works by Volkhard Dörner (1976), A. Friedrich-Liebenberg (1976), Heinz Schmitz-Maibauer (1976), Holger Hase (1989), and Jana-Maria Lehnhardt (1996), as well as Patrick Reinmöller's work *Produktsprache. Verständlichkeit des Umgangs mit Produkten durch Produktgestaltung* (1995). At the time this was probably the most painstaking contribution to the construction of a disciplinary theory in design.

Products as Messages

The Austrian psychologist Helene Karmasin published a far-reaching work on the topic of *products as messages* (1993), linking aspects of psychology (cognitive and linguistic), sociology, cultural studies, and communication sciences (semiotics) to develop a quite remarkable and highly original work. Her central thesis is the statement that what makes products and services "interesting and distinguishable on the market, 'unique,' is actually their meaning, their 'semantic added value'." For Karmasin, this meaning is imparted by signs and sign systems. From this she derived the prognosis that the success of new products would lie increasingly in the area of "sign management." The scientific theory upon which this is based can be found in semiotics.

Communication can be performed with products, and the combination of various single products results in a communication mix that can be regarded as a construct of meaning (connotation), and which can be understood (denoted) by different social groups. This describes precisely the current approach in design, aside from its omission of the important principle of connectibility.

In a further paper Karmasin (1998) made clear which methods can be used to describe cultures adequately, referring back to the cultural theory developed by Mary Douglas (1973, 1992). She describes four lifestyles of potential relevance to product design: individualistic, hierarchical, egalitarian, and isolationist. These variants may serve as the basis for design strategies.

Karmasin makes it clear that products should be seen not only in terms of satisfying needs and maximizing individual utility, but predominantly as means of communication. In other words, she draws another analogy to the communicative function of design. Karmasin describes a number of cultures – the hierarchical, the individual, the egalitarian, and the fatalistic – and derives from them different design concepts (for a detailed description of her methodology, see Karmasin 1997).

Three Scandinavian Contributions

Carl Eric Linn, a Swedish corporate consultant who worked both in product development and in marketing, published an extremely illuminating book (1992), which unfortunately was scarcely reviewed in the field of design. Linn proceeded from the assumption that products possess both material and non-material characteristics. He used the concept of the metaproduct to cover the entire range of non-material aspects like image, reputation, market niche, product positioning, and the distinctions between products, using a fitting metaphor: "The product in your hand is never the same as the product in your imagination." Also interesting in this case is that he shows how such factors as experiencing a product positively can annul the conventional price-demand relation. In other words: when the added value imparted by design is high enough, then a product will be bought for its own sake and not because of its practical functionality. The luxury automobiles that came on the market in the first decade of the twenty-first century, like the Maybach (Daimler), Bentley and Phaeton (Volkswagen), and Rolls-Royce (BMW), are vivid examples of how principles of image transfer are brought to bear. For Linn, too, the language of objects is a central impetus with which such mechanisms can be described and initiated: "An imperative demand on the functions of the product is that they be communicable. It must be possible to describe the product such that the listener understands what is meant." The task of design is brought down to the lowest common denominator: it must inform, communicate, and symbolize.

The Swede Rune Monö published a work called *Design for Product Understanding* (1997), whose subtitle designated it explicitly as a semiotic approach to product aesthetics. Monö refers to the works of such semioticians as Umberto Eco (1972), who had declared semiotics to be a universal cultural technique. Monö picks up on Linn's concept of the metaproduct, which he defines as the context behind the physical entity, including, for example, prejudices, status, nostalgia, and group belonging. His recourse to Gestalt theory (↗ p. 156 ff) refers to the shared foundation for a design theory and practice based on perception and language. Monö advocates a holistic approach; that is, he studies the effect of signs in acoustic, visual, sensory, olfactory, and tactile perspective in order to encompass all the various levels of product design. He, too, refers to Karl Bühler's linguistic theory (1931, 1965) as an important building block in a design theory and practice influenced by product language. His remarks on product semantics also connect directly to the works of Butter and Krippendorff (McCoy 1996).

With her dissertation *Products as Representations* (1995), Susann Vihma, an instructor at the UIAH in Helsinki, published an especially well-grounded study that must be regarded as one of the key contributions to the design theory of the 1990s. She proceeds from a semiotic basis (Barthes, Eco, Peirce) and discusses which signal-type effects emanate from products. In her first approach, Vihma also describes the syntactic, pragmatic, and semantic dimensions. On the basis of numerous "precedents," like irons, electric shavers, and telephone booths, she discusses their emblematic effects at great length. Her considerations, too, flow into a model in which design is understood as communication.

Vihma researched and developed "design semiotics" over a period of many years in Helsinki. Alongside product semantics and product language, this field is rightly entitled to a place as the third "school" of disciplinary design theory (Steffen 2011).

Two Dutch Contributions

Dutchman Andries van Onck studied at the Ulm School of Design at the beginning of the 1960s and then relocated to Italy; there he worked for Kartell, Olivetti, Zanussi, and a number of other companies. His deliberations, set down in *Design: il senso delle forme dei prodotti* (1994), result from theoretical studies and reflection on product examples; they are an excellent example of practice-based research in design. Van Onck dedicated a long chapter to the subject of "Una semiotica del design" (with reference to Eco, Barthes, R. Jacobsen, Lévi-Strauss, and Maldonado) and formulated a non-verbal product language. On the basis of manifold precedents from the history of twentieth-century design (including a number of his own designs) he presents a broad and practice-related spectrum. His considerations flowed into what he called an "attribution of meaning through products," which addresses what is probably the latest facet of the design theory discourse. Humans as symbol-generating beings employ their products today in an increasing variety of ways; rites and myths are determined through the respective product languages.

Finally, Wim Muller, an instructor at Delft University of Technology, published *Order and Meaning in Design* (2001), a standard work on the aspects of design discussed here. Influenced by a strong methodological background, which he developed over a period of many years at Delft, he concentrated on the creative aspects of designing. Beyond the material functions that all products possess, he is interested in the social and cultural values of design. Art theorist Ernst Gombrich's statement (1979) that form engenders order and meaning is an important point of departure. Muller, however, also picks up on the debate of the "form follows function" movement – which was presumed to be the disciplinary element of design well into the 1990s – or, in other words, the relationship between the form of the product, its function, and its use. He also confronts the debate about "sensual functions" at the Offenbach School of Design with the semiotic discourses of Umberto Eco, claiming that for some time now form has not followed function, but rather convention. What is required is no longer design knowledge about technology, but knowledge about the basics of behavioral sciences, the influences on user–product interaction. Muller therefore strongly advocates empirical research about the use of products in order to avoid conceptual errors in product development.

No Conclusion

All of the examples discussed here – which are by no means exhaustive – illustrate that in numerous countries a disciplinary design theory has indeed emerged, proceeding from similar theoretical points of departure to reach quite consistent results.

Since the transition from the twentieth to the twenty-first century, design has without doubt formed into an independent discipline with a respectable and disciplinary body of knowledge. Indeed, one could say design has grown up enough to be treated as an equal among other disciplines.

And the struggle of the camps and schools predicted by Franz Schultheis (↗ p. 137) has truly been decided: product language and product semantics represent the core of the disciplinary design theory. Claudia Mareis (2014) sees three fundamental aspects of design theory possessing special significance: product language, product semantics, and design rhetoric (visual/verbal rhetoric): "Different as these three approaches may be in detail, they are all rooted in language-based systems like semiotics, semantics, or rhetoric."

On the Communicative Function of Design

The concept of product language in the 1980s implied that design is concerned chiefly with human–object relations. This means that design knowledge focuses on the relationships between users and objects (and thus products and product systems, vehicles, interior designs, public design, technical products, etc.). Of particular importance here are the functions imparted by perception (i.e., those which are perceived through the human senses). Important progress has been made using semiotics as an explanatory model.

Today design is a phenomenon that can only be understood under technological, social, economic, ecological, and most of all cultural aspects. Human-object relations as originally discussed now play only a peripheral role. Design has become a "living socio-technical formation" (Faßler 2014); while the products themselves do not disappear, their practical use lessens, as digitalization and networking dramatically alter the way we relate to material things. And the processes surrounding the products also become ever more important, for example through new, local or networked technologies. Thus the communicative function of design increases as a whole.

Several Precursors

Among the pioneers of this approach was the American philosopher Susanne Langer. Along with Charles W. Morris, she was considered the most important representative of what was known as the semantic school of American aesthetics. In her work she picked up on the symbol theory of Ernst Cassirer, conceiving of art as a semiotic, or emblematic process. Langer described cultural expressions, language, rituals, and music as symbolic life expressions.

In her work *Philosophy in a New Key,* published in 1942, she distinguished between the basic concepts of "mark" and "symbol," which have become especially important for design. Marks in this sense are direct or unmediated signs, whereas symbols are indirect or mediated signs. Marks show the (past, present, or future) existence of a thing, an event, or a state of affairs. In her discussion, Susanne Langer differentiated further between natural and artificial marks. Wet streets are marks indicating that it has rained; the smell of smoke indicates the presence of fire; a scar is a mark for a previous wound. A whistle at the train station means that the train is about to depart; mourning dress means that someone has died. Between a mark and its object there is a logical relation, and an unambiguous relation. The mark is thus something that prompts an action, or even an agent that demands an action.

Symbols are a different case entirely. Langer regards them as instruments of thinking, which stand for something other than the object itself and refer to something beyond it. As Ernst Cassirer put it, they have "representative" character. Into this concept of symbol flow aspects like experience, intuition, values held, and cultural norms. It is important that symbols are not given by nature, but rather emerge from convention, through relevant social agreements and traditions. Another major contribution to design knowledge, which also led to the creation of new disciplinary instruments, came from Alfred Lorenzer's work on symbolic interactions (1970, 1974), which built on Sigmund Freud's psychology of the subconscious.

In his analysis of the aesthetic function, the linguist Jan Mukařovský proceeded from the assumption that aesthetics could be categorized among the social phenomena (Mukařovský 1970). Based on the linguistic (semiotic) approach, he postulated that the "concept of the beautiful," which had been the subject of aesthetics for millennia, must be replaced by the concept of function. He then proceeded from the phenomenological perspective to develop a general model of the typology of this concept: "According to our assumption, this is the typology of functions: two groups, namely the unmediated and the emblematic functions, which can be distinguished further; the unmediated into the practical functions and the theoretical function, the emblematic into the symbolic and the aesthetic function. We speak of the practical functions in the plural, but of the theoretical, symbolic, or aesthetic in the singular" (Mukařovský 1970).

A Model of Product Functions

Mukařovský understood the interactions among the individual functions as a dynamic process based on the principles of structuralism, whereas the division of product language into formal aesthetic, sign, and symbol functions in Gros's model (1983) eventually proved to be rather too restrictive.

This division built on Charles W. Morris's classical division of semiotics into syntax, semantics, and pragmatics, where syntax is the relationship between signs (grammar), semantics denotes relationships between signs and

Products and their contexts

```
                    ┌──────────────
                    │ services
                    ├──────────────
                    │ software
                    ├──────────────
                    │ hardware
 ┌──────────┐       ┌──────────┐        ┌──────────┐
 │ designer │       │ product  │        │   user   │
 └──────────┘       └──────────┘        └──────────┘
      ↑                                       ↑
                practical        product language
                functions        product semantics
                usage            meaning

            cultural, sociological, ethnological,
            technological, economical,
            ecological

                    contexts
```

their meanings, and pragmatics describes the relationship between signs and their users. The instructions for using objects (marking function) are also understood in these terms.

Critiques of Mukařovský's model focused either on its rigid separation of product language functions (known as the "Offenbach trinity" because of its propagation at the Offenbach School of Design), which makes no sense in practice, or on the model's autopoietic character, which fails to address the problematic relationship between form and context. The rapid emergence of new media and new fields of activity like strategic design, service design, and information design are opening up topics which require that the concepts be reinterpreted and developed further.

In 2012 I published a further-reaching proposal that at least represents a more up-to-date, more open, and more context-related discussion of the terminology of product language and would appear to make the "Offenbach trinity" obsolete.

From Product Language to Design Language

When the theory of product language was developed in the 1980s the emphasis was primarily on what were called human-object relations, in the sense of the interplay between product and user (form, handling, dimensions of meaning, etc.). In the tradition of functional design, that appeared to be the correct approach. With today's perspective looking less at individual products and instead increasingly regarding product design as a strategic value creation concept, this position has to be modified. In a contribution for *designaustria Mitteilungen* (Bürdek 2013), I show that it is the meanings that are ascribed to the products (in fact less by the companies that produce them than by the communities in which they are used). Today, successful products need to be desirable more than useful.

Here I build on the work of the philosopher Gernot Böhme (2001), who speaks of an "aestheticization of the real" (in other words of the world) and identifies this as an important economic factor in advanced capitalist economies. Böhme replaces the term "needs," which was so overused in the 1960s and 1970s (which were to be satisfied not least by designers) with "desire-needs" ("Begehrnisse"): "Desire-needs are needs that are heightened rather than satisfied through their fulfillment."

The electronics industry illustrates best what this means, with about one billion smartphones sold in 2014. The rapid succession of models with marginal functional improvements stokes global desire for the new. And the big players are not just Apple and Samsung, but increasingly manufacturers like HTC (Taiwan), Huawei, and Lenovo (China) and LG (South Korea), whose products differ only marginally in their product and design languages. The global sign "smartphone" stimulates desire-needs worldwide, with about half of them already sold in China, India, Latin America, and Africa.

On the New Relevance of Giving Form

Many of the often impressive attempts at enlisting design to explain the world, and indeed to change it, neglect a decisive influence on the discipline since it originated: giving form.

The Swiss Max Bill studied at the Bauhaus in Dessau. As an architect, graphic designer, artist, product designer, and author he has hugely influenced the discourses around design since the mid-twentieth century. He places the concept of "use" of buildings and products at the heart of his ideas, but sees their forms of expression – the *gestalt* – as a quasi-natural derivation: the "harmonious expression of the sum of all functions" (Bill 1956). Bill stands for a holistic approach in both architecture and product design. In both disciplines postmodernist usage of the word "design" has led to a watering down or even dissolution of the term (Bürdek 2012).

Although perception theory and Gestalt theory created important foundations in the 1930s, the concept of giving form is defined and used more broadly today. A discipline of design oriented on the postulate of form and context has focused significantly more strongly on studying the contexts than the forms. Indeed, one could almost believe that designers no longer need concern themselves with anything so trivial as giving form.

The philosopher and corporate consultant Bernhard von Mutius (2002, 2004) sees this quite differently. In a discussion with *form* magazine he outlined a new concept of design and the far-reaching perspectives it entails for design in the twenty-first century. First he advocated that material and non-material objects be put on an equal footing, so that hardware, software, and services all receive their due emphasis in the field of design. The central factor here is that the invisible (the abstract) can be made concrete (visible) through design. Mutius is also concerned with improving what Niklas Luhmann calls the "connectibility" of our communicative interactions. On the one hand, he refers to my thesis that design is also the "visualization of innovations" (Bürdek 1999), but on the other hand, he sees the necessity of getting "from the raw materials to the information," and thus to the subject of "knowledge designs."

Competency in design therefore means significantly more than giving things form. Bernhard von Mutius defines it as an entire spectrum of new topics like communication, creativity, second-order solutions, cooperation, net product, transformation, progress, globalization, polarity, synergy. For all of this, the point is to develop new languages of form that can do justice to the respective topics. In this case, design expertise could become a key competency for creatively resolving many technological, economic, and social problems of the present and future.

Generating pictures or images is indisputably a domain of design, and this is what comprises the new area of "imagineering" (↗ p. 243). This area aims to conceptualize possible futures, possible interactions, and also possible new products long before they are realized.

Bernhard von Mutius also uses Luhmann's concept of connectibility as a basis for assessing the qualities of non-material processes. As traditional frames – such as three-dimensional product design – are of little use today, it is time to ask how the new "qualities of design" should be defined and determined. A promising approach to answering this question is to pick up on the design discourses from the beginning of the twentieth century.

On Language in Design

Its enduring lack of discursivity still represents an aspect of design that should not be underestimated. Reporting about design is utterly inadequate, whether in the specialist world or in the mass media. For example, one international hotel chain writes: "Contemporary design with new interiors, creative ideas, and unique stylings. With the Ibis family almost any journey becomes a design experience: Ibis and Ibis Budget set new accents with the redesigned Avanzi lobbies, while Ibis Styles will surprise you with its unique design stories. You will be astonished" (Ibis 2014).

The great dilemma of design, its lack of a language, is one reason why there is so little serious acceptance of the discipline. Especially in interdisciplinary development projects, design displays glaring shortcomings: It has been unable to develop any discursive sovereignty because it has no terms of its own, with wealth of experience operating as the only currency (Stephan 2011). Design is still a long way from claiming a place in the academic canon. Forming a discipline is always also associated with forming a language (Maser 1972, 1976; Schultheis 2005, to name but two). Although there is a section for art and culture under the heading "humanities" in the Map of Science published by Dick Klavans and Kevin Boyack (2009) (a visualization of the global world of science and research), design simply does not feature. This highlights another case of the design's disconnect between self-perception and external perception.

Gui Bonsiepe (1992) discusses this phenomenon as follows: "What creates this crass discrepancy between the public life of the concept of design and its lack of theory and foundation? Why is design a less than earnest matter? The answer is simple: A rigorous design discourse is lacking. If we compare design with historically rooted activities and professions, we find that proper professions are based on specific discursive worlds with their own linguistic distinctions. A new medical student will learn about two thousand linguistic distinctions, known as human anatomy. Similarly the student of law or engineering. This is what distinguishes a specialist from a layperson. The achievements of the design professions are rather modest in comparison, which can be taken as an indication of lack of maturity."

The debate over product language since the 1980s has made a decisive contribution simply by establishing terms to describe the design properties of products. That said, their acceptance is in fact still rather limited. Instead of discourse, the media are full of froth when it comes to design. Whether the "tile design" or "the power of technology in sleek design" (Spiegel 2015), the road to a proper language of design is still a long and arduous one, even though practicable foundations do actually already exist.

The Formal Aesthetic Functions

The conceptual pair of shape and content has been used for many centuries to conduct discourses about the artistic (aesthetic) value and the material nature of a work. The twentieth century was characterized by a strong preoccupation with the way and manner in which artistic works emerge, and less with their values. The loss of meaning this entails was manifested similarly in architecture, in design, and in art. Aesthetic formalism (or "the aesthetics of form," in this scientific parlance) is clearly distinguished from "the aesthetics of content." The latter refers exclusively to the experience of the formal elements of sensory impressions. Rhythm, proportions, and harmony are important elements of artistic or creative works.

The formal aesthetic functions of products are those aspects that can be observed independent of their meaning. In semiotic terms, the issue here is the distinction between syntax and semantics. On the one hand, every language has rules and regulations about how signs (words and sentences) can be created and described. Applied to design, this means a grammar of design, with a syntax completely void of meaning. Not until they refer to practical functions (marking functions) or social contexts (symbolic functions) do signs take on their respective meanings in design; to what extent these meanings are then interpreted as intended cannot be definitively predicted or planned. Formalism, by contrast, is when formal devices (signs) are used indiscriminately and arbitrarily without any consideration of their meaning.

Early Perception Research

The foundations of formal aesthetics were laid in perception research, which enjoys a long-established tradition. Strictly speaking, here, too, the origins can be traced back to Aristotle, who designated the five senses as the foundation of perception.

In the eighteenth century the English philosopher George Berkeley (1685–1753) developed an independent theory of perception, in which he studied the human sense of sight and the individual components that condition it.

Decisive progress was not achieved until the nineteenth century, when Hermann von Helmholtz investigated the foundations of visual perception. For him perception was a two-step process: the starting point is sensations, whose quality and intensity are inborn and conditioned by the specific characteristics of the sensory organs. These sensations are signs that take on meaning only through associations (experiences) over the course of human development.

A further important foundation for the theory of perception was research on geometric optical illusions, the first fruits of which were published around the middle of the nineteenth century.

Pioneers of Gestalt Psychology

Wilhelm Wundt (1832–1920) is considered the founder of modern psychology, as he granted the discipline an autonomous object and method, and structured it according to the scientific model. He defined psychology as the science of inner and direct experience, which should be based on experiment and observation.

Objections to the application of scientific methods in psychology were raised by Theodor Lipps (1851 1914). He designated psychology the science of mental life, and argued that knowledge is founded on the principle of inner human experience. Lipps' work is closely connected to that of Wilhelm Dilthey (↗ p. 103), who also conceived of art and literature as expressions of life and sought to understand them in their essence. Especially important for Lipps were the formal characteristics of works of art and objects. He believed that forms evoke feelings, a view that certainly runs counter to the tenets of Gestalt psychology. Lipps' principle of "unity in multiplicity" (Schneider 1996) denotes the oppositions and common interests effective in aesthetic objects and responsible for their complexity. Generating tension or even dissonance, along with the seemingly contradictory search for the harmonic principle, are standard practice in works of art – and this is equally true for forms and colors. Lipps' concept of empathy addresses a general communicative process and even serves as the basis for his own symbol theory: "for only through empathy in sensory phenomena or life expressions can something become symbolic" (Schneider 1996).

Wundt's ideas were also opposed by the Austrian school of psychology, founded at the end of the nineteenth century, whose prominent members included not only Lipps, but also Alexius Meinong and Christian von Ehrenfels.

Alexius Meinong (1853–1920) was one of the pioneers of Gestalt psychology. He demonstrated that psychological phenomena are more complex than the sum of their individual elements. In his object theory for the science of perception (1907), he concluded that each of the basic kinds of psychological experience (imagining, thinking, feeling, wanting) conceives of itself as its own object.

The Special Influence of Christian von Ehrenfels

Christian von Ehrenfels (1859–1932), one of Meinong's students, is regarded as the actual founder of Gestalt psychology. In 1890 he published a short tract that made him famous: "About Gestalt Qualities." In this work he argued that one factor effective in perception is independent of sensations: what he calls Gestalt quality. A triangle is a triangle regardless of its color or size. The Gestalt psychology thesis, "The whole is greater than the sum of its parts" can also be traced back to Ehrenfels. In other words, a melody consists of many individual notes, but its effect arises from the combination of the individual notes. Ehrenfels thus rejected elemental psychology and its deconstructive approach, exerting a strong influence on the Gestalt psychologists David Katz, Wolfgang Köhler, and Max Wertheimer.

In 1916 Ehrenfels published a treatise about the "The Value and Purity of Form," which took on central importance for design at a much later date. He stated that there is a degree of formation, that each form demonstrates a certain value of formation. Greater forms are distinguished from lesser through a greater degree of unity and multiplicity (purity of form and value of form). The concept of unity can also be paraphrased with that of order; the concept of multiplicity with complexity. Thus the value of form can be calculated as the product of order (O) and complexity (C).

In the 1960s Max Bense proceeded from such approaches to develop the concept of an "exact aesthetics" under the motto "design is the creation of order." This view was closely connected to the functionalist approach, which aimed to develop design concepts based on simple geometric elements and solids (the square, triangle, circle, cube, pyramid, and cone). This approach followed up on just one side of Ehrenfels's dual concept, emphasizing only the concept of purity of form or, as Dieter Rams liked to say, "Less design is more design." The conflicting influences of order and complexity are always the background for developments in design, thus the "measure of design" (M) is a function (f) of order (O) *and* complexity (C).

The Great Gestalt Psychologists

A number of the individuals who performed important theoretical research in this area in the first half of the twentieth century and their approaches deserve special mention. The physician and psychologist Karl Bühler (1879–1963) is considered the founder of semantic language research (what is known as "language theory") and researched psychological processes in the holistic tradition.

The most important contributions to perception and imagination were made in the "Berlin School" during the 1930s. Among the scholars there were Max Wertheimer (1880–1943), Wolfgang Köhler (1887–1967), and Kurt Koffka (1886–1941). They believed that any processes of experience and behavior had to be researched as a whole. After World War II these approaches were pursued further, especially by Wolfgang Metzger (1899–1979) and Rudolf Arnheim (1904–2007).

Wertheimer demonstrated how perception, through a series of organizational principles (known as the Gestalt laws) is subject to a spontaneous tendency toward structuring in formal terms. He illustrated how objects are grouped and experienced spatially and temporally.

Köhler published treatises on the problem of the assumption of constancy, on figural after-effects, on the psychology of learning and memory, and on the Gestalt theory of brain physiology.

In 1935 Koffka published his *Principles of Gestalt Psychology,* at the time the most comprehensive attempt to present a broad overview of Gestalt psychology research. In his theory of learning he demonstrated that memory strives toward what he called "perfect form" (regularity, precision).

David Katz (1979) focused in particular on the perception of color and formulated a number of Gestalt laws. He followed closely in the footsteps of Wertheimer, Köhler, and Koffka.

Wolfgang Metzger was the leading Gestalt psychologist of the Berlin School. Köhler was his doctoral adviser, and his first assistantship was with Wertheimer. His research concentrated on the psychology of perception and imagination and the psychology of learning. His studies about the sense of sight and its laws were published in 1935 (*Gesetze des Sehens;* The laws of seeing) and even today are considered to be the standard works on the psychology of perception and Gestalt psychology.

Over one hundred Gestalt laws are described in the writings of the psychologists of perception and Gestalt psychologists. Each of these laws shows how perception constructs what are known as totalities. The Gestalt laws constitute important foundations for designing and creating holistic sensory impressions even today. In design they are applied to fulfill the formal aesthetic functions and marking functions.

Gestalt laws can be demonstrated more or less effectively for just about any two- or three-dimensional design object. However, as purely syntactical instruments (and thus without a specific meaning), they do not give any indication of the overall impression of a design object. Without the semantic dimension, in and of themselves, they can not proceed beyond the level of formalism.

Perceiving and Imagining

Gestalt theory approaches have been reviewed and reworked repeatedly over the course of their development. One particular new approach was formulated by Rudolf Arnheim (1972), who attempted to demonstrate that perceiving and imagining can not be separated from each other. He advocated constructing a concept based on the conceptions of perception.

Concepts do not become clear until they are processed by means of the imagination. For Arnheim, the foundation of thinking is the human capacity for abstraction. He differentiates further between two kinds of vivid thinking: intellectual and intuitive thinking. The latter is based on productive (i.e., creative) thinking in the sciences, the arts, and also in design.

On the Aspects of Order and Complexity

In connection with the investigation of Gestalt laws at the Offenbach School of Design in the 1970s, a number of formal aesthetic dichotomies were derived from Ehrenfels's categories of order and complexity, which are quite practicable for the work of designing. Among these are, for instance: simple/complicated, regular/irregular, closed/open, homogeneous/heterogeneous, symmetrical/asymmetrical, clear/unclear, in the frame/out of the frame, in equilibrium/out of balance, familiar/new, and order of experience/complexity of novelty.

The higher-order features of order and complexity, however, do not imply any valuation. In each concrete design project it must be decided anew whether a solution in the direction of greater order or higher complexity appears more appropriate to the task at hand. Of course, the formal complexity discussed here has nothing to do with the (semantic) complexity of a product's content. Even products that are simple in form can turn out to be thoroughly complex in their functionality or operation.

The long tradition of functionalism was based primarily on the formal aim of order. Attractiveness, in terms of the psychology of perception, suffered accordingly, and visual monotony resulted in such areas as architecture, urban planning, visual communication, and design.

The objective of complexity can be achieved by various creative means, for instance, with materials, surfaces, textures, structures, colors, and product graphics. But functional complexity also affects product development and design, especially in the case of electronic products ("featuritis" or "function overload"; Fischer 2001). Each of these criteria has to be discussed on the basis of a concrete design example.

On the Ecological Approach to Visual Perception

A fundamentally new approach in the science of perception was developed by the American psychologist James J. Gibson (1973, 1982). Surmounting the atomistic theory of perception, he formulated a contrasting holistic, ecological approach to visual perception. In this case, perception is studied under the natural conditions of the environment. Gibson distinguishes three main characters of the environment: the medium (atmosphere), the substance (materi-

1 **Pegasus piano**
   Design: Luigi Colani
   Fa. Schimmel Pianos
   Braunschweig (1997)

2 **Study: forklift truck
   as a tool for the Linde AG**
   Design: Fabian Kragenings
   HfG Offenbach (2012)

1

2

als and gases), and the surface (defined as the border between medium and substance, that serves as a point of orientation for sentient beings). Thus colors, the arrangement of surfaces (forms), and the given illumination become important elements in perception. Gibson defines the environment on an ecological level, comprising surroundings, objects, events and also other living beings, which are perceived in their interactions. Perception itself is defined as an activity oriented toward developing one's own consciousness about the environment and developing one's self within it.

Principles of Formal Design

A more precise description of the formal principles of design was offered by Dieter Mankau at the Offenbach School of Design as part of his studies of formal aesthetics:

Additive Design One speaks of additive design when, in the perception of a product or a form, the technical or practical functions characteristic to a product are arranged so that they largely maintain their visual independence.

Integrative Design Here the creative instruments that are employed lead to a holistic perception of the product. Visual irritations that emerge primarily through multiple or different technical and practical functions, and through the materials used for these, can be considerably reduced by formal means, including uninterrupted lines, continuity, and uniformity of materials and colors.

Integral Design What dominates here is the basic form, which is generally mathematically geometric and whose multiplicity of forms is limited to a few elementary basic shapes, including spheres, cylinders, squares, and pyramids. Cognitive and cultural imprinting make these geometric solids extremely stable in terms of the psychology of perception; they remain visually stable in our mental conceptualization even when their form is violated, for instance, through notches or clear reductions or additions to the form.

Sculptural Design This variant does not merely conform to the pure, practical, and functional requirements of the products, but rather interprets the functions individually or even artistically, generating highly symbolic expressive power.

Organic Design This method refers to biological principles (bionics); it also allows nature-like associations. The resulting sentiments not only build on a visual perception, but also integrate our spectrum of perception as a whole. Such perceptions as smells, sensations of cold and hot, tactile experience, and hearing as a spatial phenomenon are elementary experiences with only minimal differences in meaning for different cultures.

These examples show that formal aesthetic functions extend far beyond the purely syntactical sphere. The given forms are always imparted socioculturally and therefore have different meanings in their given contexts. From the design of objects it is thus possible to read the mental, technological, or social stance from which a product was designed.

An Example The "Tolemeo" lamp (designed by Michele De Lucchi and Giancarlo Fassina for Artemide in 1987) picks up both on familiar creative technical principles and on the classic Swedish desk lamp "Luxo" by Jacob Jacobsen. The high-gloss, anodized aluminum frame contrasts with the matte reflector, which appears ready to "fly away." Tightrope (association: suspension architecture), concealed springs, and screws generate a heightened functionality that is accompanied by a multiplicity of complex creative details. The black dots are not pivots, which is incorrect under the marking aspect, but the lamp is extremely simple to handle. The association with lightweight construction techniques from aircraft construction makes the Tolemeo a modern high-tech product so neutral that it can be used in a wide range of application areas; for this reason it rapidly became design icon of the 1990s. It is said that more than 350,000 Tolemeo lamps per year have now been sold worldwide.

Lampe Tolomeo, Design: Michele de Lucchi and Giancarlo Fassina
Fa. Artemide (1987)

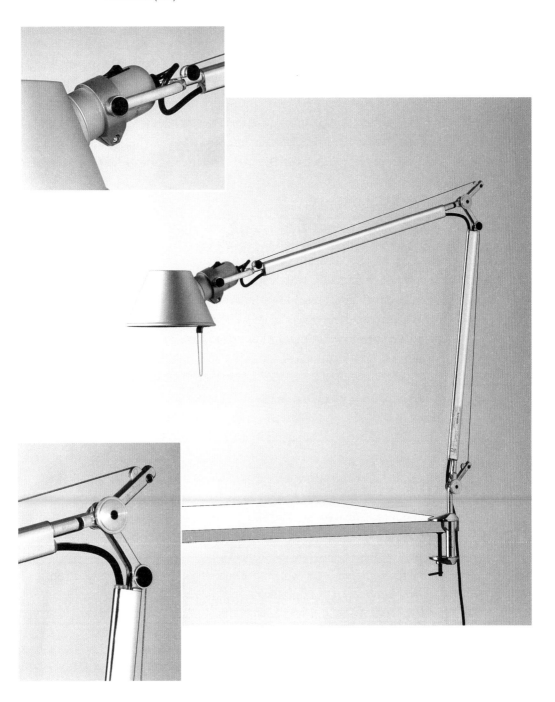

The Marking Functions

As discussed above, markings always refer to the practical functions of products. They visualize a product's technical functions, explaining how it is to be handled or operated. Markings show users how they should deal with a product. Since the design of markings is directly connected to the practical function of a product, this is the area of design which allows the least individual interpretation and personal statement. Nevertheless, the design of markings requires coming to terms with the users and their contexts and experiences.

Visualizing Practical Functions

The design of markings is part of the "classic" repertoire of design, as it was portrayed by such designers as Hans Gugelot at the Ulm School of Design in the early 1960s (↗ p. 40). Strictly speaking, however, Plato had dealt with this topic already; he recognized in every thing a "peculiar ability," and believed that the essence of an object must be comprehended directly in order to be able to identify its special significance. The tradition of "good design" is inconceivable without the design of markings, although these have not always been consciously used or perceived.

Systematic work on the marking functions was begun at the Offenbach School of Design in the 1970s using the cognitive methods of the humanities, particularly the groundbreaking works of Richard Fischer (1978). These were developed further and depicted comprehensively in 1984 by Richard Fischer and Gerda Mikosch, as well as Dagmar Steffen (et al.) (2000).

Sven Hesselgren (1980) published a study in which he reached similar findings for the fields of architecture and design. This topic was the subject of intensive study, especially in the former East Germany. In a historical discussion on the topic of signs and markings, Günther Feuerstein (1981) demonstrated the development of an "apparative semiotics," in which what was substantial about products (i.e., their meaning) makes up the preeminent principle of design: "We defend ourselves against the apparatus not by storming it or destroying it, but rather by interpreting it as an aesthetic object: a process of 'interpretative aesthetics'."

The close linkage of design in East Germany to the tradition of functionalism was also evident in a paper by Horst Oehlke (1982), in which he describes the visualization of a product's uses as a task of the functional method of design. Oehlke held the dialectics of product function and product appearance to be the central topic of design in the 1980s (↗ p. 182 f).

Work on the theory of product language soon showed that the transition from formal aesthetic functions to marking functions is often quite fluid. Here, it was also evident how new meanings can be generated systematically by applying Gestalt laws, as these exist independent of specific meanings.

Martin Gessmann (2014) proposes another example from the history of philosophy: Husserl (↗ p. 98), he says, defined an important distinction in the use of signs. On the one hand, there is the "meaningful expression," which Derrida (1967) calls the "expression" and on the other the mere "mark" which Derrida translates as "indice." Gessmann interprets this as follows: "The mark or indice represents the mere material aspect of the sign, in the sense of the conventional manner of embodying what is meant, whereas the expression (the sign understood as meaningful expression) reveals the meaning of what is meant. In the expression, the philosophical spirit is thus speaking to itself; in the mark in itself, the spirit finds only material spiritlessness." Of course the debate over marking functions in design is not quite so "spiritless," as the following examples demonstrate; in fact they remain part of the central discourses about product, whether material or immaterial.

Discussion of Precedents

In a collection of precedents from design praxis, a number of categories of markings were identified as general points of orientation (Fischer and Mikosch 1984), and remain valid even today. This work quite correctly pointed out that a holistic observation of all product language (communicative) functions must always be the first step in designing new products.

Such examples are oriented primarily toward a product world characterized by the transition from the mechanical to the electric, or even electronic world. However, they ultimately can serve as examples only for the relationship between language and its formal aesthetic visualization (portrayal, specification), as understanding always depends on the context, the cultural background, and the experiences of the users. To a somewhat lesser degree, such product categories and corresponding markings continue to exist, including:

orientation such as the orientation toward the users

idle function through which, for instance, visual information about how to use the product can be provided

stability may concern the representation of technical and physical laws

changeability and configurability markings serve to visualize ways in which the product may be adapted

operation controls should communicate to the user the details about how a device is to be used. Individual elements should be designed to make their application immediately obvious (for instance, push, turn, slide, firmly or gently)

precision concerns the visualization of how precisely certain products can be manipulated or how they can be adjusted (precision needed on a measuring device, a camera, or a medical device is functional, whereas such signs on a stereo have more of a symbolic character

reference to the human body concerns not only the direct adaptation of the product to anthropometric conditions, but also associative indications of this adaptation

These examples again make it evident that a clear delimitation of individual communicative functions is often impossible and rarely makes sense. In each individual case of design, the point is to carefully consider which emblematic categories will receive special emphasis.

Thus ticket machines for mass transportation systems require a clear operating design ("on the fly"), whereas it is quite legitimate to design a stereo system that only the owner understands how to operate.

These examples show that product language is not an end in itself, but merely a basis for discussion in the process of product development. Here designers and design managers have to present their specialized expertise to the sales and marketing experts and developers involved. From this perspective, product language can become a strategic tool which can have a major influence on the expressiveness of a product and its relation to, or acceptance by, the user.

Changes through Microelectronics

The 1980s saw the mass influx of microelectronics into the world of artifacts, which fundamentally changed marking functions. The obvious markings, originating from the mechanical world, gradually disappeared and were replaced by the interfaces used to operate digital products. This paradigmatic change meant a developmental leap for design after the postmodern obscurity of the 1980s (Bürdek, 1990a, 2001b).

CAD (Computer Aided Design) is a particularly vivid example of this process. The conceptual worlds of developers and builders were transferred almost directly to the new tools emerging at that time (CAD software).

Problems – if not a public menace – arose when these worlds of imagination entered into the development of devices for broad groups of users. In most cases, rather cryptic user interfaces resulted. As a consequence, interfaces, and also the increasingly imperative user manuals, began to receive more attention (Bürdek and Schupbach 1993).

Against a completely different background – namely, that of cognitive psychology – the American scientist Donald A. Norman (1989) obtained quite convincing findings about the real environment, which can be subsumed directly under the concept of marking functions. A multiplicity of mistakes and errors in dealing with products can be traced back not to human incompetence, but to inadequate design.

Norman referred in particular to "creeping featurism" – the tendency to raise to absurdity the number of functions a device can perform. This phenomenon – the aforementioned "featuritis" or "function overload" (Fischer 2001) – is increasingly evident in products equipped with microprocessors. In such cases, the costs of realizing ever more functions in a product are negligible, although the user cannot comprehend most of them, let alone apply them sensibly.

Control module with TFT touch display and rotary knobs, Ovens 200 series from Gaggenau
Design: Brand Design Gaggenau/HID Human Interface Design GmbH (2013)

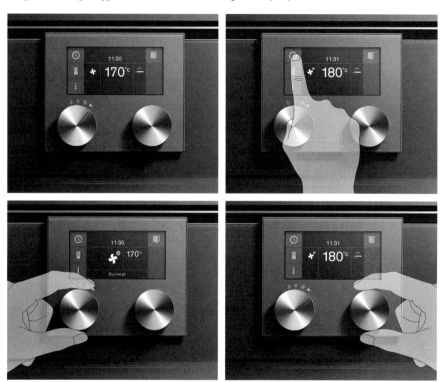

User Interface Design

This results in the design of user interfaces, which has become an ever more decisive criterion for purchasing (and is especially evident with cell phones and for software). In the case of the smartphones that are in such great demand worldwide (internet-capable cell phones with a plethora of additional functions), the interfaces and the operating systems behind them are indeed decisive selling points. Beyond the actual hardware, the emphasis is on the design of the virtual level behind it (i.e., the design of user instructions – also called interaction design – and thus access to a device's spectrum of features).

Designers of user interfaces have learned to account for differences in users' experiences and cultural backgrounds. While this is still difficult in hardware design, there are already (expanding) opportunities for individual adaptation of interfaces, signs and symbols, visibility, and size.

The Symbolic Functions

The concept of the symbol has taken on different meanings at various stages of its history. Generally speaking, it means a (distinguishing) sign that receives intercultural meaning through convention. It has the function of a sign or emblem because symbols serve as representatives for something that is not perceptible. Such symbols exist in religions, in art and literature, but also in the natural sciences, in logic and linguistic philosophy, and in countless variants in everyday life. The meanings of symbols often develop by association, and cannot be determined unambiguously: interpretation always depends on the respective context.

Susanne Langer's distinction between marks and symbols (1965) (↗ p. 148) established this concept of symbol in the process of developing a disciplinary design theory.

Symbols and Contexts

To all appearances, symbolism did not exist at all in the functionalist tradition of the twentieth century – after all, the emphasis there was on realizing the practical functions of a product to maximize creative order in keeping with the motto "form follows function." Marking functions were dealt with more or less intuitively, primarily to facilitate the optimal operation of a product by the user.

But how exactly was the practical function of a product indicated? Designers had always taken pains to analyze and interpret the respective functions. However, the answers were often more ideological than functionalist. Thus the early functionalism of the 1920s, in fact, became an "unacknowledged symbolism," because it was applied as a sign of technological progress (Venturi, Scott Brown, and Izenour 1972).

Functionalism itself was regarded as a way of overcoming style: supposedly value-free design was considered significant for mass culture, or even as a revolutionary milestone in the social history of architecture and design. However, in retrospect, it appears that the functionalism of the Bauhaus period between 1920 and 1930 was the symbol of an intellectual and progressive minority. After 1945, functionalism became the foundation of mass produc-

Symbolic language
Erich Fromm

"Ich halte die Symbolsprache für die einzige Fremdsprache, die jeder von uns lernen sollte." Erich Fromm

tion and was considered the symbol of the industrial development of Western Europe. This consensus held until the rise of postmodernism in the 1980s.

Dealing with symbolic functions in the practical work of design is complicated by the fact that there is no "dictionary of meanings" for products: symbolic meanings can be interpreted only from their given socio-cultural contexts. While marking functions are oriented primarily on the product itself (indicating its use), symbolic functions serve as background reports, representing the different contexts of each given product.

Furniture designs from the Bauhaus period had shown that the original intentions of the designers to design affordable mass furnishings for broad sectors of the population could be turned around to the opposite effect. Today, designers like Philippe Starck try to ensure their products' direct influence on mass culture by distributing their furniture designs through mail-order catalogs, and even by taking over distribution themselves.

It is impossible to arrive at generally valid propositions about the symbolic functions of products. For this reason a scientific theory of design grounded in the humanities must also allow different interpretations of one and the same object.

Semiotic Methods of Investigation

Semiotics, conceptualized as a method for studying all cultural processes (Eco 1972), is also a suitable instrument for investigating symbolism. Since one of the objectives of the process of design is to provide "accesses" between the symbolic worlds of the respective users (or groups of users) and the producers of the symbols (companies), a thorough understanding of the respective sign worlds is imperative. This form of communication can also be designated as a process of coding and decoding information. Particularly important for design are those codes that are supported by agreements, cultural traditions and conventions, and by group-specific socialization processes. From this perspective, as long as products remain within a socially compulsory sign system – a product language – it is possible to decode their lexical content (Selle 1978).

Dealing with symbolic functions means dealing intensively with the multifarious communicative functions of design. In the design process it is often necessary to produce one product version for the national market and another for the global market to ensure that each can be decoded under the conditions of the given sociocultural context.

Our critique of hermeneutics thus can be applied analogously to symbolism: further empirical studies are required to protect the interpretations of products from the consequences of speculation.

The studies by Csikszentmihalyi and Rochberg-Halton (1989) mentioned above were a major step in this direction, analyzing three generations of American households (with 315 subjects). They showed that even the instrumental utilization of products in the household is located in the symbolic domains of the given culture: "The development of symbols – signs whose relation to an object is based on a convention rather than on qualitative or physical similarities – in the context of a cultural tradition enables people to compare their modes of behavior with those of their ancestors in order to predict new experiences" (Csikszentmihalyi and Rochberg-Halton 1989). Furthermore, by pointing out that the symbolic dimensions of objects have been researched by ethnologists, Csikszentmihalyi and Rochberg Halton are able to relate their findings back to the anthropological and semiotic approaches of French structuralism: "Indeed, ethnologists have compiled an abundance of unbelievably detailed descriptions of the symbolic uses of objects from a multiplicity of different cultures" (Csikszentmihalyi and Rochberg-Halton 1989).

In addition to their function as status symbols, objects take on another role in social integration. This is especially evident among children and teenagers, for whom the use of identical products or brands is tantamount to group membership. Sporting goods manufacturers like Adidas, Nike, and Puma (↗ p. 362) are particularly adept at exploiting this phenomenon in their product development and design. The same also applies to electronics manufacturers such as Apple, Google, Nokia, LG, and Samsung. The implicit inverse is also true: not using these brands (for whatever reason) results in social exclusion: wearing shoes with two stripes guarantees complete ostracism. Decisive here is not the missing third stripe, but rather the mere fact that the cult brand – Adidas – is missing. International sporting events (such as the Olympic Games and world championships) are therefore also arenas for global sports brands, offering as they do identification opportunities for globalized participants and spectators in all age classes.

One of the best works on the symbolic functions of products was published by Tilmann Habermas (1999), who bases his methodology on both the sociological tradition of Émile Durkheim (1912) and the linguistic tradition of Ferdinand de Saussure. In this it is also reminiscent of the exemplary analysis by Roland Barthes (1985), who defined articles of clothing (fashion) as technological (pattern, textile structure), iconic (emblematic), and verbal (descriptive) systems. The codes which Barthes described have both a denotative and a connotative character. Tilmann Habermas also picks up on Eco's categories of objects of utility and symbolic objects, defining symbolic objects as things "whose explicit and primary use is to mean something," as opposed to objects of utility, which "primarily fulfill a practical task, including both manipulanda and utilitanda to be applied instrumentally."

Tilmann Habermas's approach thus dovetails neatly with the previous discussions and derivations of a design theory based on communication. He also notes the discussion of how to apply this theory to non-material products, as Donald A. Norman (1989) proposed.

With Mary Douglas's *Purity and Danger* (1966), Tilmann Habermas mentions yet another significant contribution to the disciplinary design research adopted and extended by Helene Karmasin. He identifies the process that enables social groups to take part in culture by consuming goods, suggesting that these goods (products) can even be regarded as means of communication. "The more stable the society, the more clearly objects and goods function as indicators of social position."

Hardly any such traditional systems are intact in industrialized countries today, but they are still cultivated in primitive societies. Today, the relations that products have to the social positions of their respective users are only implicit. For this reason the use of symbols is actually more similar to Baudrillard's "proliferation of signs," which, however, can also result in the loss of users' social identities.

A Few Examples

If their identity is challenged, many people retreat into their domestic environments (keyword: cocooning) and load the objects accumulated there with symbolic meaning. An individual's own apartment, house, or room (in the case of children and teenagers) becomes a place that "symbolizes social identity."

The body takes on this task all the more: clothing, shoes, jewelry, glasses, hair-styles, tattoos, are all unmediated fields of action for the construction of personal symbols. Indirect fields of action are those related to the body, such as foods, beverages, and personal accessories (pens, purses, backpacks), and also means of transport like skateboards, rollerblades, and scooters. And last but not least, all of the electronic "devices" needed to play and communicate (Fischer 2001). The worldwide cult associated with smartphones and tablets also has its source in these teenage symbolization rituals.

On the whole, individualization appears to function only through intense collective experiences. When all members of a group of teenagers have the same sneakers (or at least the same brands), backpacks, and cell phones, every member is equal – the perfect form of social individuality. One remarkably well-founded and illuminating study on teen culture (SPoKK 1997) demonstrated the multifarious spectrum of such communities of identification: the techno scene, ravers, punks, skinheads, headbangers, hip hop, inline skaters, street basketball players, acid house fans, boy groups and girl groups and their fans, snowboarders, beach volleyball players, and many, many more. What they all share is the use of identical sign systems, rituals, and clothing.

Today we refer to such subcultures as "communities," where the use or ownership of identical products creates social networks. Apple is currently the example par excellence. Steve Wozniak, one of the company's founders and Steve Jobs's technical partner, still wonders how the company became "a question of style," (Jens Höhner 2009). But the trend has spread rapidly beyond the Apple fan club, as an example from China demonstrates: "There is no doubt that the company has shaped the taste of the young Chinese middle class to a point where they are prepared to use its products as their preferred badge of identity…. A study by Stanford University at elite universities in Beijing found a higher density of i-Pads there than in Palo Alto" (Simeons 2012).

This example highlights what far-reaching communicative functions design possesses today. Users communicate their social status back into society with and through the products they acquire. Which in turn identifies the status of the users through the products they use.

Tilmann Habermas also picked up on Bourdieu (1979), claiming that membership in subcultures (with their respective value and life orientations) can be portrayed and described not with individual symbols, but only with entire systems of symbols. In the 1990s the "lifestyle discussion" this initiated became a leitmotif of both design theory and design practice.

Camper infoshop Madrid, design: Marti Guixe, Barcelona (2003)

A post-doctoral dissertation at the philosophy department of the University of Cologne provided evidence for the validity of the lifestyle approach. Friedrich W. Heubach's psychological analysis of the everyday (1987) proceeded from the different connotations possessed by, for instance, household utensils. Every culture in the world has attributed to these objects symbolic meanings – often, these have become more important than their original meanings. Without alluding directly to design – Uta Brandes (1988) charted that territory with a profound review that greatly enhanced the impact of Heubach's work – Heubach established a direct link to semiotic models of cognition, speaking of the "double objectivity of things," which is equivalent to Eco's conceptualization of first and second functions.

However, sociological research is concerned with similar questions. Paul Nolte (2001) claimed that private consumption (especially the purchase of brand products) has great importance for an individual's "self-styling;" that is, the social determination of the individual no longer occurs through prescribed patterns as when "belonging to a certain class was part of individual identity; it offered a community that granted social security." These mechanisms emerged in the nineteenth century and have definitely hit retirement age. The social definition of the individual takes place through the acquisition and possession of products. "Tell me what you buy, and I'll tell you who you are" runs the new creed. Individuals no longer define their social role through the world of work, but above all through consumption. Whether you shop at the discount supermarket or the specialized delicatessen expresses more than the traditional sociographic features used in market research: age, gender, education, profession, and income.

Consumption and the respective lifestyle thus take on a new role, not leveling social differences, but making them particularly evident. Consumption, therefore, also yields new class societies, formed and simultaneously differentiated by social behavior, sports, vacation habits, and fashionable restaurants. So design has no small role to play in the formation of such communities.

Thus it is the symbolic statements made by products that most strongly promote brand recognition (Jungen 2011). Jungen points out that the shift in consumer attitudes has considerable repercussions for product design. In particular a growing striving for self-realization means that products are today acquired less for their objective or functional properties than for their immaterial benefits, with the experience orientation shifting to the fore (Schulze 2005). This phenomenon is increasingly identifiable in Asia (especially China, where social status is demonstrated via semantically charged products).

Jungen also draws on the product language approach (↗ p. 136 ff), when he empirically investigates what connotations products may possess (a dimension that, incidentally, is otherwise largely lacking in design). The work of Patrik Jungen is a true piece of (disciplinary) design research where he explores the different product connotations that arise using series of models (product variations) produced by a single designer.

One of the most successful new categories of automobiles is the SUV (sports utility vehicle), which has secured a considerable market share since the 1990s. In 2012 over seven million were sold in the United States alone. The practical functions of these products (four-wheel drive, step-down gears, differential lock) can actually be used by very few owners (farmers, foresters, residents of mountainous areas). However, the symbolic effect of SUVs is unmistakable: their owners clearly set themselves apart from the drivers of other mass-produced vehicles; they increase the individuality of the driver. The driver sits high, looking down, not only on traffic, but on the world in general. The elevated seating position also imparts security, which is particularly valued by female drivers (Reinking 2002).

Proceeding from the classics of this market segment (Land Rover Defender, Range Rover, Mercedes G, Jeep Wrangler, Lada Niva, a number of new vehicles emerged, all of which were developed and designed with an eye to the buyers' symbolic needs. These days almost all automobile manufacturers jostle for market share in this segment. German car companies offer SUVs across the entire spectrum from luxury class to more basic, fun-orientated models like the Opel Mokka. All SUVs are conceived for cruising in the metropolis, or for trips away from the working world and suburban routine. The shift in this product class is rather nicely illustrated by a comparison of the Russian Lada Niva and the Opel Mokka. Whereas the former was a purely functional workhorse, the latter is a semantically charged fun-car for the young urbanite.

Thanks to symbolic supercharging, the manufacturers of outdoor clothes and equipment have experienced a similar boom since the 1980s. As a consequence of increasing global travel to the most remote regions of the world (Andes, Himalayas, Antarctica), demand has grown for practical, high-quality equipment. Designers have successively integrated the experiences of professional mountaineers (in the Alps, for instance) to market products to a broader clientele. In Germany, for instance, a great number of specialized stores emerged to provide selected products for globetrotting travelers. The names are symbols in themselves: Outdoor, SINE (from "sinecure" = without care), Supertramp, and many more.

These stores carry clothing and shoes, backpacks and tents, sleeping bags and mountain climbing equipment, equipment for winter sports and water sports, knives and tools, outdoor kitchens, maps and books – everything required for expeditions, safaris, survival vacations, and trekking. An autonomous, functional world of products, which stands out above all for its symbolic compactness and consistency. This is where professionals buy their equipment: only high-tech materials are used and quality is guaranteed. Most of the salespeople have outdoor experience themselves; they know what they are talking about and can give advice accordingly – which is truly necessary, for selling an item like a flashlight for about 400 euros (approx. US $900) requires a user's expert knowledge. But even people who spend time in open country only sporadically and avoid real danger can appreciate the qualities of high-tech equipment: the image transfer and symbol transfer works flawlessly (Ronke 2002).

Symbolic worlds such as these are what determine current design discourses and therefore describe anew the close interactions between products and their contexts (see Kohl 2003).

From Product Language to Product Semantics

Kant's category of reason outlined a cognitive horizon that can serve as the foundation for a consistent and logical disciplinary theory of design. In complete opposition to the beginnings of theory construction at the Ulm School of Design – the contingencies of which were discussed in a previous section – a decisive instrument has existed since the 1970s that can be applied to design for description and generation. Description here designates the processes of defining, analyzing, and criticizing design using the expedient and evident methods of the humanities. Generation means the actual process of designing, for which this instrument has proven its worth over a wide spectrum of tasks.

The Forerunners

Uri Friedländer (1981/82) stated at the beginning of the 1980s that the epoch of timeless design was over, that weariness prevailed in the face of "good design." In contrast to the postmodern tendency of groups like Alchimia and Memphis (who concerned themselves exclusively with interior design) prevalent at the time, Friedländer – and separately, but in parallel, Winfried Scheuer – attempted to apply new design tendencies to technical devices. They did not intend for products to become the carriers of practical functions; instead, symbolic functions would attain even more importance.

Friedländer's approach involved an extensive use of what he called "metaphors." He distinguished three forms:

the historical metaphor, which reminds us of earlier objects,

the technical metaphor, which contains elements from science and technology, and

the natural metaphor, in which shapes, movements, and incidents from nature appear.

The first results of these attempts were designated as sensual-expressionistic or metaphorical designs.

In the 1970s Helga and Hans-Jürgen Lannoch (1983, 1984, 1987) responded with irony to Wolfgang Fritz Haug's exposé of the dual character of the commodity by designing erotic product sculptures, which they called meta-realistic sculptures (Lannoch, 1977). While mechanical products had been designed from the interior to the exterior (form followed function), today's electronic devices possess only a user-orientated exterior; this, and the user's physical and psychological traits become form-defining. Using the example of semantic space, the Lannochs demonstrated that relationships between people can be described spatially to the extent that they are mediated by objects. They called the method thus derived "semantic transfer" and developed creative exercises that transpose words into shapes and interpret them from the perspective of the given period. Accordingly, once again semiotic and hermeneutic elements are included in this approach.

Influences from Linguistics

Design theory based on linguistics gained particular importance in the United States. In 1984 Reinhart Butter, together with the Industrial Designers Society of America, initiated a special issue of the journal *innovation* on "The Semantics of Form." With papers by Klaus Krippendorff and Butter himself, Jochen Gros, Michael McCoy, Uri Friedländer, Hans-Jürgen Lannoch, and others, this journal paved the way for a new conception of design in the United States. Butter succeeded in enlisting the enthusiastic support of American designer Robert I. Blaich, who was design director at Philips in Eindhoven from 1980 until 1992. From this point on, product semantics was propagated throughout Europe through seminars, publications, and new product lines. Philips had great success with its "design strategy of expressive forms" (Kicherer, 1987). For

1 **Elaine printer**
Design: Technology
Design, 1988

2 **Book computer**
Design: D.M. Gresham
with Hel Rinkleib,
Cranbrook Academy 1985

3 **Stereo-receiver**
Design: Robert Nakata,
Cranbrook Academy 1985

2

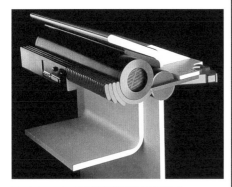

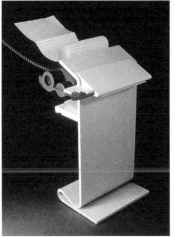

1

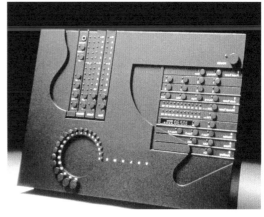

3

instance, over 500,000 units of the "roller radio" were sold shortly after its market launch.

A close relationship is evident between American product semantics and the semiotic approach of the Ulm School of Design, as Krippendorff (1984, 1985) indicates. For him, the meaning of an object constitutes the aggregate of all contexts in which the object can occur. Everything that one knows about it and can state – history, manufacturing process, users, logic of its functions, economic value – is mediated through language.

Krippendorff describes three models of product semantics. First, a linguistic model that studies the meaning of concepts, and thus language within the language. Here he makes reference to Wittgenstein's discourse analysis. Second, a communicative model in which the designer functions as the transmitter, but affects this by evoking associations in the recipient (What do consumers buy? How do they deal with a product? What impression do they want to make on others by using the product?). And third, a cultural model in which social systems of symbols are analyzed, that is, the inner structure, the elements of form, the inherent dynamics, and their representative functions. Further developments in product semantics were reported in the journal *Design Issues* (V:2, Spring 1989), and in publications on the occasion of a conference at the UIAH in Helsinki in summer 1989 (Michel 1992.

The McCoys and Cranbrook

One of the first American institutions to pick up on the concept of product semantics for training was the renowned Cranbrook Academy near Detroit. Eliel Saarinen and Charles Eames had taught there in the 1930s and 1940s; graduates included Harry Bertoia and Florence Knoll. The designer couple Michael and Katherine McCoy, who taught there from 1971 to 1995, consciously emphasized these historical roots: Harry Bertoia developed his chairs from pictures of cellular structures, and Eero Saarinen used associations of flight for his design of the Dulles Airport building. The principle of metaphors continued to play a major role: visual analogies in design improve the practical functions of the respective products (McCoy 1984).

In a very short time the McCoys and their students succeeded in developing a number of exemplary designs based on product semantics. In a paper about design in the information age (1988) they, too, picked up on the semiot-

Phonebook, Design: Lisa Krohn, Forma Finlandia (1989)

ic approaches of the French structuralists (especially of Ferdinand de Saussure), by portraying the designer as the interpreter of the product's meaning for the user, the mediator between people and the information that surrounds them. The McCoys also recalled Le Corbusier's claim that some objects function as background, whereas others come into the foreground with great expressive power. In the 1920s it had been Le Corbusier's chairs, while cabinets and tables had receded into the background.

Product semantics experienced its actual breakthrough when Cranbrook student Lisa Krohn won the Forma Finlandia design competition, demonstrating the kind of design potential the concept would release, especially for electronic products. Lisa Krohn's design was true to the traditional way of dealing with books – leafing. Each page of her electronic notebook contains a user manual, and the interplay between hardware and software makes it easy for even a computer novice to use.

This is why product semantics received special attention in a far-reaching publication about American design by Hugh Aldersey-Williams (1988). This publication even propagated the impression that product semantics was the topic of American design in the 1980s. Although it had been characterized by more pragmatic approaches in the past, here explicit reference was made to the ideas of the French semioticians Roland Barthes and Jean Baudrillard.

On the other hand, product semantics demonstrated a continuity with the great designers of the styling period, who were explicitly concerned with shaping their products (i.e., the aesthetic questions of design). Aldersey-Williams pointed out that since social, cultural, and even mythical aspects flow into design today, design had to do justice to all of them.

When the McCoys left Cranbrook Academy in 1995 (after teaching for over twenty-four years), it meant the end of product semantics at this design school. In a kind of retrospective, Michael McCoy (1996) designated this phase as one of "interpretive design," which at its core is even closer to product language. He compared the linguistic turn, which came into force in structuralism and post-structuralism, with examples from the architecture of the 1970s and 1980s – which he indicates were the conscious point of departure for his work at Cranbrook. He said he believes semiotics to be too tightly restricted to the production and reception of signs and therefore prefers the concept of interpretive design, which covers the broader field of cultural production. His idea of good design is any design suitable for the given use and context.

Product Semantics in East Germany

Product semantics was reviewed and underwent further development not only in the United States, but also in former East Germany, where its extension constituted an interesting parallel to the product language approach (↗ p. 52). From 1977 to 1996, Horst Oehlke directed the department of theory and methodology at the former Hochschule für industrielle Formgestaltung Halle, Burg Giebichenstein (Academy for Industrial Design in Halle, Burg Giebichenstein). The foundations for a new direction in design theory were laid in the regular colloquiums held there (Oehlke 1977, 1978). At a seminar on functionalism, held in February 1982 by the Office for Industrial Design in Berlin, Oehlke outlined the topic of visualization, which he identified as the central task of functional design. His definition of visualization was making the respective utility values of a product visible to the user so that the user could easily comprehend its nature. Here Oehlke followed up on Gropius's eidetic inquiry. Probably the most concrete contribution to this field was Oehlke's dissertation, submitted in 1982 and published in 1986, on the topic of "Produkterscheinung/Produktbild/Produktleitbild – ein Beitrag zur Bestimmung des Gegenstandes von industriellem Design" (Product Appearance/Product Image/Product Model: A Contribution to the Determination of the Object of Industrial Design). In further publications, especially in the journal *form + zweck,* he presented intermediate findings, follow-up studies, and the like.

Semantics in Design

A conference under that title was held in Munich in 1998, supported by BMW Design and Siemens Design & Messe GmbH. Not until 2010 was it possible to reconstruct the contributions and publish them on the website of the Offenbach School of Design (Semantics in Design). This event was the first occasion the topic was discussed in Germany among a circle of hand-selected participants, including the following experts:

Reinhart Butter Butter was one of the founders of US product semantics, alongside Klaus Krippendorff. He argued that "understanding" products always means "making sense," in other words, making plausible, recognizable, comprehensible, or visible. Butter argued for the needs and wishes of users to be prioritized in product development.

Hartmut Ginnow-Merkert Ginnow-Merkert argued for product language to be expanded to encompass a "multisensory interaction with products." The senses with which people perceive the information broadcast by a product include the acoustic, haptic, olfactory, and gustatory.

Wolfgang Jonas Jonas presented a model for design theory based on system theory. He regards things (products) as manifestations of social dynamics, rather than representations of reality. Similarly, zeitgeist (style, fashion) is generated not through the form of the product, but through specific social parameters and their transformations.

Klaus Krippendorff Krippendorff placed the concept of the "stakeholder" at the center of his argument. Terms like "user," he argued, suggest that products seek largely or exclusively to satisfy needs. He countered this with the thesis that "the user is a myth." In fact, he said, the interests of numerous users, which he referred to as "stakeholders," need to be taken into account in design processes.

Patrick Reinmöller Reinmöller, who comes from the discipline of business administration, argued for design to be liberated from the studio and relocated within management. The semantic dimension of products was increasingly acknowledged as an important economic factor in "strategic product planning," he argued, in a development for which designers were largely unprepared. At the same time, he said, the semantic approach fulfilled the conditions for possible success (of products). Product semantics defined future fields of activity and offered ambitious blueprints for an academic discipline.

Siegfried J. Schmidt As a linguist Schmidt distinguished real perceivable phenomena in communication processes (ordered surfaces or character strings, in other words, semiotic material) from the imperceivable. The imperceivable, he said, included all that is colloquially and linguistically designated "sense," "meaning," "content," etc. Product language addresses the meanings assigned to the products, so people operate with sensorily constituted experienced realities. The example of texts (by implication transferable to products) shows that not even fixed definitions possess "meaning," but instead ultimately the reader (or product user) must decide.

Erik Spiekermann Spiekermann, a typographer, demonstrated why type should play an important role in product language as the "user interface" to the product. He sought to introduce type to the discussion as a meta-language.

Although the consensus on the question of language was surprisingly clear at this point, dissemination and acceptance of this discourse was nonetheless still some way off. Dagmar Steffen (1998) wrote in a summary of the meeting: "To that extent – and there was consensus on this too – the circumstances for progress in design theory in Germany are currently not the best, as theory-formation requires a lobby and management." Yet Claudia Mareis notes today (2014): "Product semantics ... initiated the turn from a semiotics to a semantics of design, from an analysis of the relationships of signs to one of the generation of meaning." This was certainly an important step forward in design theory.

Movigear, Fa. SEW – EURODRIVE Bruchsal
Design: Hans-Jürgen Lannoch (around 2000)

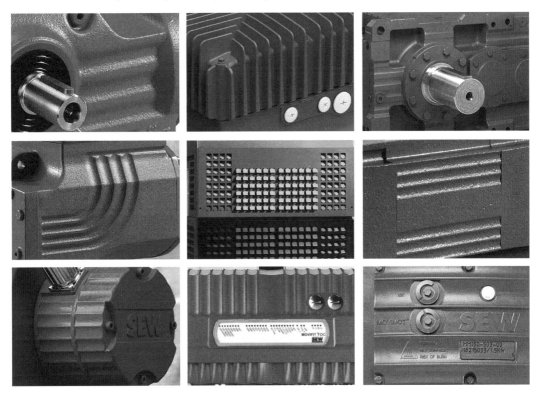

Design and Semantics

DeSForM (Design and Semantics of Form and Movement), founded in 2005 at the initiative of Loe Feijs (University of Eindhoven), Steven Kyffin (Philips), and Bob Young (Northumbria University), addressed these issues in a series of events. Comprehensive proceedings are available for the following conferences: Newcastle 2005, Eindhoven 2006, Newcastle 2007, Offenbach 2008, Taipei 2009, Lucerne 2010, Sydney 2012, Wuxi 2013, and Milan 2015.

Altogether the published papers represent an exceptional contribution to the discipline's body of knowledge about design and its theoretical foundations (design science), and to research building thereupon.

At this juncture mention must also be made of a contribution by Nathan Crilly, James Moultrie, and P. John Clarkson (2004) of Cambridge University, which was not specifically made in the scope of DeSForM but originates from the same intellectual environment. The authors describe the perception-conveying properties that users distinguish in products, identifying:

aesthetic phenomena

semantic phenomena, and

symbolic interpretations,

"which may be defined as the perception of what a product says about its owner or user: the personal and social significance attached to the design." The authors build on the product language approach, but expand it to include the socio-psychological phenomena that emanate from or can be attributed to the products. As such, they use similar terms to those coined in the "theory of product language" (↗ p. 150 f).

Product semantics in particular is now unchallenged. Deyan Sudjic (2008), director of the London Design Museum, describes this very clearly: "And design has become the language with which to shape those objects and to tailor the messages that they carry. The role of the most sophisticated designers today is as much to be storytellers, to make design that speaks in such a way as to convey these messages, as it is to resolve formal and functional problems. They manipulate this language more or less skilfully."

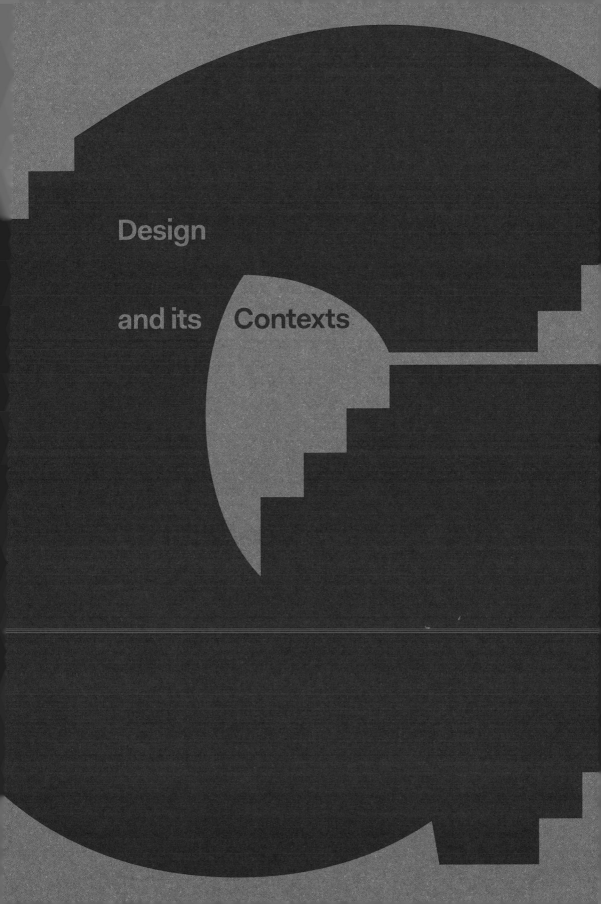

Design

and its   Contexts

189   **From Corporate Design to Service Design**

196   **From Design Management to Strategic Design**

202   **Architecture and Design**

216   **Utopias, Visions, Concepts, and Trends**

226   **Design and Society**

From Corporate Design to Service Design

Companies and organizations worldwide have increasingly come to recognize the importance of the design factor. Going beyond the design of individual products to include product systems, hardware and software, and service design means entering a sphere that is gaining more and more significance in design: corporate identity and corporate design.

How It All Began

The furniture and domestic utensils developed in the eighteenth century exhibit a shared system of ideas, values, and norms. The origins of corporate design are commonly traced to the Shakers, a religious sect of English and French origins that settled in the United States in the second half of the eighteenth century. With Protestant severity and the most sparing of means, they began to develop crafted objects for their own use (see for example Andrews and Andrew, 1964). The simplicity and functionality of their furniture and implements was rooted in their spirituality. The unity of form and function was still unbroken – unlike the mass dissemination of functionalist ideas initiated by Bauhaus, which degenerated into a lifestyle in the 1960s and 1970s. But today, Shaker objects are also marketed as lifestyle products (Donaldson 2001), a fate they share with many other historical movements.

This early brand of functionalism, which did not begin to take shape elsewhere until the nineteenth century, can be counted as an example of identity in that the functional, aesthetic, and social quality of the products was understood to express religious culture. A characteristic feature of Shaker products was the principle of equality apparent in them. Aesthetic distinctions were not used to mark any hierarchies, nor did the products reflect contemporary design fashions.

Early in the twentieth century, from 1907 to 1914, the German architect Peter Behrens (↗ p. 24) was responsible for redesigning the products, factory buildings, showrooms, graphic materials (catalogs, price lists, etc.), and the trademark of the German electrical corporation AEG (Allgemeine Elektrizitäts-Gesellschaft). He also designed exhibition stalls, sales outlets, and apartments for the workers. It is to him that we owe the notion of "industrial culture" that goes beyond the recording of objects and emphasizes the knowledge of historical contexts and living conditions (Glaser 1982). Peter Behrens, in the usage of his day, would have been called the artistic adviser of an industrial company; today, however, he would bear the title of corporate designer or even design manager.

The Italian company Olivetti introduced corporate design and corporate identity as commercial strategies and expanded corporate culture to include, in particular, social services provided by the company for its employees.

Meanwhile, in Germany, after World War II, Braun was the first company to seek to unify the visible aspects of its activities in areas ranging from product design to visual communication and architecture. "Good design" is an established term for such efforts to bring unity to the visible aspects of a corporation's activities and institute a consistent identity in the two- and three-dimensional areas of its output.

The German graphic designer Otl Aicher gave design an important impetus here when he created the visual image for the Olympic Games in Munich in 1972, but he also developed corporate design programs for Deutsche Lufthansa, the kitchen furnisher Bulthaup, Dresdner Bank, ERCO, FSB, the television station ZDF (Zweites Deutsches Fernsehen), and Westdeutsche Landesbank.

Other companies that adhere to this modernist tradition and orient their image on its principles are IBM, the writing instruments manufacturer Lamy, Siemens AG, the heating technology supplier Viessmann, and the office furniture company Wilkhahn.

Defining Terminology

So what exactly do companies mean when they talk about strategic design? The most common terms are corporate behavior, corporate communication, corporate culture, corporate design, corporate identity, corporate strategy, and corporate wording. In this context, "corporate" means unified, joint, overall. The fusion of different elements, images, and strategies is therefore the key to these important instruments of management policy.

Defining Identity

The notion of identity plays an important role in this context. Martin Heidegger discussed problems of identity and difference in two lectures (1957). Both terms today resurface at the center of the debate on questions of corporate identity or corporate design.

In Heidegger's words: "According to a common formula the axiom of identity reads: A = A. The axiom applies as the supreme rule of thinking. In the German language the identical is also called the same *(das Selbe)*. And for something to be the same, one thing is sufficient, while equivalence requires two. Hence this concept is based on a mediation, a combination, a synthesis: uniting into a unity" (Heidegger 1957).

Hence "identity" refers to the complete unity or correspondence of things or persons, to an essential consubstantiality. With regard to "identity," the question therefore is one of uniting or creating a synthesis of two different elements. Applied to the activities of corporations, organizations, or municipalities, this means that a company's internal performance profile, its specific know-how, expertise, and attitude is brought in line with its external performance profile (e.g., product design, communication, or the brand image). The degree of correspondence then represents the respective company identity. "Corporate identity" in this sense is an exact term for the unity of content, communication, and behavior of a company or organization (Bürdek 1987). The aim of all CI activities therefore must be to express the identity of a company's internal and external essence (Rieger 1989) or, to put it simply: "Be what you are."

A good way of finding out what that is, is by analyzing the personality of a company or institution. Defining the basic principles for implementing corporate identity in practice, Peter G. C. Lux (1998) explicitly pointed out that identity has to be shaped from within, and can never be imposed from the outside. To this end, Lux suggests emphasizing the respective "personality" (of the company or institution):

Its needs are a central concern in this context, while

expertise refers to particular skills and abilities, and

attitude stands for a company's philosophy and policy;

the constitution encompasses the physical, structural, organizational, and legal framework of activities;

temperament describes how results are achieved (i.e., the company's strengths, intensities, speed, and emotional state); while

origins relates current features back to the past, placing special emphasis on the principle of continuity; and

interests include the concrete mid- to long-term objectives and goals set for the future.

These, then, are the features that corporate identity experts outline, discuss, and decide. The next step is to work them into a code of conduct that is binding for all concerned and so provide the basis for design activities.

The Role of Product Design

Product design itself increasingly represents the central concern of all corporate measures. First impressions are the most lasting, and design determines the first impression that (potential) users have of the product. In 1980 Wolfgang Sarasin pointed out that, in many cases, forceful corporate identities emerged with the development of distinctive product identities. Since a company's identity-building process is primarily seen from the outside, he says, particular care has to go into aspects related to product design.

This is also an important background for the design campaigns that began in the 1990s and have only grown in importance since. Numerous European companies noticeably increased their design activities, even promoting them to the status of strategic instruments, as is especially evident in the automobile industry. In some Asian countries, such as Japan, South Korea, or Taiwan, and now especially strongly in China, design has been recognized as the crucial instrument for achieving success on a global scale, and is deployed accordingly.

Corporate Strategy

Corporate culture
Philosophy

Corporate identity
What you are or what you
want to be

Corporate image
Image to the public

Corporate
design

Corporate
communication

├ Architecture
├ Interior architecture
├ Industrial design
└ Interface design

The activities of numerous corporations and institutions illustrate the strategies employed, individually or in combination, to shape a company's image. The following areas are especially relevant in the context of design:

communication

behavior

product design

interface design

interior design and architecture

Corporate Communication

This is the area in which corporate design measures have been implemented most frequently. Following the outline mentioned above, all the elements of a company's graphic image are planned and realized on the basis of "design bibles," the design manuals that specify standards for the logotype, lettering, colors, printed materials, vehicle lettering, and similar material.

The Italian company Olivetti is both a classic and a pioneer in this field. In the early 1970s its Servizio di Corporate Identity section, headed by Hans von Klier, produced the legendary Red Books, laying down a design framework within which Olivetti's national subsidiaries could develop initiatives and variations of their own (Bachinger and Steguweit 1986). In the meantime, numerous other companies have developed similar graphic manuals, taking what is certainly an important step toward a corporate design (Schmidt 1994, 1995). From an international point of view, the design manual of the Xerox corporation is an outstanding example. Assembled in the 1980s, it sets up binding guidelines on product forms, communication materials, interfaces, and so on.

1 **Olivetti corporate design**
   shipping packages

2 **Corporate design manuals**
   (1971–1978), Olivetti

1

2

Corporate Behavior

Behavior – both inside the company and toward the outside – is an important factor in companies and institutions. It includes interaction between employees, but also their behavior toward people outside the company. A further aspect is behavior toward the media and the public. How are innovations, change, accidents, or other matters best communicated? Public-relations work in itself has become a key element of the behavior used by the public to gauge the credibility of a company or institution. A company's "image" is decisively shaped by its behavior, reflecting the way it is perceived and judged by the public. Though companies have realized that the challenge is to shape and design this image, product design has yet to address this adequately; nonetheless, it is one of the non-material aspects of design.

Corporate Design

This includes all measures aimed at shaping a company's image at the material level (i.e., its two- and three-dimensional manifestations from logo to company headquarters). This classic field of corporate activity is characterized by fixed design constants and variables that guarantee the desired unity in the visual appearance of companies and institutions. That includes binding instruments like the corporate design manuals mentioned above.

From Design Management to Strategic Design

Design Management

As design methodology emerged during the 1960s, currents sprang up, principally in the United Kingdom and North America, that were to contribute toward a positive re-evaluation of design in the context of corporate activities. Design management was the new battle cry.

Peter Behrens is once again the obvious figure to mention. His seminal work for AEG at the beginning of the twentieth century can be regarded as the first contribution to design management. The corporate design activities that Olivetti initiated during the 1930s also belong in this context. But it was only in 1966 that the Briton Michael Farr combined fundamental principles from systems theory and project management to derive a framework for handling design at the corporate level (Bürdek 1989).

These currents had a strong impact on approaches developed in Germany – which drew on British and American sources as well as methodological work done at the Ulm School of Design – especially on business economics. The main focus was on two issues:

the development of strategic planning

the problems related to systematic information management.

These early considerations centered on how companies can appropriately process the information and methodically pursue the kind of product development that successful corporate development relies on (beyond trial-and-error methods) (Geyer and Bürdek 1970). For this purpose, comprehensive checklists were compiled to aid companies in guiding processes and making decisions on a systematic and transparent basis. AW design was one of the first consulting agencies to develop corresponding instruments and implement them in the operations of a large number of companies (Geyer et al. 1970, 1972).

In the mid-1970s the DMI (Design Management Institute) was founded in Boston, Massachusetts. One of its aims was to prepare and distribute product case studies according to the method used at American business schools, investigating specific product developments to illustrate the possibilities of success and failure. The TRIAD design project, initiated together with the Harvard Business School, gained international acclaim. Fifteen case studies were outlined in a publication and a touring exhibition to draw attention to the importance of design management. Contributors included companies as diverse as the Swedish machine-tool company Bahco, the Dutch producer of ultrasound scanners Philips, as well as Braun (coffeemakers) and ERCO (gantry lighting systems) from Germany. The Design Management Institute regularly hosts seminars and conferences and also publishes the quarterly *Design Management Journal*. Over the course of the years the DMI has become a stable and influential institution. This is without doubt due to the strong business base of design in the United States (although a broader approach is pursued there today): "Design management encompasses the ongoing processes, business decisions, and strategies that enable innovation and create effectively designed products, services, communications, environments, and brands that enhance our quality of life and provide organizational success" (DMI). The DMI website points to the successful establishment of this approach at various universities, including Brunel University (United Kingdom), De Montfort University (United Kingdom), Illinois Institute of Technology Institute of Design (United States), Inholland University of Applied Sciences (the Netherlands), KAIST (South Korea), Lancaster University (United Kingdom), MIP – Politecnico di Milano (Italy), Parsons School of Design (United States), Pratt Institute (United States), Suffolk University (United States), University of Salford (United Kingdom), UMIST – University of Manchester Institute of Science and Technology (United Kingdom), and the University of Kansas (United States).

In the 1980s also in Germany the subject of design management received noticeable impetus once a small group of business economists realized that design had not only aesthetic effects, but also highly relevant economic impacts. A series of doctoral theses (e.g., Sybille Kicherer (1987), Heinrich Spieß (1993), Carlo Rummel (1995), and Hans Jörg Meier-Kortwig (1997)) exhaustively discussed related issues. Design gradually emancipated itself from its roots in the traditions of craftsmanship and gained its place as a full-fledged research discipline. In the 1970s economic considerations largely defeated efforts to shift the emphasis in design to environmental concerns.

However, it is this attitude (you could also call it an ethic) that moves companies to embrace design management. Their insecurity and ignorance of how to make design a success turned out to be a relevant gap that up-and-coming consultancy agencies in the 1990s filled by offering know-how in both design and industry, in packages covering the entire process of product development, from market analysis to the conceptual and project phase, to communication and market launch (Buck and Vogt 1996). A comprehensive approach was in order here, and companies also learned that it is possible to fill design with meaning and use it to position products in the market. This became especially evident in the European automobile industry, which garnered great success with a large number of new and differentiated vehicle types. What also became apparent was that beyond individual projects, images and brands – or the process today known as branding – play an increasingly important role.

In his anthology of case studies of German companies (Heidelberger Druckmaschinen AG, Rowenta, Vaillant, Volkswagen, Wilkhahn, Wöhner), Alex Buck (2003) clearly demonstrates that "design visualizes – everything!" and notes that "the transition from a post-functionalist world to a semantically dominated one is now finally being accomplished in industrial terms too." His theoretical ideas are deeply rooted in the product language model (↗ p. 136), which he calls the only internally consistent model on design theory.

The case studies cover the positioning of brands and companies (branding), strategic efforts to redefine these, and the required corporate design and corporate identity measures, from trade fair appearances to the aforementioned corporate design manuals (↗ p. 193 ff).

Brigitte Borja de Mozota (2003), who is associated with the DMI and teaches at the Parsons Paris School of Art and Design, published a more theoretically slanted academic study on the topic of design management. For her too, design is the driving force for companies to create identifiable differences, to coordinate all development measures, and ultimately to transform themselves for market visibility. Mozota also conducts case studies in which she uses examples of corporate activity to explain the issues of design management.

Branding

The term branding originally referred to the marking of cattle on the North American plains. A branding iron burned their owner's name into the cattle's hides for permanent identification. The same idea can be recognized today: individual products are only identifiable (and recognizable to potential buyers) if they stand out from the surrounding variety, if they are conspicuous enough to gain attention: labels such as Made by Sony, Made by Daimler, or simply Adidas, Apple, Google, Huawei, Levi's, LG, Microsoft, Nike, Nokia, Palm, Puma, Samsung, Siemens, Swatch, Vitra, and so forth. The name of a company has to have the same connotation worldwide, and economic globalization (↗ p. 69 ff) is reflected in product design.

In more and more areas, technical performance is largely identical, with products even being assembled from the same components (e.g., chips mass-produced by Asian manufacturers). So while design plays an important role for differentiation, branding (i.e., the trademark image) gains significance as the factor that, in the end, decides the purchase. Today global corporations like Google, Apple, IBM, and Microsoft lead the world brand rankings. It is characteristic of the twenty-first century that these are all from the digital sector.

Strategic Design

Since the 1990s, design has become an increasingly central concern in product development, with designers taking on an increasing number of communicative tasks for companies, ranging from corporate design to corporate culture, corporate communication, and so forth. The challenge for designers results from their position at the interface of design and business concerns, which also requires a secure sense of context: for example, the contexts of corporate cultures or target groups. The specific role of design here is to illustrate concepts and product strategies in convincing images, communicating at a non-verbal level. "Imagineering" (↗ p. 243) is the apposite term coined to describe this approach.

Strategic Design, De Tao master class for strategic design Shanghai
Hartmut Esslinger, (2010)

Close interaction with business is the heart of strategic design, which is economically successful design (Hermann and Möller 2011). The point from the perspective of business is to pursue product development processes where aspects of quality, functionality, efficiency, sustainability, and customer orientation are addressed in an integrated form.

Hartmut Esslinger's model of strategic design spans a much broader frame, relocating design in the process of globalization. Alongside technology and the economic, he argues for the so-called soft sciences such as anthropology and ethnology (↗ p. 251f) to be included in the development process, along with semantics (↗ p. 177 ff). These three fields represent a significant step forward for design in the twenty-first century. And they will be decisive for future product design, because of the need to establish core competences that describe central components of the value creation process – in contrast to DIY design (↗ p. 255), which supplies no contribution.

In her dissertation, Johanna Schönberger (2011) investigates the current anchoring of creativity and innovation in the business world and asks what action needs to be taken. She proceeds largely empirically, in the form of fifty interviews conducted in countries across the globe with academics, researchers, and practitioners. The interviews clearly reveal that "strategic design" is an indispensable factor for any globally operating corporation.

Design Thinking

The origins of design thinking can be traced back to the English designer John Woollatt, who studied under John Chris Jones and Nigel Cross in the 1960s, and later taught design at Northumbria University in Newcastle, United Kingdom. The actual concept of design thinking arose in the 1990s in the Californian IT circles (Terry Winograd) and the design firm IDEO (David Kelley, Bill Moggridge, and Mike Nuttall). The idea was that interdisciplinary working groups in companies and institutions should develop new concepts departing far from the beaten track.

This method (which is actually typical for design) was promoted especially strongly by former SAP CEO Hasso Plattner, who founded his Hasso Plattner Institute of Design at Stanford and a School of Design Thinking at the Hasso-Plattner-Institut für Softwaresystemtechnik in Potsdam. The target group of these institutes, however, is not designers, but those responsible for product and project development in corporations and institutions.

The methodological framework is undeniably based on the Anglo-American design methodology movement of the 1960s, where the individual problem solving steps were described: understand, observe, define perspective, invent, visualize or prototype, develop, and test. These were then adopted by the design thinking movement.

The hype over design thinking (which is, incidentally, not itself design, but only a step on the way there) has been massively directed to economic ends by the protagonists. But, as Donald A. Norman (2010) describes, what they presented as new is in fact banal: All disciplines have creative actors who transcend boundaries, think ahead, etc. This, he shows, is certainly not a design-specific phenomenon.

Annalena Kluge (2013) builds on Reckwitz's discussion of design as an aesthetic management (2012). She goes on to ask whether design thinking cannot in fact be understood as a management technique and as a component of an economics of the aesthetic. Here she also connects to the aforementioned dissertation by Johanna Schönberger (2011) and proposes assigning design thinking a mediating role between economics and design. Pursuing design thinking in the span between creativity and innovation would cultivate special awareness "for the sensing, perceiving, communication, and shaping of aesthetically, sensorily, and emotionally effectual atmospheres."

Architecture and Design

The history, theory, and practice of design are closely linked to developments in architecture. From Vitruvius's famous treatise on architecture, which upheld *firmitas* (solidity), *utilitas* (utility), and *venustas* (beauty) (↗ p. 18) (Bürdek 1997b) to the present, architectural theory has referred not only to function, but also to aesthetic effect and design, particularly to the meaning of buildings. But what is a matter of course in architecture is not nearly as well established in the theory of design. Wolfgang Welsch (1996) puts it pithily: "Architecture's effect is real and symbolic."

Architectural theory naturally homes in on the meanings of buildings, in a way that remains largely absent in design. Thus product presentations (at design schools) often take the form of inventors' fairs, with pseudo-functional explanations stuck in the thinking of the 1970s. Design – quite unlike architecture – has made little progress to date in establishing itself as a social and cultural discipline.

As the oldest, often designated "mother" of the arts, architecture acquired a very important role for design at the beginning of the twentieth century. Many early designers, not least Peter Behrens, Walter Gropius, Mart Stam, Le Corbusier, and Mies van der Rohe, were architects. Walter Gropius, in the 1919 Bauhaus manifesto, called building the ultimate goal of all design activities, and all classes and workshops were geared toward it. The impacts of the architecture and urban planning that triggered a critique of functionalism have already been pointed out (↗ p. 59). Building activities after World War II, especially in Europe, were so intense that they prevented a discussion of what it was that architects did. Occasional individual statements could hardly aspire to the status of architectural theory. It was only after the building boom declined in the 1970s that architects once more began to feel the need for theoretical foundations (Kruft 1985).

Important impetus came from American architects. On the occasion of an exhibition at the New York Museum of Modern Art in 1932, Philip Johnson, together with Henry-Russell Hitchcock, published *The International Style*, giving this term worldwide currency. During the 1950s, however, Johnson shed the influence of Mies van der Rohe, and turned his interest toward postmodern architecture.

Architects also had a strong influence on the emergence of Italian design. Mario Bellini, Rodolfo Bonetto, Achille and Pier Giacomo Castiglioni, Paolo Deganello, Alessandro Mendini, Ettore Sottsass, and Marco Zanuso shaped, one could even say invented, Italian *bel design* and determined its features through several decades.

In the United States the impact of French structuralism was especially strong in the field of linguistics. Though Tom Wolfe (1986) saw its roots in a kind of late-Marxist duff, its effect on the young Robert Venturi was positive and momentous. His book *Complexity and Contradiction in Architecture,* published in 1966 in the United States, is rooted in a pluralistic attitude (hence the title) and can be seen as the first argued challenge to the predominant International Style. Venturi pointed out that architectural thought in the 1960s turned exclusively on function and form, and that hardly any architects took account of the symbolism of architecture. He used the terms "ambiguity," "double-functioning," and "plurality," and integrated the frame of reference of Gestalt psychology. In architecture, the frame of reference can be employed to extend the reference of a sign to include a meaning beyond its immediate signification. This was the first mention of the symbolism of architecture, which was given much greater scope in *Learning from Las Vegas,* published in 1972 by Robert Venturi, Denise Scott Brown, and Steven Izenour. The authors focused on semiotics (↗ p. 83 ff) as an explanatory model for architectural phenomena. Looking back in 2002, Robert Venturi and Denise Scott Brown said: "We feel that it is an obsolete approach to make architecture ever more abstract, to reduce it ever farther. That was an important development, but the challenge today is to open architecture to meaning and endow it with a new symbolism." With regard to the language of architecture they refer to early church buildings which, they say, did not just stand around meaninglessly, but had much to tell people, be it by their imposing shape, the rituals celebrated inside, or the sermons and interpretations proclaimed from the pulpit.

The debate on postmodernist literature that began in the United States in the late 1960s came to Europe by two channels, through the works of Jean-François Lyotard (1982, 1985) and through actual implementation in architecture: "Architecture may not be the first, but it is certainly the most prominent manifestation of the postmodern. It was through architecture and the related debate that people learned that today there is a postmodernist agenda, and that it is not just an idea but a reality" (Welsch 1987).

The worldwide breakthrough of postmodern architecture came in 1978 when Charles Jencks published his book *The Language of Post-Modern Architecture*. The author proclaimed the death of modernity, dating its demise to 15 July 1972 at precisely 3:32 p.m. in St. Louis, Missouri. To him, the end of the International Style in architecture had come with the demolition of the dilapidated Pruitt-Igoe housing estate. The mention of language in the book's title clearly indicates the frame of reference, a renunciation of the monotony and univalence of the International Style. Postmodernism developed from semiotics, which, as a branch of linguistics and hence one of the humanities, allows very different interpretations.

In 1987 Charles Jencks described eleven emergent rules of postmodern classicism in a list that included the terms "cultural pluralism," "eclecticism," "double coding," "multivalence," and "tradition reinterpreted," and illustrated them with examples of existing buildings. This underlines how much importance architecture today attaches to semiotic debate. Wolfgang Welsch even defines postmodernism as the recourse to semiotics, and Hanno-Walter Kruft identified the symbolism of architecture as the common denominator in contemporary architectural theories. Obviously, it was no accident that in a parallel development the emphasis in design also shifted to the communicative function of objects. Architecture and design both moved from working with the notion of function to exploring the meaning of buildings or objects in order to arrive at an encompassing language of objects.

The architectural and cultural theorist Stephan Trüby (2014) calls the contemporary boom in banking architecture *architecture parlante,* where the point is to semiotically heighten the actual function to a point where banks become signs visible from far afield in the heart of the great cities. The architect Wolfgang Prix argues that the new headquarters of the European Central Bank in Frankfurt am Main, designed by Coop Himmelb(l)au from Vienna, shows that the European Union needs three-dimensional icons – what he refers to as "assigned meaning." And the bank building itself has even been compared to Ulm Cathedral at the entrance to the old city.

Due to the postmodern movement, architecture at the end of the twentieth century experienced a new boom that found expression in a wide variety of concepts, styles, and manifestations. Many architects engage in theoretical discourse on their buildings, relating them to their respective historical, philosophical, or cultural contexts. This dimension is almost entirely lacking with designers. Their widespread speechlessness ultimately attests to the discipline's lack of maturity, which, however, is hardly surprising. After all, documents of architectural theory go back more than 2,000 years, while the history of design is barely 150 years old.

The various museum buildings erected in many countries are especially illuminating, providing a broad field for experiments with a linguistic angle, while at the same time adding important traits to the identity of a city or region that contribute toward image transfer. Even more recently Asian states – China in particular, but also Hong Kong, South Korea, and Singapore – have made a name for themselves with spectacular buildings intended to visualize their progress. The 2008 Summer Olympics in Beijing, for example, provided an occasion for striking symbols of the country's international reputation with spectacular buildings like the National Stadium ("Bird's Nest"), designed by Swiss architects Herzog & de Meuron. In many cases the post-Olympic use is more than a little problematic; here symbolism has been given clear priority over sustainability.

Volker Fischer (1988b) once referred to this kind of boundary crossing between architecture and design as professional piracy of a decidedly one-sided nature. Numerous architects quite naturally move into the professional field of design by producing, incidentally it seems, furniture, lighting fixtures, door handles, accessories, and so forth.

Today globally operating architecture firms maintain their own design departments to create the fittings and furnishings they require in-house. The projects involved these days extend far beyond the classic example of doorhandles (as designed by such as Otto Wagner, Walter Gropius, Ludwig Mies van der Rohe, Ludwig Wittgenstein, Egon Eiermann, Peter Eisenman, Christoph Ingenhoven, Josef Paul Kleihues, or Santiago Calatrava; FSB 2011). Designers who build are rather rare, not least on account of the strict regulations governing admission to the profession (whereas anyone can call themselves a designer). Nevertheless, there are examples of designers encroaching into the field of architecture.

In 1994, Philippe Starck designed a wooden house near Paris for his own use and marketed the building kit through the mail-order firm Trois Suisses; and in 1999, Matteo Thun developed the low-energy house *O Sole Mio* for a German manufacturer. The London-based Israeli designer (and architect) Ron Arad designed the Bauhaus Museum in Tel Aviv (2008) and jointly with Bruno

Door-handles, FSB – Franz Schneider Brakel

from left to right:
model 1023: Max Bill / Ernst Moeckl /
Johannes Potente, (1957)
model 1106: Christoph Mäckler (2000)
model 1004: David Chipperfield (2010)

model 1034: Johannes Potente (1953)
model 1064: Nicholas Grimshaw (1996)
model 1102: Walter Gropius / Alessandro Mendini (1987)

model 1147: Ludwig Wittgenstein / FSB-Werksentwurf
model 1111: Philippe Starck (1991)
model 1224: Alfredo Häberli (2012)

Asa the Design Museum in Holon, Israel (2010). The German designer Werner Aisslinger operates successfully at the intersections of architecture, interior design, and product design. His projects include the LoftCube (2003/2007), a hotel for urban nomads inhabiting temporarily unused roof spaces (Aisslinger 2010). The Italian designer Massimo Iosa Ghini worked on the Memphis collection in the 1980s, in the fields of furniture, lighting, and lifestyle, but also works as an architect (Iosa Ghini 2013). The French designer Matali Crasset (2007) moved from designing objects to rooms and then buildings. She has designed a hotel in Nice, an oversized dovecote near Cambrai, France, as well as exhibition stands for companies.

Architects as Designers

The work of a number of architects illustrates the close connection between building and product. The aforementioned Peter Behrens (↗ p. 24 f an 190) was one of the foremost early protagonists of boundary-crossing design at the beginning of the twentieth century (Windsor 1985). And an exhibition by Barbara Mundt (1998) showed wide-ranging examples of product design by architects operating both as interior designers (furniture) and as engineers or students of nature (bionic design). Today the spectrum of their design activities is considerably wider-ranging.

Tadao Ando In projects that reflect the logic and stringency of European philosophers like Heidegger and Wittgenstein, Japanese architect Tadao Ando has been strikingly successful in using contemporary materials to reinterpret traditional conceptions of space. The seminar and conference center he built for Vitra in Weil am Rhein, for example, expresses a high degree of concentration and contemplation in untreated concrete walls and austere furnishings. It is the users who bring these spaces to life.

Alfredo Arribas Alfredo Arribas was an important representative of new Spanish design (Bertsch 1993). The restaurants, bars, and shops he created in Barcelona, Frankfurt am Main, Fukuoka, Madrid, Sapporo, and Tokyo express contemporary metropolitan lifestyles in a vivid architectural idiom, and his buildings were soon adopted as in-places by a young, trendy, and well-to-do group of customers.

Asymptote The work of the American group of architects and designers Asympote spans the gamut of traditional architecture, urban design, multi-media installations, and computer-generated environments. For Knoll they designed the A3 office system, an environment representing a congenial combination of micro- and macro-architecture. The A3 project is a good example of the way architecture, product design, and media increasingly merge into each other.

Mario Botta Based in Swiss Ticino, Botta is an important representative of an approach to design that emphasizes the regional and topographical context of a project. His furniture, living accessories, and door-handle designs for FSB rely on reduced forms characterized by geometric simplicity. The objects are icons of equal status to his buildings and represent a highly topical reinterpretation of modernism in addressing design and its relevance to all aspects of living spaces.

Santiago Calatrava Spanish architect Santiago Calatrava is one of the representatives of a structural approach to design oriented on organic models whose buildings stand out spectacularly, like icons, in their locations. His focus is on bridges and public buildings, but he also designs furniture. Important buildings he has created include train stations in Lisbon (for EXPO 1998), Lyon (TGV high-speed), and Reggio Emilia (Italy, Mediopadana high-speed), Bilbao Airport, various buildings in the City of Arts and Sciences in Valencia, and the Olympic complex in Athens. As a designer he works in the fields of drawing, sculpture, and ceramics.

Coop Himmelb(l)au This Austrian group was founded in Vienna in 1968 by Wolf D. Prix, Helmut Swiczinsky, and Rainer Michael Holzer. Under the influence of the experimental creations of Hans Hollein and the group Haus-Rucker-Co., they concentrated mostly on pneumatic structures, discussed alternative urban structures, and actively promoted a deconstructivist approach to design. Their "burning" projects (Reiss Bar, Flammenflügel, Hot Flat, and others) express opposition to postmodernism, which they see as a new Biedermeier period. Their emblematic kitchen design Mahlzeit (1990) redefined the preparation of meals as the central activity of living. Using materials like stainless steel, Coop Himmelb(l)au staged the kitchen as a professional workplace at home and anticipated the kitchen boom that was to unfold in the 1990s. Their UFA multiplex cinema in Dresden (1998) is probably one of the most idiosyncratic deconstructivist buildings ever realized.

Egon Eiermann The German architect Egon Eiermann was also a well-known designer who embraced a holistic principle of design. Important buildings include the Kaiser Wilhelm Memorial Church in Berlin, offices for Olivetti in Frankfurt am Main, the German embassy in Washington, and an office building for IBM in Stuttgart. His numerous designs for furniture sought to relate interior to exterior and to achieve a uniformity of spaces (Eiermann 1999). Apart from numerous chairs of molded plywood or wickerwork, he designed base frames for drawing tables originally intended for his own studio. Characterized by high flexibility and variability, they can support different types of worktops and became an emblematic product of the twentieth century. Legibility was an important feature of his designs, with visible construction details revealing how the pieces of furniture worked.

Norman Foster Early in his career the Briton Norman Foster (honored with a life peerage in 1999) worked with Richard Rogers, and together they developed a high-tech architecture that explored the possibilities of cutting-edge technologies. One example of their approach is his Sainsbury Centre for Visual Arts at the University of East Anglia, near Norwich, England. Foster Associates achieved its international breakthrough with the Hong Kong headquarters of the Hongkong and Shanghai Bank. Apart from numerous public buildings, Foster also designed airports (London Stansted, Hong Kong, Beijing T3), train stations, a metro system in Bilbao (for which the German graphic designer Otl Aicher created the visual image), bridges, service stations, high-rises, hotels, Two World Trade Center New York, Masdar City (the first eco-city in Abu Dhabi, presently under construction), and many others (Jenkins 2000). Foster's mentor is Richard Buckminster Fuller (with whom he worked for more than ten years); in his work he seeks to harmonize social philosophy with technology (Foster, 1999).

The mutual interdependence of exterior and interior is another of Foster's themes. For the Hongkong and Shanghai Bank, his practice created the office furniture system Nomos, which uses the same technological vocabulary as the building itself, and thus defines furnishings as architecture in miniature. Be it a tray designed for Alessi, a bathroom series for Duravit and Hoesch, lamps for ERCO, door-handle designs for FSB, desktop accessories for Helit, or office furniture for Thonet, all Foster's designs are characterized by the same rigor and dedication to quality as the buildings. No doubt the manufacturers of these products also benefit from the image transfer linked to designs by Norman Foster.

Frank O. Gehry Gehry, a Canadian-born American, started out with deconstructivist buildings (e.g., a private home in Santa Monica, California) and is today considered one of the world's most important and idiosyncratic designers. His proposal for the Vitra Design Museum in Weil am Rhein made an essential contribution to the company's overall corporate identity. With the Guggenheim Museum in Bilbao, he created one of the most spectacular museums of the twentieth century. In its wake the city itself changed profoundly from a dismal industrial port to a cultural center in northern Spain as masses of visitors attracted high-class galleries and shops. It is a development that has altered the character of the entire region. The boundaries between art, design, and architecture have begun to shift, and Gehry's congenial crossings stand for highly topical approaches that are landmarks on today's cultural map.

Zaha Hadid Born in Iraq and today based in London, Zaha Hadid is considered the architect pursuing the most expressive, but also the most deconstructivist approach of all her contemporaries. Her international breakthrough came in 1983 when her spectacular drawings won the competition for the Peak project in Hong Kong. Her large-format drawings of urban situations and buildings seek to illustrate what new, visionary concepts of construction could look like. In her work Hadid pursues a radical rediscovery and reinterpretation of modernism. Her philosophy of velocity, buoyancy, and contemporaneity is brilliantly expressed in the fire station of the Vitra company in Weil am Rhein (her first building to be completed, in 1993). Today, it houses a collection of eighty-three chairs, all of them classics of twentieth-century design. Other important works by Hadid include the Contemporary Arts Center in Cincinnati, a pavilion for the international gardening show (Landesgartenschau) in Weil am Rhein, the Mind Zone in London's Millennium Dome, the central building of the new BMW plant in Leipzig, the MAXXI Center for Contemporary Arts in Rome, and the ferry terminal in Salerno. Her most recent project, Messner Mountain Museum Corones, is nearing completion.

Hadid's designs for furniture also reflect her consistent approach. Manufactured since 1988, they embody the transition from spaces to objects. For the company Sawaya & Moroni she designed the Z-Scape furniture line of expressive tables and lounge furniture. The sofa glacier (2001) is shaped like an iceberg, made of CNC-machined wood, and weighs about 600 kilograms (1,300lb). She has also designed products for companies including Zumtobel, Artemide, Magis, and Marburger Tapetenfabrik.

Hans Hollein The Austrian Hollein was considered one of the most important representatives of postmodernism. The transition from object to space to make a gesamtkunstwerk was a characteristic feature of his creative work. Even his earliest commissions – a candle shop and a jewelry store in Vienna, and the partly state-owned tourist office based in the same city – were marked by an idiomatic expressiveness. His international breakthrough came with the Abteiberg Museum in the German city of Mönchengladbach. The works of art presented there enter into harmonious relationships with the museum's interiors and architecture. The MMK Museum of Modern Art erected in Frankfurt am Main is considered one of the highlights of postmodern architecture. The objects Hollein designed for the Memphis collection in the early 1980s are among the few examples of postmodern furniture design. Apart from various pieces of jewelry and watches, he designed tiles and sunglasses, a grand piano for Bösendorf, a crystal phial for Swarovski, and also a door-handle for the German company FSB, all of which unfold complex meanings in a tradition of narrative design.

Christoph Ingenhoven German architect Christoph Ingenhoven's projects include the RWE Tower in Essen and planning for the new subterranean railway station in Stuttgart and Google's Palo Alto campus. Ingenhoven Architekten maintains a design department for "secondary architecture," including sanitaryware, lighting, fittings (including for FSB), as well as an office container for Vitra.

Toyo Ito The Japanese architect Ito addresses the continuously changing interrelations between human beings, nature, and technology. Ito is an architect who uses new technologies extensively while at the same time emphasizing the effect and experience of space on and for users. His exploration of the topic of wind led Ito to the roots of Japanese living, with sliding walls and sparse furnishings, defining rooms characterized by a high flexibility.

Rem Koolhaas In 1975 the Dutch architect Koolhaas founded the OMA (Office for Metropolitan Architecture), which started out with artistic and experimental design projects. His design for the flagship store of Italian fashion giant Prada in New York congenially crossed the boundaries between architecture, design, and fashion (Koolhaas/OMA/AMO 2001). In extensive explorations that, among other things, yielded a voluminous book on shopping, he and his collaborators analyzed the phenomenon of shopping around the world (Koolhaas/OMA/AMO 2002). The shop itself is staged like a play. The premises include platforms, follow a dramaturgy, and are enlivened by changes of scenery, from daytime shop to nighttime space for concerts, performance, or discotheque.

Richard Meier The American Meier gives the tradition of classical modernism a contemporaneous twist. White interior and exterior surfaces endow his freestanding buildings with a brilliance that can be said to reflect back on the architect himself. Meier translates the same reduced idiom of shapes, focused on simple geometric forms, to furniture designs mostly created for the buildings he designed. His output includes designs for Alessi (tea services), Knoll International (object furniture), and Swid Powell (silver bowls). To him, design is as important an area of creative productivity as architecture (Fischer 2003).

Alessandro Mendini The Italian architect, designer, and critic Mendini is one of the pioneers of design in the second half of the twentieth century. He co-initiated the Memphis movement at the beginning of the 1980s, founded the Alchimia studio in Milan, and designed numerous artifacts. Moving effortlessly between architecture, design, fine art, literature, and music, Mendini is the prototypical boundary-crossing artist, and his work can undoubtedly be described as a *gesamtkunstwerk*.

Jean Nouvel The Frenchman Nouvel is probably one of the most intellectual architects of the present day. Strongly influenced by the philosophical and sociological currents of his country (e.g., Jean Baudrillard, Jacques Derrida, and Paul Virilio), he developed a symbolic architecture, always using the latest in high-tech materials. He aims to test the principles of statics and to disrupt sensory experience. His minimalist aesthetics juxtapose simple exteriors with often highly complex interior structures in his buildings (Nouvel 2001).

The Institut du Monde Arabe in Paris (1987) united these aspects to a high degree and added a reinterpretation of Arabic ornament in facade elements that change depending on the incidence of light. Nouvel's design for the Fondation Cartier in Paris (1995) addressed the question of materiality and non-materiality, which, with the coming of the new digital media, has also been discussed in the field of design since the late 1980s. A curtain of glass panes renders the building both visible and invisible by affecting to adhere to the existing line of buildings, while the real building, also fronted in glass, is markedly set back in a park. Nouvel is revealed as an expert player in the game of reality and unreality. For this building Nouvel designed the office system Less, which is manufactured and marketed by the Italian company UniFor. The desktops resemble two-dimensional disks; made from aluminum, their necessary third dimension is only revealed at second glance, when examined from below. All technical features, cables, and so on remain invisible, seemingly non-material.

Aldo Rossi The Italian Rossi was one of the most important representatives of the rational architecture that had its roots in the 1920s (Adolf Loos, Le Corbusier, Mies van der Rohe). Attention to ratio was recommended by Vitruvius (Bürdek 1997b) and today finds a place in the concepts of the rationalist branch of the postmodernist movement. Rossi also published a number of theoretical essays on issues of architecture and urban planning (1966, 1975). His work was represented at the 1980 Venice Biennale, which was devoted to milestones in the incipient postmodern architecture movement. His contribution, the floating Teatro del Mondo, proved him a master of allusion to a historical vocabulary. It is only consistent that the skills he perfected in manufacturing stage sets point back to his experience as a stage designer for the opera.

His project for the Bonnefantenmuseum (1995) in Maastricht (Netherlands) proposed a museum that resembles an austere, functional industrial building of the early twentieth century. A number of details give perfect expression to Rossi's delight in asceticism and his penchant for simple geometric forms: A seemingly endless flight of stairs refers to Mediterranean streets with glaring light at the end. The building's domes are clad in zinc sheets to evoke the style of industrial buildings, which the deliberate color scheme inside the building caricatures in an ironic twist. The entire building plays with shape and color in ubiquitous allusions to architecture past and present.

The distinctive independence of his buildings is reflected in the micro-architectures of the products designed by Rossi, ranging from coffee pots for Alessi, to seating furniture for Molteni, and the office system Parigi for the Italian company UniFor. His designs for the Maastricht museum provided the basis for the Cartesio bookcase, which mirrors the geometric austerity of Rossi's rationalist style of design.

James Stirling The Briton Stirling began his career with a critical examination of the late works of Le Corbusier, such as the church at Ronchamp (1957) in France, which turned his interest to brutalism, a style of design conspicuous for its use of exposed concrete *(béton brut)*. Up until the 1970s he designed numerous buildings in this style, including the Leicester University Engineering Building, the Olivetti Training School in Haslemere, buildings for Siemens AG, and the Derby Civic Centre.

At the end of the 1970s Stirling consciously embraced postmodernism and became the spokesman for a narrative approach to design that was not without ironic overtones. His method relied on the quotation of individual phenomena from the history of architecture (such as Schinkel's domed halls, the stoa of antiquity, or Palladian neoclassicism), reinterpreting them in new contexts that yielded new meanings, "teaching architecture to dance" (Pehnt 1992).

The Neue Staatsgalerie in Stuttgart (1984), for example, recalls the forms of an Italian palazzo. But at its center is a classical rotunda, the trapezoid pylon follows the Egyptian style, and the access ramps are designed to be imposing. The interior is also characterized by deliberate inconsistencies that juxtapose a bright green high-tech elevator with massive mushroom-headed pillars in the exhibition rooms. All the same, the interior provides a contemplative atmosphere that contrasts clearly with the spectacular exterior, and the museum as gesamtkunstwerk is in harmony with the works of art it houses.

With his 1992 design of factory buildings for the German medical technology company B. Braun, based in Melsungen, Stirling made an important contribution to the industrial architecture of the late twentieth century. Starting out as a functional and rational workplace, the building mutated into a postmodern ensemble that gives employees a sense of belonging and identity.

Hadi Teherani The Iranian Hadi Teherani runs an architecture, interior architecture, and design firm in Hamburg. His buildings include the airport

Swiss pavilion, Expo Hannover
Design: Peter Zumthor (2000)

high-speed rail station in Frankfurt, Zayed University in Abu Dhabi, and the Dancing Towers in Hamburg. In his architectural work he is interested in holistic design of overall architectural concepts, indirectly drawing on the early modernism of the Bauhaus. His design projects range through office chairs, kitchens (Poggenpohl), lighting, door-handles (FSB), and writing implements (Montblanc), to name but a few.

Oswald Mathias Ungers Early in the 1980s the German architect Ungers began to explore the square as a basic geometric form that was to become a characteristic feature of his design style. Ungers' designs extend to the interiors of his buildings, so it is only consistent that the chairs he created for the German Museum of Architecture (DAM) in Frankfurt am Main should translate the formal overall concept to a smaller scale. The result is a black wooden frame with square, white leather upholstery. The building's austerity has been communicated directly to the furniture.

Peter Zumthor Swiss architect Zumthor is one of the most rigorous representatives of his field, putting stringency, passion, and perfectionism into buildings that completely redefine the concept of space. Training as a carpenter in his father's workshop, he learned early on what flawless craftsmanship means, and his ten-year experience in conservation gave him an intimate knowledge of buildings. Zumthor almost exclusively uses natural materials (wood, stone, metal, or concrete) openly exposed to the eye. He uses harsh and geometric forms, and from the outside the buildings resemble solitaires. The interiors, in contrast, feel warm and comfortable. His intellectual point of reference is the philosopher Heidegger (1967), whose "longing for the primeval, for a sense of belonging, of being at home" he can well understand (Zumthor 2001). But beyond all questions of philosophy or design, he is not only interested in ideas or images, but in the things themselves, and their value as such. Their vividness is what fascinates Zumthor. Hence, the rock pool built from gray-green natural stone in the Swiss spa of Vals (1997) is a powerful symbol of nature, water, repose, and profound contemplation. Zumthor's art house in Bregenz in Austria is a translucent cube that after nightfall shines out luminously across the waters of Lake Constance.

Zumthor also designed the Swiss pavilion for EXPO 2000 in Hanover. For this temporary event he used 3,000 square meters (9,800 sq. ft.) of fir beams connected without screws, nails, or plugs. Steel braces provided the building's only supporting structure, leaving the individual beams undamaged for later reuse. The open pavilion, designed as an acoustic body, generated an intense sense of space through the scent of the wood, its untreated surfaces, and the pattern formed by the beams. Nature itself became an open room, a metaphor that seems highly appropriate for the country represented, Switzerland.

Utopias, Visions, Concepts, and Trends

The previous chapter has shown that far from revolving solely around its more immediate products – from individual buildings to the built environment – architecture tends to look beyond the everyday business of designing. Architects discuss the tasks of architecture in intellectual debates that go much deeper than any undertaken in the field of design. Moreover, the utopias and visions outlined in architecture provide room for analyzing, formulating, outlining, and simulating new concepts of living and designing. In contrast to design, architecture has taken these dimensions into account throughout its history.

The origins of utopian thought go back to antiquity and Plato's writings on the *politeia,* but the subject only began to draw wider attention when, in 1516, Thomas More published *Utopia*. Francis Bacon picked up the theme in *Nova Atlantis* (1626), and utopian, foresighted, and conceptual approaches to design have a long tradition in architecture (Kruft 1985). Some examples will serve to illustrate this.

In the eighteenth century French architect Étienne-Louis Boullée created designs not intended for realization, but for display in an imaginary museum of architecture. His compatriot and contemporary Claude-Nicolas Ledoux, an adherent of the French Revolution, designed buildings whose most important aspect was their symbolic meaning.

Mars Station, Mars One, The Netherlands (2012)

Italian futurism as it emerged at the beginning of the twentieth century was regarded as a prime example of a boundless idealization of technology, and the Russian artist Kazimir Malevich even attempted to design architecture that would articulate the tenets of a communist society.

The Japanese metabolists and Richard Buckminster Fuller are among the best-known utopians of the twentieth century, both in the field of architecture and in design. In the late 1960s Hans Hollein, among others, explored futuristic architectures, and the English group Archigram (including Peter Cook) developed projects expressive of a positivist technology cult.

Since the 1970s Léon Krier, the Site group, Coop Himmelb(l)au, Superstudio, Peter Eisenman, Rem Koolhaas, Bernard Tschumi, Daniel Libeskind, and, since the early 1980s, Zaha Hadid, in particular, have explored the future of space and time in drawings and designs (McQuaid 2003). The Viennese group Haus-Rucker-Co (Günter Zamp Kelp, Laurids Ortner, and Klaus Pinter), which drew up visionary architectural and urban planning concepts between 1967 and 1977, became especially significant. Riding the upbeat, rocket-fueled mood of the 1960s, they focused on the trendy. More than anything, they were about "mind expanding" (Blomberg 2014).

In the 1990s the Dutch MVRDV group continued the long tradition of utopian and visionary architecture. The Netherlands pavilion that MVRDV designed for EXPO 2000 in Hanover, for example, was among the most spectacular structures exhibited there: the very smallness of the country spawned the idea of carving its traits onto several thematic levels and presenting them as a stacked landscape in a horizontal building.

Early Design Utopias

Taking Thomas More as his inspiration, Jürgen Zänker's (1981) *Utopisches Design oder Utopie des Design* (Utopian design or utopia of design) examines in particular the work of William Morris (1890). Morris is regarded as one of the fathers of design and at the same time one of the last "utopian socialists," for to him, the two functions embodied in the artist and the social revolutionary were basically one and the same.

Both Bauhaus and the Ulm School of Design took up this socially oriented understanding of the utopia. The Bauhaus approach was based on a radical vision: to develop new design concepts that would overcome the petit-bourgeois fustiness of the nineteenth century.

The social vision in the Bauhaus approach, however, was also evident in the belief that new design concepts could bring about democratic change in society. Investigations into the objective, scientific conditions of design were seen as a basis for this. At the Institute for Environmental Planning, the successor to the Ulm School of Design, (↗ p. 43), there was even a working group on "needs research" to investigate the "true" needs of society (Baehr and Kotik 1972). As we have seen, needs transformed into "desire-needs" around the turn of the twenty-first century, engendering a process of dramatic change in the industrialized world. But in the second and third worlds important needs remain unfulfilled.

The German designer Luigi Colani, who in the 1960s and 1970s was a proponent of an approach to design characterized by organic and erotic forms (Dunas 1993; Bangert 2004), gained fame with futuristic visions including a spherical kitchen, a secretary's workplace, and a container truck for the year 2001. Many of his drawings of cars and airplanes were greeted with acclaim by sensationalist marketing people who presented the designs at trade shows to create an aura of progressiveness for their companies. However, few of Colani's designs were ever actually produced.

1 **Truck on a DAF-chassis**
  Design: Luigi Colani
  Karlsruhe (1985)

2 **Visiona**
  Design: Verner Panton
  Fa. Bayer AG, Leverkusen (1970)

1

2

The 1960s ushered in the age of space travel both in the USSR and in the United States, and the impact was felt in the field of design. The designs Verner Panton made for Bayer AG were not quite as abstruse as Colani's. The annual *Visiona* exhibition staged orgies of color and material that reflected the brave new world of synthetics of the late 1960s. These futuristic homes had more to do with the world of science fiction than with real human needs, and accordingly contributed little to meeting them. At that time, the Italian designer Joe Colombo also designed futuristic habitats.

One nuance of meaning worth noting is that the idea of utopia always implies an element of social change, whereas visions are no more than projections of possible – or fanciful – future buildings, spatial concepts, and products. Heinrich Klotz (1987) introduced the related concept of "fiction" into this context, saying that not only function, but also fiction is a crucial factor in the formula for postmodernist architecture.

From Conceptual Art to Conceptual Design

Sol LeWitt's claim that "ideas alone can be works of art" (first published in the May 1969 edition of *Art-Language*) marked the point of departure for a direction in art that became known as conceptual art. Its basis is a dematerialization of the art object, meaning, the fundamental abstention from physical manifestation that is so indispensable to classic forms of art (Felix 1972). If conceptual art is about stimulating creative thought processes in the viewer, it refers to categories that, deriving directly from philosophy, can be translated to the field of design.

Leaving behind the visionary synthetic euphorias of the likes of Luigi Colani and Verner Panton, the Italian design and architecture scene since the 1960s has produced a wide range of concepts and visions mainly developed by groups of designers whose work was rooted in social criticism or even political radicalism. Italian cultural developments of the 1960s brought forth countercultures that made reputations as "radical design," "counterdesign," or "antidesign." In contrast to the work of English formations like Archigram, these groups consciously sought to develop negative utopias (dystopias) by drawing attention to the devastating impacts of industrialization. Important representatives of Italian conceptual design were Gaetano Pesce, Andrea Branzi, and the Alchimia group of Alessandro Mendini.

Geröllradio, design: Kunstflug (Heiko Bartels, Hardy Fischer, Harald Hullmann), Düsseldorf (1986)

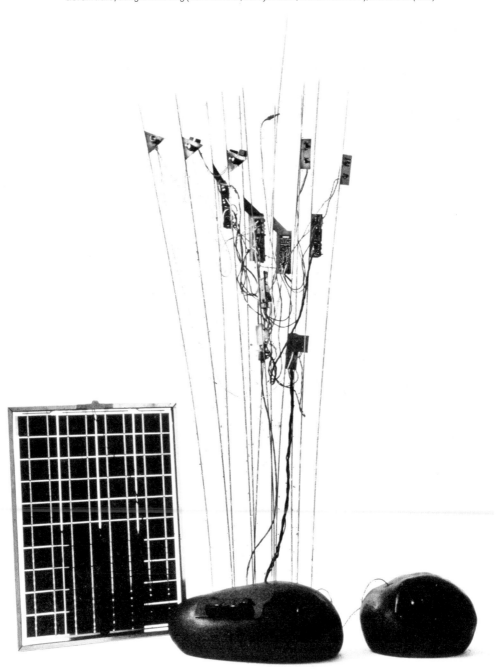

In Germany, meanwhile, the group Kunstflug, founded in 1982, saw itself in the tradition of Italian designer and architect groups like Archizoom, Superstudio, or Strum, but its influence did not outlive the comparatively short flowering of the new German design in the 1980s (Albus and Borngräber 1992; Hoffmann and Zehentbauer 2014). The point of departure for their work was a rigorous critique of the ossified forms of good design. In a provocative response they designed ironical objects that consciously alluded to the artistic traditions of Dada, ready-mades, and *objet-trouvé* art. Kunstflug (Heiko Bartels, Hardy Fischer, Harald Hullmann) started out by combining industrial semi-manufactured products (laminations, connectors, cables, lamps, transformers) with natural materials (timber). The Geröllradio ("scree radio" 1986) stands for their insight that the future of the avant-garde would lie in electronics. Their concept for a new ticket and service machine (Kunstflug 1988) pointed to the declining importance of machines and devices (hardware design) against the increasing importance of user interfaces (software design).

Operating under the colors of *GINBANDE* since 1985, the two Frankfurt-based designers Uwe Fischer and Klaus-Achim Heine followed the intellectual tradition of classical modernism through to its logical conclusion as they developed what they called creative mental leaps (Lenz 1988). Folding furniture, for example, has been a popular theme with architects and designers for centuries (Blaser 1982, Spalt 1987). *GINBANDE* used floor surfaces to fold away chairs, tables, or lamps in an interior that stands less for functional thinking than for thinking beyond function. In their folded state, these pieces of furniture come into their own as floor ornaments that use the floor to define interior space in the best Japanese sense. The Tabula Rasa project presented in 1987 at the exhibition *Un posto a tavola* (A place at the table) attracted international attention. The well-established, simple scissor principle was ingeniously applied to an extendable table measuring from 0.5 up to 5 meters (1.6 to 16 ft.). From an intimate tête-à-tête at a small bistro table to an opulent dinner at a vast board, Tabula Rasa provides hosts and guests with the space they need, whatever the occasion.

The London-based Ron Arad focused on concepts such as a hi-fi system set into broken pieces of concrete. By doing so he destroyed archetypal signifiers of high-quality technology to combine them with the ruins of modern civilization. The concept, however, also made sense technically, as concrete has excellent vibration absorption characteristics.

In the mid-1990s the Spaniard Martí Guixé began work on conceptual projects that explore the interactions between product and consumer. He playfully crosses the boundaries between design, typography, anthropology, humanities, and natural science as he outlines concepts and stages performances and happenings (Ed van Hinte 2002). His motto is, "Form follows destruction," for he intends his works to subvert traditional habits of handling and using products.

Future in the Age of Microelectronics

The most obvious use of the microchip, as the industrial index fossil of the late-twentieth century (Bürdek 1988), is in the computer itself. The permanently accelerating process whereby the computer manoeuvers itself into almost every corner of our lives is the ongoing subject of design studies and concepts.

Research projects, especially in the United States, concentrate on the integration of disparate technological possibilities. The Media Laboratory at Massachusetts Institute of Technology in Cambridge, Mass., has acquired an outstanding reputation in this field (Brand 1987; Negroponte 1995). Since the 1980s they have conducted intense research into the integration of television, computing, and telecommunications, preparing future product concepts with considerable international industrial funding. For some years the topic of "things that think" was fashionable (Gershenfeld 1999), and led to the design of numerous so-called "intelligent products."

At the end of the 1990s Media Lab opened a branch in Dublin to work on diverse new digital products. James Auger, a British product designer there, made waves with his proposal for a "phone tooth" which transgressed the bounds of "body design." Today the Media Lab in Cambridge, Mass., is interested more in developing new functions to make products attractive to potential buyers than in projecting visions of digital futures.

Anthony Dunne, a graduate of the London Royal College of Art who now teaches there, stands firmly in the tradition of concept design. His *Hertzian Tales* (Dunne 1999) is a fantastic collection of unknown electronic products, aesthetic experiments, and critical design statements. Dunne describes how designers and artists build bridges between immaterial digital worlds and the material culture of objects. Alongside a profound development history of digital technologies, he presents a series of concepts of his own, such as Electroclimate (an abstract radio), Tuneable Cities (the superposition of urban and natural environments), or the Faraday Chair (a contemplative space isolated from electromagnetic signals).

Together with Fiona Raby, Dunne (2001) presents concepts that explore the neglected narrative potential of electronic products. The Sony Walkman (1980) was already much more than a device for listening to music: it dramatically altered social relationships, and perception too. "Design noir" is a fundamental method for altering and expanding the psychological dimensions of electronic products. In their latest publication, Dunne and Raby (2014) speculate about new products, their uses, etc. Futurology, political factors, philosophies of technology, and literary fictions determine the desirable futures.

Trend Research and it's Limits

The futurology boom of the 1960s and 1970s was followed in the 1990s by the establishment of a new discipline: trend research. Rather than medium- to long-term forecasting, the point of trend research is to supply up-to-the-minute information on changes in fashions, lifestyles, and habits, as a basis for businesses to make pertinent product and design decisions.

Trends may be reflected in matters such as colors and finishes, materials or combinations thereof. But a trend may also comprise an entire market segment, as exemplified by the sports utility vehicle (SUV).

The field was quickly occupied by so-called "trend gurus" offering expensive seminars, marketing publications, and most of all seizing every media opportunity to advertise their own services. Trend scouts scour the world's great cities seeking manifestations that might indicate new trends. Whether the Americans Douglas Coupland, Faith Popcorn, and Suzi Chauvel, or the Germans Gerd Gerken, Gertrud Höhler, Matthias Horx, and Peter Wippermann – what they all share in common is breathless marketing of trends (Rust 1995/ 2002), which often last barely to the next season. Then of course new (and expensive) advice is required.

The furniture industry has turned out to be especially susceptible to – and yielding of – such trends. The annual trade fairs have mutated into spectacles of fashion and triviality, with Cologne and Milan leading the way. "Trend press conferences" instruct trade and public what to look for: "noble cocooning," "jungle in the living room," "retro wave," "new simplicity," "nomadic living," "new organic," and "furniture on casters." Every year sees new trends with new products to match, and furniture design itself dates even faster than the catchwords used to describe it.

Describing all these activities as trend research is not without a certain irony, for it has precious little to do with research. In fact very few of the existing approaches could be called serious. The economist Franz Liebl (2000) localizes the problem of business decisions about the future in strategic management: it concerns the possibilities for shaping the future. To Liebl, the term "issue" is preferable, because it serves to describe medium- and long-term processes of change, be they in society, technology, or culture, on whose basis solid statements about future developments can be made.

Outlook

Beneath all these efforts to develop visions lies a shared concept, to which Mihai Nadin (2002) has given new meaning: anticipation. To Nadin, anticipation is not a matter of probability, but a theory in the mathematical realm of the possible. Possibilities may be described and represented in the form of scenarios, of which some will come to pass, while others fall by the wayside. This, therefore, always a mental expectation of possible events. "Prediction is very difficult, especially about the future," is a pertinent aphorism here. Minimizing the uncertainties is an increasingly important function of design, where the task is less to develop visions than to visualize them.

Design and Society

The internationally renowned lifestyle designer Karim Rashid (2001) famously said: "I want to change the world." As such he joins the ranks of a multitude of voices expressing similar sentiments. The media apparently like such self-promotion, especially where the ambition of designers appears boundless: Only we can actually save the world from its doom. Which discipline speaks less credibly than that?

But it is certainly bold: *"Weil Design die Welt verändert … Texte zur Gestaltung"* (Because design changes the world) proclaims the cover of a book by two architects (Borries and Fezer 2013), only to admit just a few pages later that design can in fact at best improve it a little (Fezer). And that is hardly news.

Wolfgang Ullrich (2011) quotes Marx's eleventh thesis on Feuerbach: "Philosophers have hitherto only interpreted the world in various ways; the point is to change it," and asks ironically: "Do product designers change it too?" Not really, one might say, as they tend to concern themselves with shower gels, woolly socks, pepper grinders, perfumes, and mineral waters, all of which of course need to be designed, for which product designers are well equipped. What Ullrich is driving at is more "an understanding of consumer goods as products of aesthetic sheen." Changing the world is not on the agenda here.

Design is always embedded in a sociocultural context, so to that extent there are always social and economic circumstances that impact massively upon it (Hauffe 2014). One example is the historical decline of the porcelain industry, which is also a social history of the demise of a bourgeois way of life (Grossarth 2009). The alternative is not "coffee to go," but the ability of designers to identify social transformation processes and develop new product concepts out of them.

Young designers like to sidestep this issue by retreating individually into a new "craft design." But unfortunately "think global – act local" is interpreted rather one-sidedly here. The same applies to the currently so popular new "digital crafts" of 3-D printing (↗ p. 255 f). And the results of "digital crafts in the hands of amateurs" can also be problematic: Many of the presented products (Warnier, Verbruggen, Ehmann, and Klanten 2014) are simply amateurish.

On the other hand it is indisputable that the role of design has changed since the 1980s, since the onset of postmodernism. Therefore I would now like to turn to a number of social models whose relevance for design is uncontested. Being a European, I naturally discuss them against the backdrop of the European context.

The Theory of the Leisure Class *The Theory of the Leisure Class* (1899) by Thorstein Bunde Veblen (1857–1929), an American sociologist and economist, represents one of the earliest sociological studies describing the efforts at differentiation of the upper classes in nineteenth-century societies. During this period, the consumption of expensive goods (today we would say "products") gradually replaced leisure as the emblem of success and status. Here we already see products being developed, designed, and purchased not only for their functionality, but especially for their symbolic (semantic) properties.

The "conspicuous consumption" described by Veblen shaped nineteenth-century ways of life: "Conspicuous consumption of valuable goods is a means of reputability to the gentleman of leisure. As wealth accumulates in his hands, his own unaided effort will not avail to sufficiently put his opulence in evidence by this method." The goods (products) thus become vehicles for visualizing individual ownership, and "visible consumption" represents more or less the foundation of commodity-producing societies. At the same time: "The aesthetic serviceability of objects of beauty is not greatly nor universally heightened by possession." Veblen was also one of the first to formulate principles of design theory, for example: "Beauty of form seems to be a question of facility of apperception," and "... among objects of use the simple and unadorned article is aesthetically the best." Electronics manufacturers like Apple are indeed still working to those rules.

Social Differentiation and Money Like the work of Veblen, the analyses of the sociologist and philosopher Georg Simmel (1858–1918) also retain their validity today. One of his main works is the *Philosophy of Money* (1900), in which he describes how money defines and changes society, how it assumes ever more importance and a life of its own.

Simmel recognizes that societies are characterized by growing social differentiation that permits individuals to distinguish themselves from one another to an ever-increasing extent. The decisive aspect, as we know, is the amount of money available to the individual, because individualization processes are promoted through the acquisition of products.

The Distinction On the basis of empirical investigations conducted during the 1970s, the French sociologist Pierre Bourdieu published a comprehensive analysis of society, *La Distinction* (1980). He describes the study as a kind of "ethnography of France." Bourdieu's interest is in the interactions between economic and social conditions and the lifestyles he finds. In the process he explicitly used the term "taste."

Bourdieu argues that works of art (and also products) possess classifying or class-granting properties. In other words, they distinguish their owners by marking differences. Bourdieu ties these phenomena to the social classes existing in France in the 1960s and 1970s, and identifies coexisting cultures of taste, for example for particular styles of music, painting, or film as legitimate, middlebrow, and popular. And he ties them to typical social classes.

While Bourdieu regarded the classes in 1960s and 1970s France as largely immutable, the positions they represent, as reflected in cosmetics, clothing, or household furnishing for example, can today serve only as a rough orientation. The German sociologist Gerhard Schulze (2005) notes a distancing from the "altar of Bourdieu," in the sense of the final dissolution of social classes. And thus the long-established "target groups" based upon them become obsolete. Both product development and product design have now moved on a long way from Bourdieu's categories.

The System of Objects In *The System of Objects,* Jean Baudrillard (1991) presents not only a semiotic investigation of the product worlds (↗ p. 89), but also a social and economic analysis of special significance for design.

What Baudrillard sets out to identify those processes that create relationships between people and objects and thus generate human (social) behavior and relations. He also stresses that the description of the system of objects cannot be conducted without an applied ideological critique of that system. The "language of objects," he writes, must also expose the contradictions experienced by the user.

The objects themselves get detached from their practical function and become signs of something other (in a manner exploited especially by advertising). The growth of social networks over just the past decade highlights this very clearly. The required (and designed) products (hardware and software) become reduced to vehicles for the functioning and maintenance of social systems. This means that they may become thoroughly unmodern despite still

Das Parlament der Dinge, Stylepark Frankfurt am Main (Christmas 2013)

being completely usable. The sale of about ten million of the iPhone 6 and iPhone 6 Plus within one week (September 2014) illustrates this perfectly: While all the older models still function just as well, the social pressure of innovation is so strong that particular groups simply "must" acquire the new product.

"A scene in a Beijing store recently made waves in China. A new student demanded that her exasperated mother buy her what she called the obligatory Apple study set: iPhone 4s, iPad 3, and MacBook. Otherwise she would lose face at college" (Siemons 2012). In Asian cultures to "lose face" is a catastrophe, and in that sense Baudrillard's observation that the rhetoric of the real reveals the form of social relations is very pertinent. Today product design is life design.

The Experience Society *The Experience Society* (1992) by the German sociologist Gerhard Schulze is a far-reaching analysis of society that can more or less be regarded as a comprehensive diagnosis of Germany at the end of the twentieth century and remains relevant for the twenty-first. This "cultural sociology of the present" (according to the subtitle) concentrates largely on the aestheticization of everyday life and its consequences, including for product design. Already in 1992 he noted that: "Design and image become the prime concern, usefulness and functionality are accessories. The incidentalness of purposes unconnected to the immediate experience function becomes especially clear in the marketing of utility, robustness, and technical perfection." Using the example of the SUVs that began to appear at that time, he demonstrates that their off-road functions are almost irrelevant in the urban centers (where they are mostly purchased and driven) and that instead the symbolic functions are clearly uppermost. The lasting success of these vehicles (which represent about 15 percent of vehicles sold in Germany) endures not only in the West: they also enjoy great popularity in China. Design becomes an expression of social values. And in the introduction to his second edition (2005), Schulze writes explicitly of the "designer furniture" that shapes our everyday lives, alongside the shopping malls, wellness oases, theme parks, etc.

Schulze's socioeconomic finding of growing wealth disparities in our societies is also important, and has consequences for product design. Luxury goods and cheap products (often imported, also as a consequence of globalization) exist side by side, with vigorous demand for both. The so-called middle class is being increasingly squeezed, not only in Germany. This also boosts demand for distinction and differentiation of products, which is not least a semantic issue.

The significant point is that people in different milieus attribute meanings to things; products do not speak on their own. One common product with such a semiotic function, visualizing the social position of the wearer, is the wristwatch: it makes a difference whether someone wears a Swatch or a Rolex.

Roger Häußling (2010) draws a striking conclusion for design from the ideas of Schulze and others: "Designed objects are always also symbolic objects of milieus. Today the sociocultural constitution of the individual occurs to a great extent through the acquisition and possession of products. Designed objects function as providers of social identity."

Methodologically Schulze combines quantitative data (about the members of a society) with hermeneutic interpretation of the same. Ulrich Oevermann (see www.agoh.de) calls this area of research "objective hermeneutics," whose significance for design has yet to be even acknowledged.

The aestheticization of everyday life occupies a special place in Schulze's investigations. The economic stabilization observed in European states since the 1980s has led to an increasingly pronounced differentiation of products, with "the experiencing of life" becoming central. In relation to products, Schulze writes: "The abandonment of use value occurs during the transition to the mere symbolization of newness through accessories like new design, new packaging, new brands. Over the years one learns that the latest achievements, innovations, and trends will never be the last. Again and again one must make room, internally and externally, for whatever is coming next." The electronic gadget industry supplies numerous examples of this.

Deyan Sudjic (2008) describes how he purchased his first laptop at the Apple Store in New York in 2003, believing he would grow old with it. To him it was an investment in the future, a possession that would last a lifetime. What a mistake, he was quickly to learn.

At this point however, we must remind ourselves of the aforementioned ideas of Gernot Böhme (2001), which I discuss in detail elsewhere (Bürdek 2012). In increasingly saturated societies, the crux is no longer the satisfaction of needs, but of desire-needs: "Desire-needs are needs that are heightened rather than satisfied through their fulfillment." As socioeconomic phenomena, desire-needs today determine design to a great extent. Closely connected with this are processes of aestheticization of buildings, events, products, to name but a few. Schulze writes: "Distinction is the symbolization of social difference."

One important methodological contribution of Schulze's is his description of social milieus. In order to understand this one must explore "social semiotics," in other words pursue questions where "the relationship between situation and subject is understood as a sign/meaning relation. The situation is read as a configuration of signs." Here again, a pointer to semiotics is useful, given that it serves as the central epistemological model, not only for design: "For describing the relationship between object and experience, the sign and meaning model is not only appropriate, but necessary."

In his "theory of milieu segmentation" Schulze argues that milieus are not constant variables (like, for example, Bourdieu's social classes), but designate social groups whose boundaries are always shifting. So this is a discontinuous but not static model of society: "People form social milieus, social milieus form people."

Sinus Milieus
Publisuisse, Bern (2014)

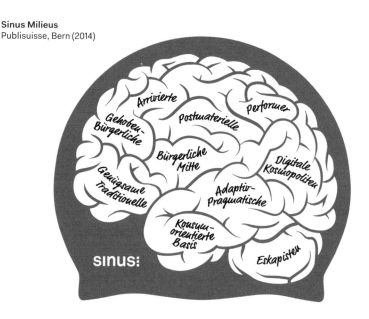

Schulze differentiates five milieu-specific existential perspectives, the first three of which are externally, the last two internally rooted:

Sophisticated Milieu This is characterized by social hierarchies. Social positions (especially profession) shape taste, education, verbal competence, etc.

Integration Milieu Social expectations are characterized by categories like conformity and deviation.

Harmony Milieu This concerns polarities between good and evil, harmless and dangerous, trusted and suspicious.

Self-realization Milieu The perspective turns inward, where self-rootedness is decisive for the self/world relation.

The Entertainment Milieu The self, to whose external characteristics the external world is adapted, is placed at the center of the perspective on reality.

Altogether, Schulze argues, social milieus are communities of interpretation of the world. Different horizons of experience and diverging routines of processing perceived social realities mean that there are always multiple worlds within societies. The roles that individuals play in them are always changing, and this is another indication that there are no longer "target groups" for design in the classical sense. Schulze describes these worlds in great detail, and altogether this approach transpires to be exceptionally useful for design, given that he describes the shifting product contexts in socioeconomic terms (↗ p. 83 ff).

The Aestheticization of the World The emergence of postmodernism at the beginning of the 1980s initiated a phase of societal aestheticization that endures to this day, with considerable ramifications for design. This phenomenon has not a little to do with the functional and aesthetic shaping (design) of products.

Anna Calvera illustrates this very well in two Spanish-language volumes. In *Arte¿?Diseño* (2003) Bruno Munari, André Ricard, Isabel Campi, and others discuss how design has much to do with aesthetics, but nothing to do with art (↗ p. 63 ff). In the second volume, *De lo bello de las cosas: Materiales para una estética del diseño* (2007), Jordi Mañá, Fátima Pombo, Jordi Pericot, and many others use concrete examples to discuss the role aesthetics plays in the design of products. The thinkers Anna Calvera cites include Martin Heidegger, whose discussion of "things" she updates for today's conditions. Jordi Pericot builds on Ludwig Wittgenstein, whose philosophy of language he expands semiotically. Both volumes represent essential contributions to design theory, which have unfortunately never been translated.

The German philosopher Wolfgang Welsch has edited three volumes of essays (1990, 1996, 2012) presenting important contributions that have decisively influenced not only the design discourse but also architecture, urban planning, etc. Welsch's lecture at the World Design Congress in Nagoya, Japan, in 1989 has achieved legendary status. In it he declared: "And with this expanded concept of design, the twenty-first century could become a century of design, as the twentieth was a century of art." His prediction has come true sooner than expected, with the 1990s already experiencing a hitherto unprecedented design boom. At an international conference in Hanover in 1992, Welsch noted: "Design is becoming a universal category" (1993). And François Burkhardt (1993) went so far as to predict: "Design in the twenty-first century faces a hard but important task." To date it has performed only patchily.

The following ideas of Wolfgang Welsch have been especially significant for the design theory discourse: "The transition from object design to frame design promoted by postmodernism also corresponds with the demands of ecology. And today the task of design shifts increasingly from object design (which modernism concentrated on) to frame design. The thing – whether postmodern or ecological – is to change the circumstances (or frame) of our living conditions." At the end of the twentieth century, at the latest, design left behind the narrow definition of product coined at the beginning of the century, and turned to more complex questions of lifestyle, with thoroughly positive outcomes for the development of the discipline.

But there are also critical voices on the discipline question: "A design sociology seeks to answer questions of form and representation under aspects of power, identity, ritual, work, mass media, technology, protest, and resistance. The radical sociological argument within complementary design research reveals itself in participation, participant observation, solidarity, and empathy, and ultimately in the formative power of survival in social fields" (Milev 2014). Here, "design" is nothing but an empty shell that can be applied to practically anything in the world. Yana Milev consciously frees herself from a design research based on technology and economics, and seeks to turn Joseph Beuys's "extended definition of art" into an "extended definition of design." Beuys understood this as the route from traditional (including modern) art to an anthropological art, with the concept of the "social sculpture" representing the expansion of the specialist discourse into a societal one. Such interventions were central to Beuys. Milev does not even try to connect to the design under discussion here (product design): "An anthropological/sociological design research distances itself from the concept of design tied to industrial and technological processes of use-oriented manufacture and marketing of objects, products, and things that has become established both in academic society and popular understanding" (Milev 2014).

Let us now return to Wolfgang Welsch. The aesthetic boom that broke out in the 1980s ranged from individual styling and body design to urban design, it draws in all lifeworlds and becomes the dominant principle of the "culture society." Welsch (1990) even uses the term "postmodern facelifting," to characterize the prettification of cities and shopping malls, which he calls "anestheticization" because it involves superficial phenomena whose atmospheric effects serve nothing other than stimulating consumption. At the same time, a "general condition of aestheticization" arises (Welsch 1993), that has promoted design nationally and internationally. Thus it is less the aesthetic theories of Alexander Gottlieb Baumgarten than the social forces that have largely economically co-opted aesthetics. Incidentally, not only in relation to design, but also in particular in connection with art.

Welsch reminds us that modernism (at the beginning of the twentieth century) turned against the excesses of industrialization and sought "a sweeping artistic design process throughout society." In the 1980s aestheticization became a differentiation strategy in saturated global markets, for cities and regions as well as for products.

In his second anthology (1996), Welsch investigates the "broad field" of aesthetics, distinguishing between a superficial aestheticization (to which design definitely belongs) and a deep aestheticization affecting philosophical and societal levels. One influence he cites is, again, the work of Gerhard Schulze (1992). Welsch's ultimate diagnosis is: "The world becomes an experience space." Aesthetics "should be to do not primarily with art, but a branch of epistemology." It freed itself some time ago from art and now serves only economic ends, which is one place where the roots of the aforementioned design boom are to be found. The marketability of all types of goods, especially products for everyday use, increasingly occupies center stage. Like fashion in the narrower sense, aesthetic fashions are short-lived and demand constant innovation. Here we find the visible expression of Böhme's thesis that it is desire-needs rather than needs that shape our existence.

Welsch introduces the rather zeitgeisty concept of the "aesthetic turn." From the philosophical perspective the aesthetic has penetrated "the basal dimension of truth and knowledge." And further: "In the modern understanding truth is steeped in aesthetic premises. Our recognition is in fundamental respects aesthetically configured. Aesthetic categories have become fundamental categories." This immensely enhances the status of design, although this has been largely overlooked in design theory. The claim to ubiquity obviously collides with the reality of design practice. *Homo oeconomicus* has become *homo aestheticus*. But it is precisely in the connection of the two that the actual (disciplinary) field of design – or more precisely product design – lies.

In his third anthology (2012), Welsch focuses on design in the electronic age. He, too, regards interface design (↗ p. 248 f) as a central issue of the twenty-first century: "Mostly we still think only of interactivity between user and device or between user and user, and forget communication between machines, which may perhaps become as important or even more so." Welsch also describes the duality of immaterialization and rematerialization that explains the growing divergence between industrial design and a new (art and) craft design. According to Welsch we should be able to "move lustfully in the electronic worlds – but not only there, also in other worlds."

The Invention of Creativity The subtitle of Andreas Reckwitz's *Die Erfindung der Kreativität* (The invention of creativity; 2012), "on the process of societal aestheticization," makes it clear where he stands: aesthetics has today moved far beyond the art discourses. It has become a generalized cultural model affecting architecture, design, fashion, urban design, and advertising. "The societal regime of the aesthetic new" has become an important phenomenon especially promoting design. Reckwitz names as the latest phase: "the merging of management and design and the establishment of 'design economics'."

Gert Selle (1994) was one of the first to describe the effects of this massive over-aestheticization: "But, not only in the media, design has become a general means of representation, communication, and life, where by the traditional bounds of the form-giving disciplines have long been transgressed and given way to an aesthetic overstructuring, be it in the effort expended, be it in the opening up of new fields of application. The spectrum of what can be designed – visible and invisible, material and fantasy, behavior and emotion – is designed, without quarter."

Actor-Network Theory In the 1980s the French sociologists Michel Callon, John Law, and Bruno Latour developed Actor-Network Theory, originally to explain the impact of science and technology. In the meantime it has been applied to various societal questions; the discussion about the extent to which it could be applicable to design is only just beginning.

The starting point is the idea of transcending the classical division between "object" and "subject" and instead introducing the concept of networks. Methodologically, ANT sets out to: "treat all entities – people and technical apparatus – as social actors" (Bellinger and Krieger 2006). Treating human and non-human actors (actants) as equals completely reinterprets the concept of communication. This cutting-edge sociological theory is highly contested, but stands in the tradition of "thinking things" (Gershenfeld, 1999), of "ubiquitous

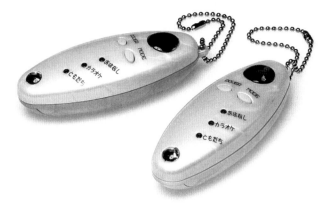

Lovegety (1998), Photo: Museum für Angewandte Kunst Frankfurt am Main (Donation Bürdek)

computing," of virtual reality, of artificial intelligence and robotics. Together these projects can be said to represent the avant-garde of digital technologies.

Madeleine Akrich (2006) begins by considering "the way in which technical objects define actants and relations between actants. I demonstrate that the simplicity with which the actants assumed in the design of the object become associate with those that exist in practice is partially a function of decisions made by the designers." In contrast to the human-object relations described in the 1970s (↗ p. 148), Actor-Network Theory attributes autonomous function to the objects themselves. Networks can "consist of machines, animals, texts, money, architecture, de facto of any material one wishes" (Law 2006).

The sociologist Albena Yaneva (2012) seeks to relate Actor-Network Theory to design: "Considering ANT from the perspective of ANT, on the other hand, would mean researching not the theories and ideologies of designers but their culture and their practices. In other words, focussing on what designers and users do in their everyday routine activities rather than their ideas and interests. This thus prioritizes the pragmatic content of actions over discourses ... ." This is relevant, she argues, in the sense that it is worth at least doing a little empirical testing on the idea that design must orientate on society (↗ p. 226 ff).

Another approach to applying ANT consists in examining the social impacts of products. One early example of this phenomenon were the "Lovegety" devices manufactured in the 1990s in Japan, which sold extremely successfully (more than 1.3 million). Their function was to facilitate the initiation of contact between individuals, their three available functions being: "Let's just chat," "Let's go sing some karaoke" and "Get2" (also named "Looking for love"). Lovegeties were thus actants in social situations with a reach far beyond their – modest – technical functions. The ANT model could therefore be applied successfully to product development processes – but further methodological treatment is still awaited. That would certainly be a topic for design science.

The interaction of technology, economics, and the social framework appears to be the central and most viable subject for a future design theory and design practice. Deyan Sudjic (2008) writes: "Design in all its manifestations is the DNA of an industrial society – or of a post-industrial society, if that's what we now have. It's the code that we need to explore if we are to stand a chance of understanding the nature of the modern world. It's a reflection of our economic systems. And it shows the imprint of the technology we have to work with. It's a kind of language, and it's a reflection of emotional and cultural values."

Design and Technology

No other topic has changed design like technology has. The nineteenth-century world exhibitions were already gigantic inventors' fairs and presentations of wares (whose designerly manifestations, however, were rather poor). In the second half of the nineteenth century it was hoped that involving artists in product development would rectify these shortcomings.

But not until the twentieth century did an explicit division of technology and design come about, when the latter set off on the road to an independent discipline. The Werkbund and Bauhaus eras saw close cooperation between designers and engineers. After World War II it was in particular at the Ulm School of Design that a close linkage of the two spheres was discussed. In the still largely mechanical and electrical world, designers took on ever more of the tasks of engineers, and more or less became inventors of products. Not until the 1980s, with the rise of microelectronics and digitalization, did the spheres separate once again. The visuality of product worlds declined sharply and new forms of visualization had to be developed to enable users to handle the technology. The use of the proverbial hammer can be elucidated empirically or even purely visually in a way that is simply not the case with a cell phone.

Furthermore, digitalization has spawned a multitude of new technologies, such as rapid prototyping or the now legendary 3-D printing, both of which open up new fields for design. And the new technologies have massively promoted globalization.

From Invention to Visualization

In the 1980s two important events exerted a huge influence on the architecture and design discourses. The 39th Venice Biennale (curated by the Italian architect Paolo Portoghesi under the motto "La presenza del passato") presented a city of facades where architects like Frank O. Gehry, Rem Koolhaas, and Robert Venturi presented postmodernist projects that were to define the architecture of the 1980s. This opened the way for postmodernism (Jencks 1978) to enter European architecture.

At the "Forum Design" in summer 1980 in Linz, Austria, both designers and architects presented their ideas. The presentation by Ettore Sottsass was ground-breaking, showing furniture designs that were to reappear in the legendary 1981 Memphis collection (Radice 1981).

While these two events were driven by a new visuality, the Swiss sociologist Lucius Burckhardt declared: "Design is invisible." That lecture title was also used to name the voluminous catalog of the Linz exhibition (Gsöllpointner, Hareiter, and Ortner 1981), from where it wandered the design discourses for decades. Burckhardt was not talking about the emerging debate over microelectronics, but seeking to point out that architects, urban planners, and designers too needed to think about action contexts and user interests and wishes before they set about drafting or realizing their projects (Bürdek 2012). This criticism hit designers as hard as those of Victor Papanek (1972). Under "invisible design" Burckhardt understood conventional design unaware of its own social function.

While events in Venice and Linz were dedicated to the new visuality, technology, driven by microelectronics, was increasingly moving in the opposite direction – toward a new invisibility. But the digital world demands its own new new visuality, for man is and remains an analog being. The sociologist Manfred Faßler (2002), who has developed an advanced media theory, describes this process absolutely in line with actor-network theory: "Visibility, too, consists in what one has made visible, in what one sees, and in how meaning is attributed to the visible form. In this constructivist understanding made visibility depends upon actors and structures."

Seen that way, one could certainly argue that designers today are no longer inventors (in the sense Leonardo da Vinci was), but visualizers of a world that has become increasingly invisible. Design is not invisible, but makes visible. Moreover, visualization has already become a field for architects and designers, whose specializations represent completely new tasks in product development (hardware design) and interface design (software design). In both architecture and design, preparing visualizations from CAD data shortens the processes and is a good deal cheaper than making three-dimensional models.

It is reported that a certain Swedish furniture retailer already uses computer-generated visualizations for 75 percent of the product illustrations in its catalogues (factodesign 2014).

Imagineering

The ongoing "visual turn" is producing considerable substantive changes in design, as the example of new visualization technologies underlines. The term "imagineering" emerged in the 1990s to describe a combination of "image" and "engineering" (Disney and Eisner 1996). What it refers to is the "artificially constructed imaginary worlds" (Mutius, 2000) now used especially in development processes to depict new products and systems and allow others to see and experience the (often diffuse) ideas involved. In that sense imagineering is one of the new methods with great untapped potential for design management and strategic design.

It is expected that three main technologies will shape the twenty-first century (Faßler 2012):

Molecularization (post-genomic biology)

Miniaturization (nanotechnology and biotics

Micrologization (changes relating to data and information technologies)

Thus it is clear that increasing complexity and specialization leave designers no longer the inventors of products, but the interpreters or visualizers of new technologies. As the example of the Daimler study group shows (↗ p. 119 f), the designers of the future will more likely be found in the engine room than on the bridge.

Out of the three aforementioned areas, changes in information technology are likely to influence design most heavily, so the further discussion here is restricted to those. While molecularization has little to do with the field of design, material research does play a significant role in both architecture and design. Numerous publications demonstrate that here, too, the "inventions" occur at the level of research and technology, while architects and designers are the visualizers of new applications.

**Visualization of a
business racer**
Design: Julian Hallberg,
Serious3d, Thun (2008)

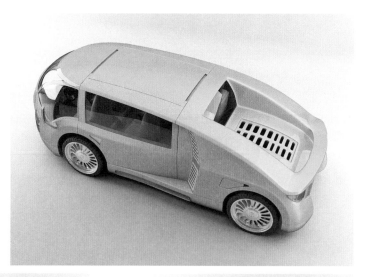

Microelectronics and Design

There are two good reasons for calling the 1980s an epoch-making decade for design. First, the influences of postmodernism triggered a fierce stylistic eclecticism (as promoted, for example, by Memphis and Alchimia), which, however, soon lost its bearings in the fog of what Jürgen Habermas called the "new obscurity" (Habermas 1985). Second, the chip, which was to become the index fossil of the 1990s, opened up completely new horizons (Bürdek 1988). In 1982, for the first time ever, *TIME* magazine's Man of the Year was not a man at all, but a machine. The computer was seen as the symbol of the new technological age. *TIME*, however, did not give the title to the big, complex mainframe computers used since the 1970s (manufactured by companies like IBM or Bull), but to the desktop personal computer that had only really come into existence after Stephen Wozniak and Steven P. Jobs invented the Apple II in 1977 It was estimated that by the end of the 1980s more than 100 million PCs were in use worldwide (Hahn 1988). The US consulting firm Gartner (www.gartner.com) estimates there were one billion by 2008, by 2014 it was perhaps two billion. A truly breakneck development, if one remembers that in 1943 IBM CEO Thomas J. Watson guessed "I think there is a world market for maybe five computers." And in 1949 it was predicted that: "Computers in the future may weigh no more than 1.5 tons."

According to researchers in cultural studies, the history of Western civilization only includes two real technological revolutions:

1. The invention of movable type by Johannes Gutenberg in the fifteenth century, which paved the way for the triumph of book printing around the world.

2. The massive spread of personal computers since the early 1980s.

Both revolutions triggered profound changes in human behavior, communication, centralization and decentralization, education and training, work and leisure, health services and public transportation, and many other domains. The past three decades have affected the lifeworlds of wide segments of the population more deeply than ever before in such a short period: the transition from analog to digital technology marked not only a technological, but also a cultural, revolution.

One of the early media theorists, the Canadian Marshall McLuhan, pointed out in his studies on *The Gutenberg Galaxy* (1962) that the invention of the printed book did much to foster individualism: "Just like easel painting emancipated painting from institutions, book printing broke the monopoly of libraries." The analogy in our world today is the computer. It has become a personalized tool, breaking the monopoly of computer centers in companies and administrations, as globally linked networks give most people in industrialized countries access to theoretically unlimited stores of data and processing power. Cloud computing is a case in point.

Microelectronics Meets Design

As the personal computer proliferated in the 1980s, designers began taking an interest in the new technology. Three very different levels were addressed:

1. Microelectronic products were soon recognized as opening up new terrain to design. The practice, frog design, that Hartmut Esslinger headed in California is a textbook example with its legendary designs for Apple (Bürdek 1997a; Kunkel 1997; Esslinger 2014).

2. Rapid progress in the dematerialization of products carried totally new challenges in its wake. Interaction and interface design grew into important fields, especially for product designers (Bürdek 1990b, 1996a).

3. The breakneck speed at which computers' graphic performance improved soon caused great hopes to be placed in CAD (Computer Aided Design). Once considerable teething problems had been overcome, paradigmatic changes in the processes of designing, constructing, and manufacturing followed (see Rapid Prototyping, p. 256).

More Leeway for Hardware Design

The first overview of the influence and impact of digital phenomena on design was compiled by Richard Fischer, who had also launched the debate on marking functions at the Offenbach School of Design. Fischer (1988) identified a total of nine areas in microelectronics that are relevant for design:

1. As the use of microprocessors does not allow a product's technology to be revealed, the design of the remaining controls has to achieve a high degree of legibility. The increasing dominance of electronics in many product areas requires more concentrated efforts to be put into marking functions in the remaining operating elements. It is not only with electronic products that the relationships between user and product are of particular importance, for the "nature" of products is increasingly ephemeral.

2. Miniaturization entails a dematerialization of products in a process that is reflected in increasingly two-dimensional design concepts. Jürgen Hitzler's study of a train tracking terminal conspicuously drew attention to the new design options that microelectronics opened up. Today's tablet PCs, flat screens, and smartphones are cases in point.

3. The falling prices of microelectronics present regular opportunities to bring products back to a human scale. The costs for realizing appropriate dimensions and sizes are low. The minute calculator watches whose operation required a special stylus illustrate how far developments in this area had veered off course. An equal absurdity is evident when fingernails have to be manicured to a sharp point in order to operate cell phones weighing less than 50 g.

4. LCDs, in fact all sorts of displays, and monitors in combination with membrane keyboards have become emblems of progress. Be it in airplanes, automobiles, medical equipment, or machine tools, visual elements are the most important interfaces between person and product.

5. The technology is programmable to a high degree; more and more fully automated products are being developed. The visualization of technical features often makes way for an exaggerated emphasis on ergonomic aspects (hand-shaped casings).

6. Remote controls gain increasing importance as an interface between user and product (Schönhammer 1997). The actual products fulfill their functions in the background while remote controls direct and regulate their operations. Centrally located, freely programmable remote controls direct entire households: TV, stereo and video, domestic appliances, data terminals, front door, garage door, and more.

7. Microelectronics add a new dimension to the modular principle, which opens up endless possibilities for arranging and employing the individual components of a product system.

8. Light-conducting materials come to stand for dematerialization or even symbolize the mystique of products.

9. Product graphics gains increasing importance for electronic products (user interfaces).

Yotaphone 2, Smartphone, Fa. Yota
Devices, St. Petersburg (2014)

Yotaphone 2, Smartphone, Fa. Yota
Devices, St. Petersburg (2014)

This analysis points to the direction that many product areas have already followed. The area of user interfaces developed at a particularly rapid pace, and became an important field of activity for product designers (Bürdek 2002).

Interaction and Interface Design

The transition from the mechanical to the electric and then to the electronic world of objects confronted designers and product developers with a host of new challenges and problems. By the late 1980s it was clear just how unwise it was to leave engineers and programmers to deal with the interfaces between digital products and human beings. Mathematics and physics determined the way their minds worked. Made by technical experts for technical users, the solutions they proposed clashed violently with the innocent expectations of lay users. The operating instructions, handbooks, and user manuals that come with digital products tell an obvious tale: to put it in hermeneutical terms, developers and users have widely divergent horizons and act accordingly (Bürdek 1992, 1994, 1996a+b, 1999).

As indicated in the discussion of marking functions, however, experience gathered in analog product design has been of undeniable relevance for the new digital product worlds. One aspect was the transition from matter to language, and the subsequent visualization of that transition. This was also associated with proposals to bring insights from design theory, for example on product language or communication, to bear on these new challenges. At an early date Stephan Schupbach and Frank Zebner published some fundamental ideas on the topic and designated "language as the most important criterion in design strategy" (Schupbach and Zebner 1990). The digital media play a special role here since, on the one hand, they multiply communication channels and the amount of information communicated, while on the other, they have an almost autopoietic character in that they proliferate and distribute information whose usefulness is rarely challenged.

A Clear Terminology

Bill Moggridge, co-founder of the global design practice IDEO, and Bill Verplank of Interval Research introduced the following definitions:

"Interaction design" relates to the way we handle a digital product (be it hardware or software) and to the behavior patterns that are determined by a specific operating procedure.

"Interface design" refers to screen layout on the monitor, display, and so on (i.e., the visual representation and user interfaces of hardware and software) (Spreenberg 1994).

This distinction neatly falls in with the above-mentioned linkage of analog and digital product worlds, for communicative functions are equally relevant to the development and design of non-material products.

The principles of aesthetic form, for example, also apply to user interfaces (i.e., in screen design), including grid formation, regular-irregular, symmetrical-asymmetrical, clear-obscure, all of which resurface on websites and displays. Annika Graf (2012) demonstrates how little-known (or neglected) such design fundamentals are in practice: optics played no role for Microsoft until Apple came onto the scene. Questions related to corporate design (↗ p. 189 ff) play an important role when it comes to designing and harmonizing the visible aspects of a company's operations, from printed materials to websites. This cross-media dimension is highly relevant, in that it is the basis for creating and communicating the identity of companies and institutions.

Terms like "interaction" and "navigation" gain figurative meanings as experiences gathered in the three dimensional product world are transferred to the handling and use of two-dimensional interfaces. The figurative, however, is firmly rooted in the literal, in the underlying operational structures (interaction), the functionalities, and their visualization. Not every interface is necessarily and immediately self-explanatory. There is, after all, a difference between a public terminal (e.g., for tickets) and a computer game, not least because the amount of time they can reasonably expect users to invest is vastly different. Interfaces open doors to vast stores of information, users crave new discoveries, boredom means failure – at least with game applications. In most other cases, in contrast, users demand efficient, self-explanatory functions. The modernist, functional understanding of design therefore has a considerable explanatory and productive value for this area.

The concept of symbolic function comes into play where interfaces are in immediate contact with their respective user groups: for example, young and hip, professional, or for experts or senior citizens only. Simple software, in particular, allows a plethora of different personalized user interfaces.

A Growing Complexity

As mentioned above, developers, designers, and users all have very different horizons – just how different became strikingly clear when the early CAD/CAM systems were launched in the mid-1980s. Designers blithely expected to be supplied with handy tools for the designing process. Even the assumption that "CAD" stood for "computer-aided design," however, was somewhat optimistic, for what the new tools did, at first, was no more than computer-aided drawing. However, early examples from the CAD working group at the Offenbach School of Design show that the quality of the resulting technical drawings was astonishingly high (Bürdek, Hannes, and Schneider 1988b).

Even at this early stage it was clear that the potential of the new CAD/CAM technologies lay not in image generation, but in the profound changes they would bring to the design and manufacturing processes.

A more serious aspect emerged as rapid growth and falling prices in microelectronics triggered a veritable boom in new functions ("features"). Microprocessors grew ever more powerful, and the range of tasks they could fulfill grew ever wider and more universal. This was associated with an accelerating complexity of products. Designers were called upon to rectify this and restore products to easy usability, without the need to study operating instructions.

In this context it makes sense to take a look at the operating structures of individual product categories. A high degree of inconsistency is evident here. Some strange predilection results in changes in keyboard configuration from one program version to the next, in the integration of ever new, awkward "features" in hardware (such as cell phones), and an overall tendency to equip each product with "distinctive" operating structures.

Worldwide standardization in the automobile industry, for example, means that while most drivers are able to control just about any vehicle in its basic functionality, they are confused by electronic upgrades like on-board computers, navigation systems, and audio and video systems (Bürdek 1998, 1999). Moreover, the updatability of electronic systems is limited, whereas the lifespan of vehicles extends to fifteen to twenty years.

Fundamentally, product developers promote new cultural and product standards that are then implemented (visualized) by software designers. Today even small children know how to use a smartphone, and this has become a standard cultural technique. But there is little discussion of the question raised by Frank Schirrmacher (2014): "How to avoid the smartphone operating us." This general phenomenon of digital technology is becoming increasingly pressing. In his speech on receiving the Peace Prize of the German Book Trade on October 12, 2014 in Frankfurt am Main, Jaron Lanier went yet a step further: "We especially love our gadgets, and are still discovering new facets. But there is plenty to suggest that if we were to open our eyes a little further we would find ourselves staring into the abyss." There is currently no sign of practicing designers, design theory, or still less design studies seriously tackling such questions.

Anthropology and Evolution

The end of the twentieth century confronted designers with completely new challenges, namely those related to human development. So rapid was the spread of microelectronics that users could hardly master the new possibilities, much less apply them. Developers had their sights firmly set on whatever was technically feasible while designers kept their eyes on the user, and suddenly both realized how dire their mistakes were in terms of the history of development. The human ability to learn cannot keep up with inexorable leaps in technology.

Stephen Jay Gould (1998) argued convincingly that the history of development provides no trace of proof for the alleged need to perpetually increase complexity. In doing so he identified a grave misconception that microelectronics, in general, seems to promote. The basic shape of the human body and brain, Gould says, have not changed at all over the past one hundred thousand years, while technical change hurtled along at breakneck speed – especially since the twentieth century. Though the design of every single artifact should ultimately address this conflict, it has a special significance for interaction and interface design. A collection of essays published by Susan Squires and Bryan Byrne (2002) impressively illustrates that the anthropological perspective has reached design research and practice. It is here to stay. Alison Jane Clarke, who teaches and researches at the University of Applied Arts in Vienna, has published extensively on this (Clarke 2010).

Globalization creates a necessity to address the different circumstances of different users: "Ethnologists have over recent years become increasingly aware of subtle changes in the design and use of global consumer goods" (Hahn 2011). Ethnology can apparently be harnessed as a useful basis for design (Hahn 2013). For instance, the Nike "Air Native N7" trainer was developed specially for Native Americans, for whom conventional shoes simply do not fit. "N7" refers to the Native American philosophy of the seventh generation, which means thinking about the effects of today's actions on the coming seven generations. As such it is an ethnological product with implied sustainability.

From Hardware Design to Software Design

Apart from a considerable reduction in the size of electronic devices, dematerialization also entails a shift to what actually makes these products tick: the programs, otherwise known as software. At the end of the 1970s we described a similar development (Bürdek and Gros 1978), predicting that in the future design quality would no longer rest on constructive achievements, but, to use the words of the followers of Udo Koppelmann in Cologne, on its "allusive qualities." In other words, this means product language or the communicative functions of products.

Giving a twist to the "linguistic turn" that had exerted such a decisive influence on design theory in the 1970s, talk in the 1980s was of a compelling "visual turn." Writing and alphabetization had a profound effect on our civilization and culture. The rapid development of digital products and systems, meanwhile, has generated even more visual images, so that today we live in what is basically a "post-alphabetic society." Our perceptions are increasingly determined by categories of visual representation: photographs, illustrations, diagrams, pictograms, icons, typography, and symbols. Literate culture is turning into visual culture, but whether that is a sign of progress is debatable.

With a background in chaos research, Roger Lewin (1992) presented a number of ideas that are very helpful in this context. Order and chaos are the two poles that determine our behavior, with chaos usually meaning coincidence. Lewin referred to studies undertaken at the American Santa Fe Institute, which has been researching this field for many years. The Institute's Murray Gell-Mann has a good phrase for it: "Surface complexity arising out of deep simplicity" (Lewin 1993). Translated to interface design this means: "Deep complexity requires surface simplicity" (Bürdek 1999). So the more complex the structures underlying a product are, the less complex its operation has to appear on the surface. This can be regarded as a general maxim for the design of digital products.

Design and Software Ergonomics

Ergonomists were just as quick as designers to tackle the challenges arising from the digitalized product world. Though their attention traditionally focused on anthropometrics or workplace physiology, they soon realized that electronics posed totally new problems. American researchers were pioneers in this field, and throughout the 1990s a host of publications appeared; their value for design, however, was extremely limited.

Donald A. Norman's works (1989, 1993, 1998) are an exception. His contributions have reached the status of standard works and have proved highly useful for designers. A psychologist and scholar in cognitive science, Norman not only did research, but also advised well-known IT corporations like Apple and Hewlett-Packard. His interest in users and their habits has yielded many insights that are of special relevance to design processes. Today his ideas about what he calls human-centered development are widely accepted, even if designers and engineers still come up with wildly different interpretations of what he actually meant.

Ben Shneiderman (1992, 1998) produced what is probably the most comprehensive work on the foundations of interface and interaction design. It includes all those scientific insights, tools, and methods that designers, developers, product managers, and all the various laborers in the field of designing digital products (hardware and software) should have at their fingertips. For example, Shneiderman is in favor of making computer performance disappear from sight, so that a system's intelligence lies not in its user interface but in the system itself. This view largely coincides with the ideas presented above.

In discussing electronic hardware design, Konrad Baumann and Bruce Thomas (2001) address a topic particularly significant for questions of design. Be it in telecommunications, audio and hi-fi systems, medical and measurement products, office communication, home, leisure, transport – nearly all products today are controlled by chips, and microprocessors rule our everyday lives. Baumann and Thomas discuss the fundamentals, covering the wide range of topics from input and output to controlling, evaluation, and usability, from the methodology of interaction design and mental user models to product language, design guidelines, and how to promote the "joy of use" (i.e., the fun to be had with products).

The Change in Processes

The rapid and pervasive spread of microelectronics in the 1990s effected a sea change in design, construction, and manufacturing processes. What are known as c-techniques (i.e. computer-aided simulation, digital construction, prototyping, and customized mass production) had a particularly profound impact on work processes in design.

It soon became clear that totally new possibilities were opening up for design. The American economists Michael J. Piore and Charles F. Sabel (1984) predicted at an early date that flow manufacturing would permit made-to-order production on a grand scale. In their view the principle of personalization, now called mass customization, would open up new opportunities for design. These opportunities are exploited today in the most diverse product fields, ranging from customized jeans to shirts, automobiles (Smart, for example, offers more than 10,000 personalized versions), and CNC-machined furniture (Steffen 2003, 2011). Computerization has wrought a permanent effect on the form and content of design processes.

The arrival of computer technologies resulted in parallel processes of design, model construction, prototyping, and manufacturing, while since the mid-1990s a growing interconnectedness has offered totally new possibilities for integrating users into the design process. Thus customers today can generate personalized products on the internet; the data are transmitted to decentralized factories, where the product is built and sent directly to the customer. Stocks are reduced to a minimum and distances are short, adding an ecological dimension to this manufacturing model.

3-D Printing

At the beginning of the 2000s a new technology came onto the market, which the American researcher Neil A. Gershenfeld (2007) at MIT proclaimed a revolution in *Fab: The Coming Revolution On Your Desktop – from Personal Computers to Personal Fabrication*. Just as the laser printer transformed conventional printing in the 1980s, it was now possible to print all kinds of products from a personal computer. Originally thought up as stereo lithography for rapid prototyping, the process gave rise to 3-D printing for one-offs and miniseries.

The "maker generation" was proclaimed (Chris Anderson 2012), with digital DIY even hailed as a new industrial revolution. The media frothed with new applications: household appliances, clothing, furniture, medical devices (dentures, joints, organs), food (you can even print a pizza; Leyla Basaran 2014), complete car bodywork, whole bicycles, and even houses. The future seemed boundless. In Japan a man has already been convicted for printing firearms. In that sense Peter Sloterdijk's take on terrorism and product design (↗p. 8) might not actually be so far off the mark.

Questions of copyright and product piracy appear to become irrelevant: "I print the world I want." Designers are especially susceptible to uncritical enthusiasm here: The old wish to produce individualized products (Bürdek 1988a) can at last become reality. At the same time the possibilities of this new technology are limited, and home printing remains an illusion. 3-D print shops to which user data can be sent are certainly conceivable (MIT researcher Neil Gershenfeld calls them Fab Labs). The printed products would then arrive by post. Amazon is already examining the possibilities of this new field of business. But nobody will be producing a new smartphone this way, at best a fancy personalized cover. And certainly not car bodywork: there is still a world of difference between model or prototype and fully functioning product. So the idea that everybody is now a designer is true only in a very limited sense. Claire Warnier, Dries Verbruggen, Sven Ehmann, and Robert Klanten (2014) demonstrate a mixed bag of applications that they also call "digital crafts in the hands of amateurs."

But it is all too easy to overlook that applications are extremely limited by the size of the available machines and the materials used. What is suitable for modelling is not necessarily appropriate for series. The euphoria about a new "maker generation," proclaimed in 2013 by the Deutsche Gesellschaft für Designtheorie und -forschung (DGTF), must therefore be taken with a great pinch of salt. In the words of Martin Gessmann (2013): "You certainly cannot print a better world with 3-D."

Industrie 4.0 – The Internet of Things

The rapid development of the internet from communication between computers through social networks and the learning machine to total networking of development, design, manufacturing, distribution, service, etc. transforms business models and value chains across the board. "Industry 4.0" has even been called a new industrial revolution.

The mechanization that took off at the beginning of the twentieth century with the rapid spread of the steam engine and industrial mass production, and the digitalization we have experienced since the 1980s, are now being succeeded by "informatization." This fourth revolution affects all aspects of products: development, design, and manufacture through to distribution and finally recycling, everything is digitally controlled. The internet becomes the all-determining meta-structure.

As product cycles shrink, globalization throws up ever new challenges. The robots integrated in the process program themselves. Brave New World. In the internet of things, the things themselves become intelligent (through embedded computers) and networked. In the meantime numerous manufacturers are bringing their production operations back to Europe from the low-

3-D-Printer and endless pulse low chair
Design: Studio Dirk Vander Kooij
Zaandam/the Netherlands (2010)

wage countries. The supposed cost advantage evaporates, speed, quality, and location become more important (Germis/Giersberg 2015).

The growing gap between industrial and non-industrial design outlined at the beginning becomes glaring at this point. The fields of play become ever larger and one must decide individually in which one wishes to operate.

Outlook

At the beginning of the twenty-first century design can clearly no longer be imagined – still less successfully practiced – without technology and economics. Only through the interplay of the three was it possible to develop and shape the product cultures that today attract increasing interest in the social and cultural sciences. There, design has moved center stage (at last, one might say).

The profession of designer emerged at the turn of the twentieth century, in the course of an industrialization characterized by a growing division of labor. At the transition from twentieth to twenty-first century craft, design is experiencing a revival. This supposedly holistic approach to creating, producing, and marketing is a step backwards in historical terms. Socially, however, this is a sphere where the supposed "avant-garde" comes to the fore (and not only in the West): design, art, and fashion are the subject of innumerable fairs and exhibitions where one-offs and mini-series are on sale. Furthermore, we have a rapidly digitalizing world where value-creation pressures alter design globally and massively influence lives.

At the same time – like certain other disciplines – design suffers from an enormous overestimation of its own achievements. This becomes glaringly obvious "where the latent suspicion arises that intolerable conditions in the world can be resolved with design alone" (Groll 2014). And that is associated with a simultaneous underdevelopment of its own disciplinary canon of knowledge. If you can only articulate yourself interdisciplinarily – and between all disciplines –you all too easily end up with none.

In design itself, awareness of this is not very pronounced. The old "inventor myth" remains alive (suffice it to say, Leonardo da Vinci). But in design theory today it is indisputable that products "speak" or "mean." Design as a discipline may be developing slowly, but the process is steady: "Different as these approaches may be (product language, product semantics, design rhetoric), they are all rooted in linguistic systems (semiotics, semantics, rhetoric)" (Mareis 2014).

Qualified and subject-specific discourse ("speaking") about design also develops rather slowly in practice. What is communicated about design in general speech is often shameful, the aforementioned "tile design" being only one example among many. Peter Eckart (2014) demands: "Theory in design should develop increasingly out of the knowledge of designing, and orientate less on the theories of other disciplines." Correct as that statement may be, it also reveals the glaring shortcomings: knowledge generated through design is and remains marginal.

Even the crucial topic of ecology has been pursued only tentatively thus far. Isolated award-winning product designs do not really move matters forward. They are more suited to attracting media attention – and they do no end of good to the consciences of the designers. Taking ecology seriously, however, is an entrepreneurial matter. Vitra for example, known for its office furniture, pursues this with professional ecology management. From the raw materials through manufacturing, to packaging, transportation, and recycling, all the steps are organized for sustainability. Only with such a sustainable strategy can ecology and design be reconciled.

Nobody doubts that digitalization will remain an important topic in the twenty-first century. But the processes of design, development, production, distribution, and recycling are subject to rapid and global change.

Design can certainly contribute to value creation. The central question for the process remains the question of "identity" and "difference," as formulated by Martin Heidegger. It is worth continuing to work on that – in theory and in practice.

Spider Dress 2.0
Design: Anouk Wipprecht
Vienna/Amsterdam (2014)

Bibliography

Adorno, Theodor W. 1967. "Funktionalismus heute." In *Ohne Leitbild: Parva Aesthetica*. Frankfurt am Main.

Aicher, Otl 1991. *Die Welt als Entwurf*. Berlin.
– 1991. *analog und digital*. Berlin.

Aisslinger, Werner 2010. *Fast Forward*. Ludwigsburg.

Akrich, Madeleine 2006. "Die De-Skription technischer Objekte." In *ANThology: Ein einführendes Handbuch zur Akteur-Netzwerk-Theorie*, edited by Andréa Belliger and David J. Krieger. Bielefeld.

Albers, Josef 1963. *Interaction of Color*. New Haven.
– Interaction of Color. Grundlegung einer Didaktik des Sehens. Mit einem Vorwort von Erich Franz. Köln 1997

Albus, Volker, and Christian Borngräber 1992. *Design Bilanz: Neues deutsches Design der 80er Jahre in Objekten, Bildern, Daten und Texten*. Cologne.

Albus, Volker, Michel Feith, Rouli Lecatsa, et al. 1986. *Wohnen von Sinnen: Gefühlscollagen*. Cologne.

Aldersey-Williams, Hugh 1988. *New American Design: Products and Graphics for Post-Industrial Age*. New York.

Alexander, Christopher 1964. *Notes on the Synthesis of Form*. Cambridge, Mass.
– 1979. *The Timeless Way of Building*. New York.

Alexander, Christopher, Sara Ishikawa, and Murray Silverstein 1977. *A Pattern Language*. New York.

Alger, John R. M., and Carl V. Hays 1964. *Creative Synthesis in Design*. Englewood Cliffs, New Jersey.

Ambasz, Emilio, ed 1972. *Italy: The New Domestic Landscape*. New York.

Anderson, Chris 2012. *Makers: The New Industrial Revolution*. New York.

Andrews, Edward D., and Faith Andrews 1964. *Shaker Furniture: The Craftsmanhip of an American Communal Sect*. New York. (1-1937)

Archer, Bruce 1963–64. "Systematic Method for Designers." *Design* 172, 174, 176, 179, 181.
– 1979. "Whatever Became of Design Methodology?" *Design Studies* 1 (1).

Arnheim, Rudolf 1972. *Anschauliches Denken: Zur Einheit von Bild und Begriff*. Cologne.

Arnold, Florian Die Logik des Entwerfens. Methode, Geschichte und Gegenwart eines umstrittenen Designkonzepts. Offenbach 2015 (Dissertation an der HFG Offenbach)

Asimov, Morris 1968. *Introduction to Design*. Englewood Cliffs, New Jersey.

Baacke, Rolf-Peter, Uta Brandes, and Michael Erlhoff 1983. *Design als Gegenstand: Der neue Glanz der Dinge*. Berlin.

Bachinger, Richard, and Christian Steguweit 1986. "Corporate Identity und Corporate Image der Firma Olivetti." In *Marktfaktor Design*, edited by Ludwig, G. Poth and Gudrun S. Poth. Landsberg am Lech.

Baehr, Volker, and Jan Kotik 1972. *Gesellschaft – Bedürfnis – Design*, Arbeitsbericht 4. Ulm: Institut für Umweltplanung der Universität Stuttgart.

Bangert, Albrecht 1980. *Möbel und Interieur*. Munich.
– 2004. *Colani: Das Gesamtwerk*, exh. cat. Schopfheim.

Bartels, Daghild 2014. "Hoffnung am Kap." *Neue Zürcher Zeitung*, August 3.

Barthes, Roland 1985. *Die Sprache der Mode*. Frankfurt am Main. (original: *Système de la mode*. Paris, 1967)

Basaran, Leyla 2014. "Wir drucken uns eine Pizza." *Stylepark*, October 17. http://www.stylepark.com/de/news/wir-drucken-uns-eine-pizza/354901

Baudrillard, Jean 1972. *Pour une critique de l´ économie politique du signe*. Paris.

— 1985. *Die fatalen Strategien*. Munich.

— 1991. *Das System der Dinge: Über unser Verhältnis zu den alltäglichen Gegenständen*. Frankfurt am Main (Vienna, 1974). (original: *Le système des objects*. Paris, 1968)

Bauer, Birgit 2013. "Unruhestand: Erlhoff und Bürdek mit neuen Büchern." *Designkritik*, November 13. http://www.designkritik.dk/unruhestand-erlhoff-und-burdek-mit-neuen-buchern/

Bauer-Wabnegg, Walter 1997. "Kleine Welten: Design muß auch in Zukunft Geschichten erzählen können." *Formdiskurs* 3 (2).

— 2001. "Logische Tiefen und freundliche Oberflächen: Neue Mythen des Alltags." In *Der digitale Wahn*, edited by Bernhard E. Bürdek. Frankfurt am Main.

Baumann, Konrad, and Bruce Thomas 2001. *User Interface Design for Electronic Appliances*. London and New York.

Becher, Ursula A. J. 1990. *Geschichte des modernen Lebensstils*. Munich.

Beck, Ulrich 1997. *Was ist Globalisierung?* Frankfurt am Main

Belliger, Andréa, and David. J. Krieger, eds. 2006. *ANThology: Ein einführendes Handbuch zur Akteur-Netzwerk-Theorie*. Bielefeld.

Bense, Max 1954–1960. *Aesthetica I–IV*. Baden-Baden.

1967. *Semiotik: Allgemeine Theorie der Zeichen*. Baden-Baden.

— 1969. *Einführung in die informationstheoretische Ästhetik*. Hamburg.

— 1971. *Zeichen und Design*. Baden-Baden.

Berndt, Heide, Alfred Lorenzer, and Klaus Horn 1968. *Architektur als Ideologie*. Frankfurt am Main.

Bertsch, Georg *Alfredo Arribas: Architecture and Design: Arquitectura y diseño: 1986–1992*. Tübingen and Berlin, 1993.

— 2008. "Undisciplined? Design in an Age of Massive Change". In *Design Research*, edited by Hans Höger. Milan.

Bertsch, Georg, and Ernst Hedler 1990. *SED: Schönes Einheits Design*. Cologne.

Bill, Max 2008. "[form, funktion, schönheit] = [gestalt], 1956." In *Max Bill: Funktion und Funktionalismus: Schriften 1945–1988*, edited by Jacob Bill. Bern and Sulgen.

Birkigt, Klaus, Marinus Stadler, and Hans Joachim Funck 2003. *Corporate Identity: Grundlagen – Funktionen – Fallstudien*, 11th ed. Landsberg am Lech.

Bittner, Regina, ed. 2003. *Bauhausstil: Zwischen International Style und Lifestyle*. Berlin.

Blank, Michael 1988. "Wir müssen aufhören, in Tassen und Tellern zu denken: Ein Gespräch mit Klaus Thomas Edelmann." *Design Report*, no. 6.

Blaser, Werner, ed. 1982. *Klappstühle*. Basel, Boston, and Stuttgart.

Bloch, Ernst 1985 [1918]. *Geist der Utopie*. Frankfurt am Main.

— 1980. *Abschied von der Utopie? Vorträge*, edited by Hanna Gekle. Frankfurt am Main.

Blomberg, Katja, ed. 2014. *Haus-Rucker-Co: Architekturutopie Reloaded*. Cologne.

Bochenski, Joseph Maria 1954. *Die zeitgenössischen Denkmethoden*, 8th ed. Bern and Munich.

Bochynek, Martin 1989. "Das möblierte Museum." *Wolkenkratzer Art Journal*, no. 4.

Böhme, Gernot 2001. "Zur Kritik der ästhetischen Ökonomie." *Zeitschrift für kritische Theorie* 7 (12).

— 2007. "Atmosphäre als Grundbegriff einer neuen Ästhetik." In *Einfühlung und phänomenologische Reduktion. Grundlagentexte zu Architektur, Design und Kunst*, edited by Thomas Friedrich and Jörg H. Gleiter. Berlin et al.

Bonsiepe, Gui 1963. "Gestammelter Jargon: Industrial Design und Charles Sanders Peirce." Ulm, no. 8/9.

— 1974. *Design im Übergang zum Sozialismus: Ein technisch-politischer Erfahrungsbericht aus dem Chile der Unidad Popular (1971–73)*. Hamburg.

— 1975. *Teoria e pratica del disegno industriale: Elementi per una manualistica critica*. Milan.

— 1978. *Teoría y práctica del diseño industrial: Elementos para una manualística crítica*. Barcelona.

— 1992. "Die sieben Säulen des Design." *Form und Zweck*, no. 6.

– 2009. *Entwurfskultur und Gesellschaft: Gestaltung zwischen Zentrum und Peripherie.* Basel, Boston, and Berlin.

Boom, Holger van den 1994. *Betrifft: Design: Unterwegs zur Designwissenschaft in fünf Gedankengängen.* Alfter.

Boos, Frank, and Heinz Jarmai 1994. "Kernkompetenzen – gesucht und gefunden." *Harvard Business Manager,* no. 4.

Borchers, Jan 2001. *A Pattern Approach to Interaction Design.* Chichester et al..

Borries, Friedrich von, and Jesko Fezer 2013. *Weil Design die Welt verändert … Texte zur Gestaltung.* Berlin.

Bosoni, Giampiero, ed. 2001. *Italy – Contemporary Domestic Landscapes.* Milan.

Bourdieu, Pierre 1982. *Die feinen Unterschiede.* Frankfurt am Main. (original: *La distinction: Critique sociale du jugement.* Paris, 1979)

Brand, Steward 1987. *The Media Lab: Inventing the Future at MIT.* New York.

Brandes, Uta 1988. "Das bedingte Leben: Heubachs Untersuchung der psychologischen Gegenständlichkeit der Dinge: Eine Rezension." *Design Report,* no. 6.

– 2001. "Die Digitalisierung des Büros." In *Der digitale Wahn,* edited by Bernhard E. Bürdek. Frankfurt am Main.

Brandes, Uta, Michael Erlhoff, and Nadine Schemmann 2009. *Designtheorie und Designforschung.* Paderborn.

Brändle, Christian, Renate Menzi, and Arthur Rüegg 2014. *100 Jahre Schweizer Design.* Zürich.

Branzi, Andrea 1985. "La tecnologia nuda: Interview mit Tomás Maldonado und Ettore Sottsass." *Modo,* no. 76.

Braun GmbH and Peter Schneider, eds. 2002. *Braun Design.* Kronberg.

Braun Design Team 2012. Kronberg. www.braun.com

British Council and Nick Barley 1999. *Lost and Found.* Basel, Boston, and Berlin.

Buck, Alex, ed. 2003. *Design Management in der Praxis.* Stuttgart.

Buck, Alex, Christoph Herrmann, and Dirk Lubkowitz 1998. *Handbuch Trendmanagement: Innovation und Ästhetik als Grundlage unternehmerischer Erfolg.* Frankfurt am Main.

Buck, Alex, and Matthias Vogt 1996. *Design Management: Was Produkte wirklich erfolgreich macht.* Frankfurt am Main and Wiesbaden.

Burckhardt, Lucius 1981. "Design ist unsichtbar." In *Design ist unsichtbar: Forum Design Linz,* edited by Helmuth Gsöllpointner, Angela Hareiter, and Laurids Ortner. Vienna.

– 1987. "… in unseren Köpfen." In *Design der Zukunft,* edited by idem and IDZ Berlin. Cologne.

Bürdek, Bernhard E. 1971a. *Design-Theorie: Methodische und systematische Verfahren im Industrial Design.* Ulm. (Italian: *Teoria del design: Procedimenti die problem-solving: Metodi di pianificazione: Processi di strutturazione.* Milan, 1977)

– 1971b. "Modelle für die Praxis: Design-Theorien, Design-Methoden." *Form* 56.

– 1975. *Einführung in die Designmethodologie.* Hamburg.

– 1980. "Produktgestaltung heute." *Format* 83 (1).

– 1987. "Keine CI ohne CD." *Absatzwirtschaft* (special issue), October.

– 1988a. "Der Chip – Leitfossil der neunziger Jahre? Der Einfluss der Mikroelektronik: Die Rolle des Designs in der individualisierten Massenfertigung." *FAZ – Blick durch die Wirtschaft,* December 2.

– 1989 "Design-Management in der Bundesrepublik Deutschland: Renaissance nach Jahren der Stagnation." *FAZ – Blick durch die Wirtschaft,* August 25. (reprinted in: Richard Bachinger, ed., *Unternehmenskultur: Ein Beitrag zum Markterfolg.* Frankfurt am Main, 1990a)

– 1992. "Produkte im Zeitalter der Elektronik." In *Design-Innovationen Jahrbuch 92,* edited by Design-Zentrum Nordrhein-Westfalen. Essen.

– 1994. "Human Interface Design." In *Jahrbuch 94, Technische Dokumentation,* edited by Jürgen H. Hahn. Frankfurt am Main.

– 1996a. "Künstler und Navigator: Der Designer als Führer durch Raum und Zeit." *FAZ-Magazin,* June 14.

– 1996b. "Missing Link with GUI." *Design News,* no. 235 (September).

– 1996c. "Ein Gespräch mit Rolf Fehlbaum." *Design* (CD-ROM). Cologne.

– 1997a. *Der Apple Macintosh.* Frankfurt am Main.

– 1997b. *Vom Mythos des Funktionalismus,* edited by FSB Franz Schneider Brakel. Cologne.

– 1997c. "Form und Kontext." In *Objekt und Prozess, 17. Designwissenschaftliches Kolloquium Burg Giebichenstein, Hochschule für Kunst und Design, Halle 28.–30.11.1996.* Halle.

– 1997d. "Über Sprache, Gegenstände und Design." *Formdiskurs: Zeitschrift für Design und Theorie/Journal of Design and Design Theory* 3 (2).

– 1998. "Die elektronische Aufrüstung des Autos." *Form Spezial* 2. (reprinted as: "Die Digitalisierung des Autos," in *Automobility: Was uns bewegt*, edited by Alexander von Vegesack and Mateo Kries. Weil am Rhein, 1999 [Vitra Design Museum])

– 1999. "Design." In *100 Wörter des Jahrhunderts*, edited by Wolfgang Schneider. Frankfurt am Main

– 2001a. "Design: Von der Formgebung zur Sinngebung." In *Werbung, Mode und Design*, edited by Guido Zurstiege and Siegfried J. Schmidt. Wiesbaden

–, ed. 2001b. *Der digitale Wahn*. Frankfurt am Main.

– 2002. "Theorie und Praxis im Design." Designreport, no. 6 (June).

– 2003. "Zur Methodologie an der HfG Ulm und deren Folgen." In *Ulmer Modelle – Modelle nach Ulm: Zum 50. Gründungsjubiläum der Ulmer Hochschule für Gestaltung*, exh. cat., ed. Ulmer Museum and HfG-Archiv. Stuttgart.

– 2009. "Hingucker: Theorie und Methodik: Anmerkungen zu einem reich bestellten und weitgehend unbekannten ostdeutschen Wissenschaftsfeld." In *Die geteilte Form: Deutsch-deutsche Designaffären 1949–1989*, edited by Günther Höhne. Cologne.

– 2011. "Design ist (doch) eine Disziplin." In *Design, Anfang des 21. Jh.*, edited by Petra Eisele and Bernhard E. Bürdek. Ludwigsburg.

– 2011. "Design in Kalifornien." In *Apple Design*, edited by Sabine Schulze and Ina Graetz. Ostfildern.

– *Design auf dem Weg zu einer Disziplin*. Hamburg, 2012.

– 2013. "Von der Produktsprache zur Designsprache." *Mitteilungen Designaustria: Designwissenschaft*, no. 2.

Bürdek, Bernhard E., and Jochen Gros 1978. "Der Wandel im Design-Verständnis: Form-Gespräch mit Vertretern der Koppelmannschule Köln." *Form* 81 (1).

Bürdek, Bernhard E., Georg Hannes, and Horst Schneider 1988b. "Computer im Design." *Form* 121 (1).

Bürdek, Bernhard E., and Yana Milev, eds. 2014. "Design Kulturen." *Form*, no. 252 (March/April)

Bürdek, Bernhard E., and Stephan Schupbach 1992. "Klarheit mit Hypermedia: Human Interface Design: Konstruktion von Benutzungsoberflächen." *KEM Konstruktion Elektronik Maschinenbau*, no. 7 (July).

– 1993. "Human Interface Design: Über neue Aufgabengebiete des Designs und ein praktisches Beispiel im Zeitalter der Elektronik." *Form* 142 (2).

Bürdek, Bernhard E., and Typographische Gesellschaft, eds. *Design und Qualität*. Munich, 1996b.

Burkhardt, François 1973. "Vorwort." In *Design als Postulat am Beispiel Italiens*, edited by IDZ Berlin. Berlin.

– 1993. "Das neue Design: Vom experimentellen Gestalten des einzelnen Objekts zur Schaffung künstlerischer Umwelten." In *Die Aktualität des Ästhetischen*, edited by Wolfgang Welsch. Munich.

Burkhardt, François, and Inez Franksen, eds. 1980. *Design: Dieter Rams*. Berlin.

Buzan, Tony, with Barry Buzan 1991. The Mind Map Book. New York.

Buzan, Tony, and Barry Buzan 2002. *Das Mind-Map-Buch*. Munich.

Byrne, Bryan, and Susan Squires, eds. 2002. *Creating Breakthrough Ideas: The Collaboration of Anthropologists and Designers in the Product Development Industry*. Westport, Conn.

Calvera, Anna, ed. 2003 *Arte¿ ?Diseño*. Barcelona.

–, ed. 2007. *De lo bello de las cosas: Materiales para und estética del diseño*. Barcelona.

CETRA (China External Trade Development Council) 1994. *Industrial Design in Taiwan 1959–1994*. Taipei.

Clarke, Alison Jane, ed. 2010. *Design Anthropology: Object Culture in the 21st Century*. Vienna.

Cook, Peter *Archigram*. 1974. London and New York.

Cooper, Alan 1999. *The Inmates Are Running the Asylum: Why High-Tech Products Drive Us Crazy and How to Restore the Sanity*. Indianapolis.

Crasset, Matali 2007. *Spaces 2000–2007*. Cologne, London, and New York.

Crilly, Nathan, James Moultrie, and P. John Clarkson 2004. "Seeing Things: Consumer Response to the Visual Domain in Product Design." *Design Studies* 25.

Cross, Nigel 1984. *Developments in Design Methodology*. Chichester.

– 1989. *Engineering Design Methods*. Chichester.

– 2001. "Design/Science/Research: Developing a Discipline." Keynote speech, International Symposium on Design Science, 5th Asian Design Conference, Seoul, October.

Curdes, Gerhard http://www.club-offulm.de/Curdes-Geschichte-des-IUP.pdf

Csikszentmihalyi, Mihaly, and Eugene Rochberg-Halton 1989. *Der Sinn der Dinge: Das Selbst und die Symbole des Wohnbereichs*. Munich and Weinheim. (original: *The Meaning of Things: Domestic Symbols and the Self*. Cambridge, Mass., 1981)

Czemper, Achim, ed. 2008. *Hfg Ulm: Die Abteilung Produktgestaltung: 39 Rückblicke*. Dortmund.

Davis, Meredith 2012. *Graphic Design Theory*. London.

Decker, Edith, and Peter Weibel, eds. *Vom Verschwinden der Ferne: Telekommunikation und Kunst*. Cologne, 1990.

Der Apple-Check 2013. *ARD* television report, broadcast February 4, 2013, repeated August 13, 2014, on *HR3*.

Derrida, Jacques 1979. *Die Stimme und das Phänomen: Ein Essay über das Problem des Zeichens in der Philosophie Husserls*, translation and foreword by Jochen Hörisch. Frankfurt am Main. (original: La voix et le phénomène. Paris, 1967)

Design Forum Finland 1998. *Yrityksen muotoilijayhteydet*. Helsinki.

Design Thinking https://www.google.de/search?q=design+thinking&source=lnms&tbm=isch&sa=X&ei=zm3rU425DvDY4QT6yYHQDA&sqi=2&ved=0CAYQ_AUoAQ&biw=1044&bih=908

Diebner, Hans, Timothy Druckrey, and Peter Weibel 2001. *Science of the Interface*. Tübingen.

Dietz, Georg 2002. "Begegnung mit einem Monster." *Frankfurter Allgemeine Sonntagszeitung*, November 11.

DMI. www.dmi.org

Donaldson, Stephanie 2001. *Der Shaker-Garten: Von der Schönheit des Nützlichen*. Munich.

Dörner, Volker 1976. *Die Produktform als Mittel der Anmutungsgestaltung unter besonderer Berücksichtigung der Quantifizierung und Dynamisierung anmutungshafter Formleistung*. Cologne.

Douglas, Mary 1973. *Rules and Meaning*. New York.

– 1988. *Reinheit und Gefährdung: Eine Studie zu Vorstellungen von Verunreinigungen und Tabu*. Frankfurt am Main.

– 1992. *Risk and Blame: Essays in Cultural Theory*. London.

Dunas, Peter 1993. *Luigi Colani und die organisch-dynamische Form seit dem Jugendstil*. Munich.

Dunne, Anthony 1999. *Hertzian Tales: Electronic Products, Aesthetic Experience and Critical Design*. London.

Dunne, Anthony, and Fiona Raby 2001. *Design Noir: The Secret Life of Electronic Objects*. Basel

– 2014. *Speculative Everything: Design, Fiction and Social Dreaming*. Cambridge, Mass.

Durkheim, Emile 1981. *Die elementaren Formen religiösen Lebens*. Frankfurt am Main. (original: *Les formes élémentaires de la vie religieuse*. Paris, 1912)

Dyson, James 2001. *Against the Odds: An Autobiography*. London.

Eckart, Peter 2014. "Design studieren: Der Wandel bleibt." In *Design identifizieren*, edited by Deutscher Designer Club. Frankfurt am Main.

Eckstein, Hans 1985. *Formgebung des Nützlichen: Marginalien zur Geschichte und Theorie des Design*. Düsseldorf.

Eco, Umberto 1972. *Einführung in die Semiotik*. Munich. (original: *La struttura assente*. Milan, 1968)

Edelmann, Thomas 2014. "Visionen von Gestern." *Stylepark*, April 13. http://www.stylepark.com/de/news/visionen-von-gestern/350403

Ehrenfels, Christian von 1890. "Über Gestaltqualitäten." *Vierteljahrsschrift wissenschaftliche Philosophie* 14:249–92.

Eisenman, Peter 1995. *Aura und Exzeß: Zur Überwindung der Metaphysik der Architektur*. Vienna.

– 1991. "Schwache Form." In *Architektur im AufBruch: Neun Positionen zum Dekonstruktivismus*, edited by Peter Noever. Munich.

Eisner, Michael D. 1996. *Walt Disney Imagineering: A Behind the Dreams Look at Making the Magic Real*. New York.

Ellinger, Theodor 1966. "Die Informationsfunktion des Produktes." Offprint from *Produktionstheorie und Produktionsplanung*, Festschrift for the 65th birthday of Karl Hax. Cologne and Opladen.

Engell, Lorenz, Oliver Fahle, and Britta Neitzel, eds. 2000. *Kursbuch Medienkultur: Die maßgeblichen Theorien von Brecht bis Baudrillard*. Stuttgart.

Erlhoff, Michael 1987. "Kopfüber zu Füßen: Prolog für Animateure." In *Documenta 8*, vol. 1, Kassel.

– 2013. *Theorie des Designs*. Munich.

Escherle, Hans-Jürgen 1986. *Industriedesign für ausländische Märkte*. Munich.

Esslinger, Hartmut 2011. "im Gespräch mit Bernhard E. Bürdek." In *Design, Anfang des 21. Jh.*, edited by Petra Eisele and Bernhard E. Bürdek. Ludwigsburg

Esslinger, Hartmut 2014. *Genial Einfach: Die frühen Design-Jahre von Apple*. Stuttgart. (original: *Keep it Simple: The Early Years of Apple*. Stuttgart, 2014)

Farr, Michael 1966. *Designmanagement*. London.

Faßler, Manfred 2002. *Bildlichkeit: Navigation durch das Repertoire der Sichtbarkeit*. Vienna, Cologne, and Weimar.

– 2011. *Kampf der Habitate: Neuerfindungen des Lebens im 21. Jahrhundert*. Vienna and New York.

– 2014. "Design – Statuskunst?" In *Design identifizieren*, edited by Deutscher Designer Club e.V. Frankfurt am Main.

Fehlbaum, Rolf 1997. "Vitra: Eine pluralistische Identität." In *Kompendium Corporate Identity und Corporate Design*, edited by Norbert W. Daldrop. Stuttgart.

Feldenkirchen, Wilfried, ed. 1997. *150 Jahre Siemens: Das Unternehmen von 1847 bis 1997*. Munich: Siemens Forum.

Felix, Zdenek 1972. *Konzept-Kunst*, exh. cat Kunstmuseum. Basel.

Feuerstein, Günther 1981. "Zeichen und Anzeichen." *Form und Zweck*, no. 5.

Feyerabend, Paul 1976. *Wider den Methodenzwang: Skizze einer anarchistischen Erkenntnistheorie*. Frankfurt am Main and New York.

Fiebig, Wilfried 1986. "Zum Begriff der Vernunft. Ringveranstaltung zur „Theorie der Produktsprache"." Lecture, Hochschule für Gestaltung Offenbach am Main, November 13.

Fiedler, Jeannine, and Peter Feierabend, eds. 1999. *Bauhaus*. Cologne.

Figal, Günter 1996. *Der Sinn des Verstehens: Beiträge zur hermeneutischen Philosophie*. Stuttgart.

Fischer, Richard 1978. "Zur Anzeichenfunktion." In *Fachbereich Produktgestaltung*, edited by Hochschule für Gestaltung Offenbach am Main.

– 1988. "Design im Zeitalter der Mikroelektronik." Lecture, Hochschule für Gestaltung Offenbach am Main, October 13.

Fischer, Richard, and Gerda Mikosch 1984. *Grundlagen einer Theorie der Produktsprache*, vol 3: *Anzeichenfunktionen*. Offenbach am Main.

Fischer, Volker, ed. 1988a. *Design heute: Maßstäbe: Formgebung zwischen Industrie und Kunst-Stück*. Munich.

– 1988b. "Produktstrategie als Kulturstrategie." *Perspektive: Zeitschrift der Vorwerk & Co. Teppichwerke KG*, no. 1.

– 2001. "Emotionen in der Digitale" Eine Phänomenologie elektronischer „devices"." In *Der digitale Wahn*, edited by Bernhard E. Bürdek. Frankfurt am Main.

– 2003. *Richard Meier: Der Architekt als Designer und Künstler*. Stuttgart and London.

Fischer, Volker, and Andrea Gleiniger 1998. *Stefan Wewerka: Architekt, Designer, Objektkünstler*. Stuttgart and London.

Fischer, Wend 1971. *Die verborgene Vernunft: Funktionale Gestaltung im 19. Jahrhundert*. Munich.

Flierl, Bruno, and Heinz Hirdina 1985. *Postmoderne und Funktionalismus: Sechs Vorträge*. Berlin.

Foraita, Sabine *Borderline: Das Verhältnis von Kunst und Design aus der Perspektive des Design*, diss. HfBK. Braunschweig, 2005.

– 2011. "Grenzgänge: Über das Verhältnis von Kunst und Design." In *Design, Anfang des 21. Jh.*, edited by Petra Eisele and Bernhard E. Bürdek. Ludwigsburg.

Formdiskurs: Zeitschrift für Design und Theorie / Journal of Design and Design Theory 1997. Vol. 3 (2). Special issue "Über Sprache, Gegenstände und Design."

Foster, Norman 1999. *Architecture Is about People*, exh. cat. Museum für Angewandte Kunst. Cologne.

Frank, Manfred 1984. *Was ist Neustrukturalismus?* Frankfurt am Main.

Friedländer, Uri 1981. "Wir sind in einer Phase der Umorientierung …" *Form* 96 (4).

Friedrich-Liebenberg, Andreas 1976. *Anmutungsleistungen von Produkten: Zur Katalogisierung, Strukturierung und Stratifikation anmutungshafter Produktleistungen*. Cologne.

Friemert, Chup 1984. *Die gläserne Arche: Kristallpalast London 1851 und 1854*. Munich.

Fritenwalder, Henning 1999. *Kann Design eine Theorie haben?* degree diss., HdK Hamburg.

FSB Franz Schneider Brakel 2011. *Begreifbare Baukunst: Die Bedeutung von Türgriffen in der Architektur, mit Texten von Bettina Rudhof*. Brakel.

Gadamer, Hans-Georg 1960. *Wahrheit und Methode: Grundzüge einer philosophischen Hermeneutik*. Tübingen.

– 1988. "Der Mensch als Naturwesen und Kulturträger." Opening lecture in the series "Mensch und Natur," November 28, Frankfurt am Main.

Garnich, Rolf 1968. *Konstruktion, Design, Ästhetik*. Esslingen.

Gershenfeld, Neil 1999. *Wenn die Dinge denken lernen*. Munich and Düsseldorf. (original: *When Things Start to Think*. New York, 1999)

– 2007. *Fab: The Coming Revolution on Your Desktop – from Personal Computers to Personal Fabrication*. New York.

Gessmann, Martin 2010. *Was der Mensch wirklich braucht: Warum wir mit Technik nicht mehr zurechtkommen und wie sich aus unserem Umgang mit Apparaten wieder eine sinnvolle Geschichte ergibt*. Munich.

– 2012. *Zur Zukunft der Hermeneutik*. Munich.

– 2013. "Kann man die bessere Welt in 3D drucken?" DGTF Tagung. www.dgtf.de/tagungen/tagung2013

– 2014. *Wenn die Welt in Stücke geht: Warum wir philosophieren*. Paderborn.

Geyer, Erich 1972. *Marktgerechte Produktplanung und Produktentwicklung: Teil II: Produkt und Betrieb*. Heidelberg.

Geyer, Erich, and Bernhard E. Bürdek 1970. "Designmanagement." *Form* 51 (3).

Geyer, Erich, Jupp Frerkes, and Manfred Zorn 1970. *AW Design Kompendium 70*. Stuttgart.

Gibson, James J. 1979. *Die Wahrnehmung der visuellen Welt*. Weinheim and Basel.

– 1982. Wahrnehmung und Umwelt. Munich.

Giedion, Sigfried 1948. *Mechanization Takes Command*. Oxford. (German: *Die Herrschaft der Mechanisierung. Ein Beitrag zur anonymen Geschichte*, edited by Henning Ritter, special edition, Frankfurt am Main, 1987)

Ghini, Massimo Iosa 2013. *Palazzo della Triennale, Milano*. Milan. (Italian, English)

GK Design Group 2003. *GK Design 50 Years 1952–2002*. Tokyo.

Glaser, Hermann 1982. "Industriekultur oder die Sache mit den Knopflöchern." In *Industriekultur: Expeditionen ins Alltägliche*, edited by Klaus-Jürgen Sembach, Manfred Jehle, and Franz Sonnenberger. Nuremberg.

Göbel, Lutz 1992. "Den „Integralisten" gehört die Zukunft." *VDI Nachrichten*, no. 13.

Golde, Chris M., and George Walker 2001. *Overview of the Carnegie Initiative on the Doctorate. Draft 2.1*, August 19, 2001.

Gombrich, Ernst H 1979. *The Sense of Order*. Oxford.

Gorgs, Claus 2003. "Gemeinsamer Nenner." *Wirtschaftswoche*, January 9.

Gorsen, Peter 1979. "Zur Dialektik des Funktionalismus heute." In *Stichworte zur „geistigen" Situation der Zeit*, vol. 2, edited by Jürgen Habermas. Frankfurt am Main.

Gould, Stephen Jay 1998. *Illusion und Fortschritt: Die vielfältigen Wege der Evolution*. Frankfurt am Main (original: *Full House: The Spread of Excellence from Plato to Darwin*. New York, 1996).

Graf, Annika 2012. "Microsofts neuer Sinn fürs Schöne." *Financial Times Deutschland*, November 2.

Groll, Sandra 2014. "The Words for Design." *Form*, no. 256, November/December.

Gropius, Walter 1925. "Grundsätze der Bauhaus-produktion." In *Neue Arbeiten der Bauhauswerkstatt*, Bauhausbücher 7, edited by Walter Gropius and László Moholy-Nagy. Munich.

Gros, Jochen 1971. *Dialektik der Gestaltung*, Schriftenreihe des IUP – Institut für Umweltplanung der Universität Stuttgart. Ulm.

– 1976. "Sinn-liche Funktionen im Design." *Form* 74 (2) (part 1) and *Form* 75 (2) (part 2).

– 1983. *Grundlagen einer Theorie der Produktsprache*, vol. 1. Offenbach am Main.

– 1987. *Grundlagen einer Theorie der Produktsprache*, vol. 4: *Symbolfunktionen*. Offenbach am Main.

Grossarth, Jan 2009. "Das neue Bürgertum kauft kein teures Porzellan." *Frankfurter Allgemeine Sonntagszeitung*, January 18.

Gsöllpointner, Helmuth, Angela Hareiter, and Laurids Ortner, eds. 1981. *Design ist unsichtbar.* Vienna.

Gugelot, Hans 1984. "Design als Zeichen (Vortrag, gehalten am 13.10.1962 bei dem Industrieunternehmen CEAD in Dortmund)." In *System-Design Bahnbrecher: Hans Gugelot 1920–1965*, edited by Hans Wichmann. Munich.

Habermas, Jürgen 1968. *Erkenntnis und Interesse.* Frankfurt am Main.

– 1981. *Theorie des kommunikativen Handelns*, vol. 1: *Handlungsrationalität und gesellschaftliche Rationalisierung*. Frankfurt am Main.

– 1981. *Theorie des kommunikativen Handelns*, vol. 2: *Zur Kritik der funktionalistischen Vernunft*. Frankfurt am Main.

– 1985. *Die neue Unübersichtlichkeit*, Kleine Politische Schriften 5. Frankfurt am Main.

Habermas, Tilmann 1999. *Geliebte Objekte: Symbole und Instrumente der Identitätsbildung*. Frankfurt am Main.

Hackenschmidt, Sebastian, and Klaus Engelhorn, eds. 2011. *Möbel als Medien: Beiträge zu einer Kulturgeschichte der Dinge*. Bielefeld.

Hahn, Erwin 1988. "Amerika, Du hast es besser." *Computer Persönlich*, no. 26.

Hahn, Hans Peter 2005. *Materielle Kultur: Eine Einführung*. Hamburg.

– 2011. "Ethnologie und Konsum: Eine globale Perspektive." In *Design, Anfang des 21. Jh.*, edited by Petra Eisele and Bernhard E. Bürdek. Ludwigsburg

– 2013. *Ethnologie: Eine Einführung*. Berlin.

Hase, Holger 1989. *Gestaltung von Anmutungscharakteren: Stil und Looks in der marketingorientierten Produktgestaltung*. Cologne.

Hauffe, Thomas 1994. *Fantasie und Härte: Das Neue deutsche Design der achtziger Jahre*. Gießen.

– 2014. *Geschichte des Designs*. Cologne.

Haug, Wolfgang Fritz 1970. In *Design? Umwelt wird in Frage gestellt*, edited by IDZ Berlin. Berlin

– 1971. *Kritik der Warenästhetik*. Frankfurt am Main.

– 1972. *Warenästhetik, Sexualität und Herrschaft: Gesammelte Aufsätze*. Frankfurt am Main.

– 1986. *Critique of Commodity Aesthetics: Appearance, Sexuality, and Advertising in Capitalist Society*. Minneapolis.

Häußling, Roger 2010. "Zum Design(begriff) der Netzwerkgesellschaft: Design als zentrales Element der Identitätsformation in Netzwerken." In *Relationale Soziologie: Zur kulturellen Wende der Netzwerkforschung*, edited by Jan Fuhse and Sophie Mützel. Wiesbaden.

Heidegger, Martin 1957. *Identität und Differenz.* Pfullingen.

– 1967. *Vorträge und Aufsätze*, vols. 1 and 2. Pfullingen. (specifically "Das Ding," "Die Frage nach der Technik,", "Bauen Wohnen Denken")

– 1968. *Phänomenologische Analysen zur Kunst der Gegenwart*. The Hague.

Henseler, Wolfgang 2001. "Interface-Agenten: Der Wandel in der Mensch Objekt Kommunikation oder Von benutzungsfreundlichen zu benutzerfreundlichen Systemen." In *Der digitale Wahn*, edited by Bernhard E. Bürdek. Frankfurt am Main.

Herrmann, Christoph, and Günter Moeller 2011. "Strategisches Design: Ökonomisch erfolgreiches Design?" In *Design, Anfang des 21. Jh.*, edited by Petra Eisele and Bernhard E. Bürdek. Ludwigsburg.

Herzogenrath, Wulf, and Alexander Wewerka, eds. 2010. *Nahaufnahme Stefan Wewerka*. Berlin.

Heskett, John 1980. *Industrial Design*. London. (new edition 2000)

Heß, Andreas (Porsche AG) 1997. "Produktkliniken als Instrument der Marktforschung in der Automobilindustrie." In *Auto-Motive 97*, edited by Wolfgang Meinig. Bamberg.

Hesse, Petra, and Gabriele Lueg 2012. *Architektenmöbel: von Aalto bis Zumthor / Furniture by Architects: From Aalto to Zumthor*. Cologne

Hesselgren, Sven El hombre y su percepción del ambiente urbano. Una teoria arquitectónica. México. D.F. 1980

Heubach, Friedrich W. 1987. *Das bedingte Leben: Entwurf zu einer Theorie der psychologischen Gegenständlichkeit der Dinge*. Munich.

Hierholzer, Michael 2014. "In der Handlung liegt die Kunst." *Frankfurter Allgemeine Zeitung*, September 16.

Hinte, Ed van 2002. *Marti Guixé*. Rotterdam.
– 1996. *Wim Rietveld: Industrieel Ontwerper*. Rotterdam.

Hirdina. Heinz 1988. *Gestalten für die Serie: Design in der DDR 1949–1985*. Dresden.

Hirsch, Sandra 2014. *Gestaltung und Umbruch: Industrie Design als Mittel sozioökonomischer Wertschöpfung*. Hamburg.

History of Industrial Design Vol 1: 1750-1850, Vol2: 1851-1918, Vol 3: 1919-1990, Milan 1990/1991

Hitchcock, Henry-Russell, and Philip Johnson 1966. *The International Style*. New York and London. (originally published as *The International Style: Architecture since 1922*, New York, 1932)

Hitzler, Jürgen, and Siemens Design Studio 1988. "Studie Gleisbildterminal 1986." In *Design heute: Maßstäbe: Formgebung zwischen Industrie und Kunst-Stück*, edited by Volker Fischer. Munich.

Hoffmann, Tobias, and Markus Zehentbauer 2014. *Schrill Bizarr Brachial: Das Neue Deutsche Design der 80er Jahre*. Cologne.

Höhne, Günter 2001. *Penti, Erika und Bebo Sher: Die Klassiker des DDR-Designs*. Berlin.
– 2007. *Das große Lexikon DDR-Design*. Cologne
– 2009. *Die geteilte Form: Deutsch-deutsche Designaffären 1949–1989*. Cologne.

Höhner, Jens 2009. "Computer brauchen Fans." *Wirtschaftswoche*, September 7.

Hofter, Sibylle 1997. *Modell: Aurora: 500 000 000 Plastikstühle*. Munich.

Hosokawa, Shuhei 1987. *Der Walkman-Effekt*. Berlin. (original: "The Walkman Effect," *Popular Music* 4/1984)

HTR (HighTech Report) DaimlerChrysler AG, ed. 2003, no. 1

Hüetlin, Thomas 2015. "Cool mit Zertifikat." *Spiegel*, no. 2.

Husserl, Edmund 1913. "Ideen zur reinen Phänomenologie und phänomenologischen Philosophie (1900/01)." *Jahrbuch für Philosophie und phänomenologische Forschung*.

IBIS.com E-Mail vom 11.07.2014

ICSID Daily Day 4, 11.10.2001. Seoul 2001

IDZ Berlin, ed. 1970. *Design? Umwelt wird in Frage gestellt*. Berlin.
–, ed. 1973. Design als Postulat am Beispiel Italien. Berlin.

if (Industrie Forum Design Hannover) 1990. *Kriterien einer guten Industrieform* (Herbert Lindinger). Hannover.

Ingher, Lea, and Nadine Jürgenssen 2014. "Nutzen statt besitzen." *Neue Zürcher Zeitung*, September 6.

Italia diseño 1946/1986 Katalog Museo Rufino Tamayo. Mexiko 1986

Jencks, Charles 1978. *Die Sprache der postmodernen Architektur*. Stuttgart. (original: *The Language of Post-Modern Architecture*. London, 1978)
– 1987. *Die Postmoderne: Der neue Klassizismus in Kunst und Architektur*. Stuttgart. (original: *Post-Modernism*. London, 1987)

Jenkins, David 2000. *On Foster – Foster On*. Munich.

Jonas, Wolfgang 1994. *Design – System – Theorie: Überlegungen zu einem systemtheoretischen Modell von Design-Theorie*, habilitation diss., BUGH Wuppertal. Essen.

Jones, Christopher J. 1969. "The State-of-the-Art in Design Methods." In *Design Methods in Architecture*, edited by Geoffrey Broadbent and Anthony Ward. London.
– 1982. *Design Methods: Seeds of Human Future* 9th ed. Chichester.

Julier, Guy 2000. *The Culture of Design*. London.

Jungen, Patrik 2011. *Wirkung der symbolischen Aussage einer Produktgestaltung auf die Markenbeurteilung*. Hamburg.

Kachel-Design (http://www.uni-trier.de/index. php?id=49884, abgerufen im Oktober 2014)

Kahn, Herman 1977. *Vor uns die guten Jahre: Ein realistisches Modell unserer Zukunft*. Vienna et al. (original: *The Next 200 Years: A Scenario for America and the World*. Boulder, Col., 1976)

– 1980. *Die Zukunft der Welt 1980–2000*. Vienna et al. (original: *World Economic Development*. Boulder, Col., 1979)

Kaku, Michio 1998. *Visions: How Science Will Revolutionize the 21st Century*. New York.

Karmasin, Helene 1993. *Produkte als Botschaften: Was macht Produkte einzigartig und unverwechselbar?* Vienna

– 1998. "Cultural Theory und Produktsemantik: Cultural Theory and Product Semantics." *Formdiskurs: Zeitschrift für Design und Theorie / Journal of Design and Design Theory* 4 (1).

Karmasin, Helene, and Matthias Karmasin 1997. *Cultural Theory: Ein neuer Ansatz für Kommunikation, Marketing und Management*. Vienna.

Kassner, Jens 2002. *Clauss Dietel und Lutz Rudolph: Gestaltung ist Kultur*. Chemnitz.

– 2009. *Ostform: Der Gestalter Karl Clauss Dietel*. Leipzig.

Katz, David 1979. *Gestalt Psychology: Its Nature and Significance*. Westport, Conn. (original: Gestaltpsykologi. Stockholm, 1942)

Keller, Rudi 1986. "Interpretation und Sprachkritik." *Sprache und Literatur in Wissenschaft und Unterricht* 17 (57).

Kerckhove, Derrick de 2002. *Die Architektur der Intelligenz: Wie die Vernetzung der Welt unsere Wahrnehmung verändert*. Basel, Boston, and Berlin (original: L´architettura dell´intelligenza. Turin, 2001)

Kicherer, Sibylle 1987. *Industriedesign als Leistungsbereich von Unternehmen*. Munich.

– 1990. *Olivetti: A Study of the Corporate Management of Design*. New York.

Kiemle, Manfred 1967. *Ästhetische Probleme der Architektur unter dem Aspekt der Informationsästhetik*. Quickborn.

Kiefer, Georg R. 1970. *Zur Semiotisierung der Umwelt*, diss. Stuttgart.

Kirsch, Karin 1987. *Die Weißenhof-Siedlung: Werkbund-Ausstellung „Die Wohnung", Stuttgart 1927*. Stuttgart.

Klar, Michael 1968. *Kritik an der Rolle des Design in der Verschwendungsgesellschaft*, degree diss., HfG Ulm.

Klatt, Jo, and Hartmut Jatzke-Wigand, eds. 2002. *Möbel-Systeme von Dieter Rams*. Hamburg.

Klavans, Dick, and Kevin Boyack 2009. *Map of Science*. www.mapofscience.com

Klemp, Klaus, and Keiko Ueki-Polet 2011. *Less and More: The Design Ethos of Dieter Rams*. Berlin.

Klinikum-Stuttgart *Interdisziplinarität in der Medizin*. http://www.klinikum-stuttgart.de

Klotz, Heinrich 1986. *Vision der Moderne: Das Prinzip der Konstruktion*. Munich.

– 1987. *Moderne und Postmoderne: Architektur der Gegenwart 1960–1980*, 3d ed. Braunschweig and Wiesbaden.

– 1989. *Architektur des 20. Jahrhunderts*. Stuttgart.

– 1995. *Geschichte der Architektur: Von der Urhütte zum Wolkenkratzer*. Munich.

– 1996. *Die Zweite Moderne: Eine Diagnose der Kunst der Gegenwart*. Munich

– 1996. *Schriften zur Architektur: Texte zur Geschichte, Theorie und Kritik des Bauens*. Ostfildern.

– 1997. *Contemporary Art: ZKM. Center for Art and Media Karlsruhe*. Munich.

– 1999. *Kunst im 20. Jahrhundert: Moderne – Postmoderne – Zweite Moderne*. Munich.

– 1999. *Architektur der Zweiten Moderne: Ein Essay zur Ankündigung des Neuen*. Stuttgart.

– 2000. *Geschichte der deutschen Kunst*, 3 vols. Munich.

Kluge, Annalena 2013. *Design Thinking: Im Spannungsfeld von Kreativität und Innovation im Kontext der ästhetischen Ökonomie*, degree diss. Hochschule für Gestaltung Offenbach am Main, Fachbereich Produktgestaltung.

Knop, Carsten 2003. "Die Zauberer der schnellen Chips." Frankfurter Allgemeine Zeitung, June 21.

Kohl, Karl-Heinz 2003. *Die Macht der Dinge: Geschichte und Theorie sakraler Objekte*. Munich.

Köhler, Manfred 2002. "Made in Kronberg: Scherköpfe für Schanghai." *Frankfurter Allgemeine Zeitung,* August 13.

Koolhaas, Rem 2001. Harvard Design School Guide to Shopping. Cologne.

– 2001. *OMA/AMO: Projects for Prada Part 1.* Milan.

Koppelmann, Udo 1978. *Grundlagen des Produktmarketing: Zum qualitativen Informationsbedarf von Produktmanagern.* Stuttgart et al.

Krauch, Helmut 2002. "Maieutik." In *Angewandte Systemforschung: Ein interdisziplinärer Ansatz,* edited by Tom Sommerlatte. Wiesbaden.

Krippendorff, Klaus, and Reinhart Butter 1984. "Product Semantics: Exploring the Symbolic Qualities of Form." *Innovation: The Journal of the Industrial Designers Society of America* 3 (2).

Krippendorff, Klaus 1961. *Über den Zeichen- und Symbolcharakter von Gegenständen: Versuch zu einer Zeichentheorie für die Programmierung von Produktformen in sozialen Kommunikationsstrukturen,* degree diss. HfG Ulm.

– 1985. "Die Produktsemantik öffnet die Türen zu einem neuen Bewußtsein im Design." *Form* 108/109 (1).

– 1989. "Design muß Sinn machen: Zu einer neuen Design-Theorie." *HfG Forum,* no. 14.

– 2006. *The Semantic Turn: A New Foundation for Design.* Boca Raton, Fla., London, and New York.

– 2013. *Die semantische Wende: Eine neue Grundlage für Design.* Basel.

Kruft, Hanno Walter 1985. *Geschichte der Architekturtheorie.* Munich.

Kuby, Thomas 1969. *Zur gesellschaftlichen Funktion des Industrial Designs,* degree diss. HfG Ulm.

Kühte, Erich, and Matteo Thun 1995. *Marketing mit Bildern.* Cologne

Kuhn, Thomas S. 1977. *Die Struktur wissenschaftlicher Revolutionen.* Frankfurt am Main.

Kümmel, Birgit, ed. 1998. *Made in Arolsen. HEWI und die Kaulbachs: Zwischen höfischem Handwerk und Industriedesign: Museum Bad Arolsen und Museumsverein.* Bad Arolsen.

Kunkel, Paul 1997. Apple Design: The Work of the Apple Industrial Design Group. New York.

Lang, Alfred 1989. Editor's foreword to Mihaly Csikszentmihalyi and Eugene Rochberg-Halton, *Der Sinn der Dinge: Das Selbst und die Symbole des Wohnbereichs.* Munich and Weinheim. (original: *The Meaning of Things. Domestic Symbols and the Self.* Cambridge, Mass., 1981)

Langenmaier, Arnica-Verena 1993. *Der Klang der Dinge: Akustik – eine Aufgabe des Design.* Munich.

Langer, Susanne 1965. *Philosophie auf neuem Wege: Das Symbol im Denken, im Ritus und in der Kunst.* Frankfurt am Main. (original: *Philosophy in a New Key.* Cambridge, Mass., 1942)

Lanier, Jaron 2014. "Der „High-Tech-Frieden" braucht eine neue Art von Humanismus." Acceptance speech on receiving the Peace Prize of the German Book Trade, Frankfurt am Main, October 12.

Lannoch, Hans-Jürgen 1983. Überlegungen zu einer neuen Formensprache. *Form* 104 (4).

– 1984. "How to Move from Geometric to Semantic Space." *Innovation: The Journal of the Industrial Designers Society of America* 3 (2).

Lannoch, Helga, and Hans-Jürgen Lannoch 1987. Vom geometrischen zum semantischen Raum. *Form* 118 (2).

– 1977. "Metarealistisches Design." *Form* 79 (3).

Latour, Bruno 2014. *Existenzweisen: Eine Anthropologie der Modernen.* Berlin. (original: *Enquête sur les modes d'existence: Une anthropologie des modernes.* Paris, 2012)

Law, John 1992. "Notes on the Theory of the Actor-Network: Ordering, Strategy and Heterogeneity." *Systems Practice* 5.

Lee, Kun-Pyo 2001. *Culture and its Effects on Human Interaction with Design: With the Emphasis on Cross-Cultural Perspectives between Korea and Japan,* Ph.D. project at the University of Tsukuba, Japan.

Lehnhardt, Jana-Maria 1996. *Analyse und Generierung von Designprägnanzen: Designstile als Determinanten der marketingorientierten Produktgestaltung.* Cologne.

Leithäuser, Thomas, and Birgit Volmerg 1979. *Anleitung zur empirischen Hermeneutik: Psychoanalytische Textinterpretation als sozialwissenschaftliches Verfahren.* Frankfurt am Main.

Leitherer, Eugen 1991. *Industrie-Design: Entwick-lung – Produktion – Ökonomie.* Stuttgart.
Lenz, Michael 1988 "Gedankensprünge: Zur experimentellen Arbeit der Gruppe Ginbande." Design Report, no. 5 (May).
Leuschel, Klaus, ed. 2009. *Swissness: 43 helve-tische Errungenschaften und 7 prägende Persönlich-keiten der Designgeschichte.* Sulgen.
Lewin, Roger 1993. *Die Komplexitätstheorie: Wissenschaft nach der Chaosforschung.* Hamburg. (original: *Complexity: Life at the Edge of Chaos.* New York, 1992)
Libeskind, Daniel 1995. *Kein Ort an seiner Stelle: Schriften zur Architektur – Visionen für Berlin.* Dresden and Basel.
Liebl, Franz 2000. *Der Schock des Neuen: Entste-hung und Management von Issues und Trends.* Munich.
Lindinger, Herbert, ed. 1987. *Hochschule für Gestaltung Ulm: Die Moral der Gegenstände.* Berlin.
Linn, Carl-Eric 1992. *Das Metaprodukt: Produkt-entwicklung und Marketing von Markenartikeln.* Landsberg am Lech. (original: *Metaprodukten och det skapande företaget.* Malmö, 1985)
Loos, Adolf 1908. "Ornament und Verbrechen" In *Sämtliche Schriften,* vol. 1, edited by Franz Glück. Vienna and Munich, 1962.
Lorenzer, Alfred 1970. *Kritik des psychoanaly-tischen Symbolbegriffs.* Frankfurt am Main.
– 1974. *Die Wahrheit der psychoanalytischen Erkenntnis.* Frankfurt am Main.
Lueg, Gabriele, ed. 1994. *Made in Holland: Design aus den Niederlanden.* Tübingen and Berlin.
Luhmann, Niklas 1984. *Soziale Systeme:. Grundriß einer allgemeinen Theorie.* Frankfurt am Main.
Lux, Peter G. C. 2003. "Zur Durchführung von Corporate Identity Programmen." In *Corporate Identity: Grundlagen – Funktionen – Fallstudien,* edited by Klaus Birkigt, Marinus Stadler, and Hans Joachim Funck. Landsberg am Lech.
Lyotard, Jean-François 1982. *Das postmoderne Wissen: Ein Bericht,* edited by Peter Engelmann. Bremen. (new edition Graz and Vienna, 1986)
–, Jacques Derrida, François Burkhardt, and Marianne Karbe 1985. *Immaterialität und Postmoderne.* Berlin.

MacQuaid, Matilda, ed. 2003. *Visionen und Utopien: Architekturzeichnungen aus dem Museum of Modern Art,* exh. cat Schirn Kunsthalle. Frank-furt am Main.
Maldonado, Tomás 2007. "Ist Architektur ein Text?" In *Digitale Welt und Gestaltung: Aus-gewählte Schriften,* edited and translated by Gui Bonsiepe. Basel, Boston, and Berlin.
Maldonado, Tomás, and Gui Bonsiepe 1964. "Wissenschaft und Gestaltung." *Ulm* 10/11.
Manske, Beate, and Gudrun Scholz 1987. *Täglich in der Hand: Industrieformen von Wilhelm Wagenfeld aus sechs Jahrzehnten.* Worpswede.
Manzini, Ezio, and Marco Susani 1995. *The Solid Side: The Search for a Consistency in a Changing World – Projects and Proposals.* Eindhoven.
Mareis, Claudia 2010. "Experimente zu einer Theorie der Praxis: Historische Etappen der Designforschung in der Nachfolge des Bauhauses." website *Kunsttexte,* no. 1.
– 2011. *Design als Wissenskultur: Interferenzen zwischen Design- und Wissensdiskursen seit 1960.* Bielefeld.
– 2014. *Theorien des Designs zur Einführung.* Hamburg.
Margolin, Victor 2015. *World History of Design,* 2 vols. London et al.
Martin, Marijke, Cor Wagenaar, and Annette Welkamp 1995. *Alessandro & Francesco Mendini! Philippe Starck! Michele de Lucchi! Coop Himmel-b(l)au! in Groningen!* Groningen.
Marx, Werner 1961. *Heidegger und die Tradition.* Stuttgart.
Marzano, Stefano 1998. *Creating Value by Design: Thoughts.* London.
Maser, Siegfried 1970. *Numerische Ästhetik,* Arbeitsberichte 2. Stuttgart: Institut für Grund-lagen der Modernen Architektur.
– 1971. *Grundlagen der allgemeinen Kommunika-tionstheorie: Eine Einführung in ihre Grundbegriffe und Methoden (mit Übungen).* Stuttgart.
– 1972. *Einige Bemerkungen zum Problem einer Theorie des Designs.* Braunschweig.
– 1976. "Design und Wissenschaft: Theorie ohne Praxis ist leer, Praxis ohne Theorie ist blind." *Form* 73 (1).

Mayr-Keber, Gert M. 2003. "Strukturelemente der visuellen Erscheinung von Corporate Identity." In *Corporate Identity: Grundlagen – Funktionen – Fallstudien*, edited by Klaus Birkigt, Marinus Stadler, and Hans Joachim Funck. Landsberg am Lech.

McCoy, Michael 1984. "Defining a New Functionalism in Design." *Innovation: The Journal of the Industrial Designers Society of America* 3 (2).
– 1996. "Interpretive Design." In *New Thinking in Design: Conversations on Theory and Practice*, edited by C. Thomas Mitchell. New York.

McCoy, Michael, and Katherine McCoy 1988. Design in the Information Age. In *New American Design*, edited by Hugh Aldersey-William. New York.

McLuhan, Marshall 1968. *Die Gutenberg-Galaxis: Das Ende des Buchzeitalters*. Vienna. (original: *The Gutenberg Galaxy*. Toronto, 1962)

McQuaid, Matilda 2003. *Visionen und Utopien*. Munich.

Meadows, Dennis, Donella Meadows, Erich Zahn, and Peter Milling 1972. *Die Grenzen des Wachstums*. Stuttgart. (original: *The Limits of Growth*, New York, 1972)

Mehlstäubler, Arthur 1999. *Egon Eiermann: Die Möbel*, exh. cat. Badisches Landesmuseum Karlsruhe.

Meier-Kortwig, Hans Jörg 1997. *Design Management als Beratungsangebot*. Frankfurt am Main.

Meinong, Alexius 1907. *Über die Stiftung der Gegenstandstheorie im System der Wissenschaften*. Leipzig.

Meller, James, ed. 1970. *The Buckminster Fuller Reader*. London.

Menne, Katrin 2010. "Kunst, Design und Nutzbarkeit. Die Cafégestaltung von Tobias Rehberger auf der Biennale von Venedig und in der Kunsthalle Baden-Baden." website *Kunsttexte*, no. 1.

Metzger, Wolfgang 1999. *Gestalt-Psychologie: Ausgewählte Werke aus den Jahren 1950 bis 1982*, edited and with an introduction by Michael Stadler and Heinrich Crabus. Frankfurt am Main.
– 2007. *Gesetze des Sehens*. Magdeburg.

Meyer-Eppler, Wolfgang 1959. *Grundlagen und Anwendungen der Informationstheorie*. Berlin.

Michl, Jan 1992. "A Review of Two Product Semantics Conference Proceedings." website Jan Michl. www.janmichl.com/eng.prodsem-helsinki.html

Milev, Yana, ed. 2013. *Design Kulturen: Der erweiterte Designbegriff im Entwurfsfeld der Kulturwissenschaft*. Paderborn.
– 2014. *Designsoziologie: Der erweiterte Designbegriff im Entwurfsfeld der Politischen Theorie und Soziologie*. Frankfurt am Main et al.

Miller, R. Craig, Rosemarie Haag Bletter, et al. 2001. *US Design 1975–2000*, exh. cat. Denver Art Museum. Munich, London, and New York.

Minx, Eckard P 2001. "Zukunft in Unternehmen – Strategiefindung: Methoden und Beispiele." Lectures in the scope of the Leitner endowed chair New Economy – New Design, HfG Offenbach, June 13.

Minx, Eckard P., Christian Neuhaus, Michael Steinbrecher, and Thomas Waschke 1994. "Zu Ansatz und Methode im interdisziplinären Forschungsverbund Lebensraum Stadt / Stadt, Mobilität und Kommunikation im Jahre 2020: Zwei Szenarien." In *Mobilität und Kommunikation in den Agglomerationen von Heute und Morgen*, edited by Forschungsverbund Lebensraum Stadt. Berlin.

Mitscherlich, Alexander 1965. *Die Unwirtlichkeit unserer Städte*. Frankfurt am Main.

Moles, Abraham 1965. Theorie der Komplexität und der technischen Zivilisation. *Ulm* 12/13.
– 1968. "Die Krise des Funktionalismus." *Form*, no. 41 (March).

Monö, Rune 1997. *Design for Product Understanding: The Aesthetics of Design from a Semiotic Approach*. Stockholm.

Morris, William 1974. *Kunde von Nirgendwo: Eine Utopie der vollendeten kommunistischen Gesellschaft und Kultur aus dem Jahre 1890*, new edition edited by Gert Selle. Cologne. (original: *News from Nowhere*, first published in serial form in the socialist magazine *Commonweal* in 1890, printed as a book in 1892)

Mozota, Brigitte Borja de 2003. *Design Management: Using Design to Build Brand Value and Corporate Innovation*. New York. (original: Paris, 2001)

Mukařovský, Jan 1970. *Kapitel aus der Ästhetik*. Frankfurt am Main.

Muller, Wim 2001. *Order and Meaning in Design*. Utrecht. (original: Vormgeven ordening en betekenisgeving. Utrecht, 1997)

Müller-Krauspe, Gerda 1969. "Opas Funktionalismus ist tot." *Form*, no. 46.

– 1978. "Designtheorie aus der Sicht einer zu verändernden Praxis." In *Designtheorien I*, edited by IDZ Berlin. Berlin.

Mundt, Barbara 1998. *Architekten als Designer: Beispiele aus Berlin*. Munich.

Muranka, Tony, and Nick Rootes 1996. *"Doing a Dyson"*. Malmesbury.

Mutius, Bernhard von 2000. *Die Verwandlung der Welt: Ein Dialog mit der Zukunft*. Stuttgart.

– 2002. "Gestaltung neu denken. Form-Gespräch mit Bernhard E. Bürdek." *Form*, no. 184 (July/August).

– 2004. *Die andere Intelligenz: Wie wir morgen denken werden*. Stuttgart.

Nadin, Mihai 2002. *Anticipation: Die Ursache liegt in der Zukunft: The End Is Where We Start From*. Baden, Switzerland.

Naisbitt, John 1984. *Megatrend: 10 Perspektiven, die unser Leben verändern werden*. Bayreuth. (original: *Megatrends*. New York, 1982)

– 1995. *Megatrends Asien: 8 Megatrends, die unsere Welt verändern*. Vienna et al. (original: *Megatrends Asia*. New York, 1995)

– 1999. *High Tech – High Touch: Auf der Suche nach Balance zwischen Technologie und Mensch*. Vienna. (original: *High Tech – High Touch*. New York, 1999)

Negroponte, Nicholas 1995. *Total Digital: Die Welt zwischen 0 und 1 oder Die Zukunft der Kommunikation*. Munich (original: *Being Digital*. New York, 1995)

Nehls, Werner 1968. "Die Heiligen Kühe des Funktionalismus müssen geopfert werden." *Form*, no. 43.

Nolte, Paul 2001. "Unsere Klassengesellschaft: Wie könnten die Deutschen angemessen über ihr Gemeinwesen sprechen? Ein unzeitgemäßer Vorschlag." *Zeit*, January 4.

Norman, Donald A. 1989. *Dinge des Alltags*. Frankfurt am Main and New York. (original: *The Psychology of Everyday Things*. New York, 1988)

– 1993. *Things That Make Us Smart. Defending Human Attributes in the Age of the Machine*. Reading, Mass., et al.

– 1998. *The Invisible Computer. Why Good Products Can Fail, the Personal Computer Is so Complex, and the Information Appliances Are the Solution*. Cambridge, Mass., and London.

– 2010. http://www.core77.com/blog/columns/design_thinking_a_useful_myth_16790.asp, June 25.

Nouvel, Jean 2001. *Exposition présentée au Centre Georges Pompidou*, exh. cat. Paris.

Oehlke, Horst 1977. "Zur Funktionsbestimmung der industriellen Formgestaltung." In *1. Kolloquium zu Fragen der Theorie und Methodik der industriellen Formgestaltung*. Halle.

– 1978. "Der Funktionsbegriff in der industriellen Formgestaltung." In *2. Kolloquium zu Fragen der Theorie und Methodik*. Halle.

– 1982. *Produkterscheinung / Produktbild / Produktleitbild – ein Beitrag zur Bestimmung des Gegenstandes von industriellem Design*, diss. Humboldt-Universität. Berlin.

Ohl, Herbert 1977. "Design ist meßbar geworden." *Form* 78 (2).

Olivetti, ed. *Ergonomie und Olivetti*, vol 1: *Der Mensch im Mittelpunkt: Zusammenfassung des aktuellen Wissenstandes im Bereich der Ergonomie*.

–, **ed.** 1981. *Ergonomie und Olivetti*, vol 2: *Olivetti Datensichtgeräte und Arbeitsplätze*. Milan.

–, **ed.** 1983. *Design Process Olivetti 1908–1983*. Milan.

–, **ed.** 1986. *Olivetti Corporate Identity Design*, published by Neue Sammlung München in conjunction with Olivetti GmbH, Frankfurt am Main. Munich.

Onck, Andries van 1994. *Design – il senso delle forme die prodotti*. Milan.

Papanek, Victor 1972. *Das Papanek Konzept: Design für eine Umwelt des Überlebens*. Munich. (original: *Design for the Real World*, with an introduction by R. Buckminster Fuller. London, 1972

Pehnt, Wolfgang 1988. *Karljosef Schattner: Ein Architekt aus Eichstätt*. Stuttgart.

– 1992. "Der Architektur das Tanzen beigebracht" Frankfurter Allgemeine Zeitung, June 27.

Pevsner, Nikolaus 1957. *Pioneers of Modern Design: From William Morris to Walter Gropius*. London.

Piore, Michael J., and Charles F. Sabel 1985. *Das Ende der Massenproduktion*. Berlin. (original: *The Second Industrial Divide: Possibilities for Prosperity*. New York, 1984)

Plüm, Kerstin 2007. *Glokalisiertes Design: Design-wissenschaftliche Überlegungen zu Phänomenen der Weltgesellschaft*. Berlin.

Prahalad, Coimbatore. K., and Gary Hamel 1992. "Nur Kernkompetenzen sichern das Überleben." *Harvard Manager*, no. 1.

Radice, Barbara, ed. 1981. *Memphis: The New International Style*. Milan.

– 1985. *Memphis: Research, Experience, Result, Furnitures and Successes of New Design*. Milan.

Rashid, Karim 2011. *I Want to Change the World*. London.

Rat für Formgebung, ed. 1990. *Design Management*. Frankfurt am Main.

Read, Herbert Edward 1935. *Art and Industry: The Principles of Industrial Design*. London.

Reck, Hans-Ulrich 1996. "Vom „unsichtbaren Design" zum unsichtbaren Design." *Formdiskurs: Zeitschrift für Design und Theorie / Journal of Design and Design Theory* 1 (1).

Reckwitz, Andreas 2012. *Die Erfindung der Kreativität: Zum Prozess gesellschaftlicher Ästhetisierung*. Berlin.

Reimers, Karl Friedrich 1983. Brückenschläge zwischen den Disziplinen. In Zeichenentwicklung – Bedeutungswandel – Handlungsmuster, edited by idem. Munich.

Reinking, Guido 2002. "Offroad: Wer ihn braucht und wer ihn kauft." *Financial Times Deutschland*, February 7.

Reinmöller, Patrick 1995. *Produktsprache: Verständlichkeit des Umgangs mit Produkten durch Produktgestaltung*. Cologne. (Fördergesellschaft Produkt-Marketing e.V.)

Richard, Birgit 2001. "2001 – Odyssee in Fashion. Electro-textiles and Cargo-mode." In *Vergangene Zukunft: Design zwischen Utopie und Wissenschaft*, edited by Carl Aigner and Uli Marchsteiner. Krems.

Rieger, Bodo 1989. "Das Januskopfproblem in der CI-Praxis." *Markenartikel*. (abridged version in Frankfurter Allgemeine Zeitung, June 6, 1989.

Rifkin, Jeremy 1998. *Das Biotechnische Zeitalter*. Munich.

Rittel, Horst 1973. "Bemerkungen zur System-forschung der „ersten" und „zweiten" Generation." *Der Mensch und die Technik: Technisch-wissen-schaftliche Blätter der Süddeutschen Zeitung*, November 27.

– 1992. *Planen, Entwerfen, Design*, edited by Wolf D. Reuter. Stuttgart.

– 2013. *Thinking Design*, edited by Wolf D. Reuter and Wolfgang Jonas. Basel.

Roericht, Nick H. 1982. *HfG-Synopse: Die syn-chron-optische Darstellung der Entstehung, Entwicklung und Auswirkung der Ulmer Hoch-schule für Gestaltung*. Ulm.

Ronke, Christiane 2002. "Das Abenteuer beginnt gleich um die Ecke." *Financial Times Deutschland*, December 16.

Roozenburg, N. F. M., and J. Eekels 1995. *Product Design: Fundamentals and Methods*. Chichester.

Rossi, Aldo 1966. *L'Architettura della città*. Padua. (English: *The Architecture of the City*. Cambridge, Mass., 1982)

– 1975. *Scritti scelti sull'architettura e la città*. Milan. (English: *A Scientific Autobiography*. Cambridge, Mass., 1981)

Rübenach, Bernhard 1987. *Der rechte Winkel von Ulm* (1-1958/59), edited and with an afterword by Bernd Meurer. Darmstadt.

Rummel, Carlo 1995. *Designmanagement*. Wiesbaden.

Ruppert, Wolfgang 1993a. *Fahrrad, Auto, Fernseh-schrank: Zur Kulturgeschichte der Alltagsdinge*. Frankfurt am Main.

– 1993b. *Chiffren des Alltags: Erkundungen zur Geschichte der industriellen Massenkultur*. Marburg.

– 1997. "Der verblassende Reiz der Dinge." In *Alltag und soziales Gedächtnis: Die DDR-Objektkul-tur und ihre Musealisierung*, edited by Gerd Kuhn and Andreas Ludwig. Hamburg.

– 1998. *Um 1968: Die Repräsentation der Dinge*. Marburg.

Rusch, Gebhard 1994. "Kommunikation und Verstehen." In *Die Wirklichkeit der Medien*, edited by Klaus Merten, Siegfried J. Schmidt, and Siegfried Weischenberg. Opladen.

Sachs, Angeli, ed. 2010. *Global Design: Interna-tionale Perspektiven und individuelle Konzepte*, exh. cat. Museum für Gestaltung. Basel.

– 2011. "Global Design." In *Design, Anfang des 21. Jh.*, edited by Petra Eisele and Bernhard E. Bürdek. Ludwigsburg.

Sarasin, Wolfgang 2003. "Produktdesign, Produktidentität, Corporate Identity." In *Corporate Identity: Grundlagen – Funktionen – Fallstudien*, edited by Klaus Birkigt, Marinus Stadler, and Hans Joachim Funck. Landsberg am Lech.

Schägerl, Christian 2002. "Die Scham des Futuristen: William Gibson, Großmeister des Zukunftsromans, kapituliert vor der technischen Entwicklung und beschreibt nur noch die Gegenwart." *Frankfurter Allgemeine Sonntagszeitung*, December 15.

Schirrmacher, Frank 2014. "Seine Waffe: Aufklärung." *Frankfurter Allgemeine Zeitung*, June 6.

Schmidt, Burghart 2010. "Kunst und Forschung." Transcript of lecture in series "Theorien der Gestaltung," HfG Offenbach, May 27. (see also "Fragen nach der Wissenschaftlichkeit des Forschens in den Künsten und im Gestalten überhaupt," in *Theorien Ästhetischer Praxis. Wissensformen in Kunst und Design*, edited by Hans Zitko. Cologne, Weimar, and Vienna, 2014)

Schmidt, Klaus, ed. 1994. *Corporate Identity in Europa: Strategien – Instrumente – Erfolgreiche Beispiele*. Frankfurt and New York. (English: *The Quest for Identity: Corporate Identity – Strategies, Methods and Examples*. London, 1995)

Schmidt, Siegfried J., ed. 1987. *Der Diskurs des radikalen Konstruktivismus*, 7th ed. 1996. Frankfurt am Main.

– 1992. *Kognition und Gesellschaft: Der Diskurs des Radikalen Konstruktivismus 2*. Frankfurt am Main.

Schmitz-Maibauer, Heinz H. 1976. *Der Stoff als Mittel anmutungshafter Produktgestaltung: Grundzüge einer Materialpsychologie*. Cologne.

Schneider, Norbert 1996. *Geschichte der Ästhetik von der Aufklärung bis zur Postmoderne*. Stuttgart.

Schnell, Ralf, ed. 2000. *Metzler Lexikon Kultur der Gegenwart: Themen und Theorien, Formen und Institutionen seit 1945*. Stuttgart and Weimar.

Schoenberger, Johanna 2011. *Strategisches Design: Verankerung von Kreativität und Innovation in Unternehmen*. Wiesbaden.

Schönberger, Angela 1990. *Raymond Loewy: Pionier des amerikanischen Industriedesigns*. Munich.

Schöner Wohnen, ed. 1994. *Moderne Klassiker: Möbel, die Geschichte machen*, 16th ed. Hamburg.

Schönhammer, Rainer 1988. *Der „Walkman": Eine phänomenologische Untersuchung*. Munich.

– 1997. "Zur Anthropologie der Fernbedienung: Zur Wirkungsweise eines magischen Werkzeugs." Formdiskurs 3 (2).

Schultheis, Franz 2005. "Disziplinierung des Designs." In *Zweites Design Forschungssymposium: Forschungslandschaften im Umfeld des Designs*, edited by Swiss Design Network. Zürich.

Schulze, Gerhard 1992. *Die Erlebnisgesellschaft: Kultursoziologie der Gegenwart*, 2d ed. 2005. Frankfurt am Main and New York.

Schupbach, Stephan, and Frank Zebner 1990. "Gerätedesign im Computer-Zeitalter." *Elektronik* no. 22.

Schwer, Thilo 2014. *Produktsprachen: Design zwischen Unikat und Industrieprodukt*. Bielefeld.

Seckendorff, Eva von 1986, 1989. *Die Hochschule für Gestaltung in Ulm: Gründung (1949–1953) und Ära Max Bill (1953–1957)*. Dissertation Hamburg 1986, Marburg 1989.

Seeling, Hartmut 1985. *Geschichte der Hochschule für Gestaltung Ulm 1953–1968: Ein Beitrag zur Entwicklung ihres Programmes und der Arbeiten im Bereich der visuellen Kommunikation*, diss. Cologne.

Seiffert, Helmut 1983, 1985. *Einführung in die Wissenschaftstheorie*, vol. 1 (1983), 10th ed.; vol. 2 (1983), 8th ed.; vol. 3 (1985). Munich.

Selle, Gert 1973. *Ideologie und Utopie des Design: Zur gesellschaftlichen Theorie der industriellen Formgebung*. Cologne.

– 1978, 1987. *Die Geschichte des Design in Deutschland von 1870 bis heute*. Cologne. (new edition Frankfurt am Main and New York, 1994)

– 1994. "Ist Design noch modern? Überästhetisierung als Ersatz von Utopie – ein summarischer Erinnerungsversuch." *Werk und Zeit – Perspektiven*, no. 2.

– 2007. *Design im Alltag: Vom Thonetstuhl zum Mikrochip*. Frankfurt am Main.

Semantics in Design www.hfg-offenbach.de/w3php?nodeId=3392&page=3

Sembach, Klaus-Jürgen 1971. "Das Jahr 1851: Fixpunkt des Wandels." In *Die verborgene Vernunft: Funktionale Gestaltung im 19. Jahrhundert*, edited by Wend Fischer. Munich

Shneiderman, Ben 1992. *Designing the User Interface: Strategies for Effective Human-Computer Interaction*, 2d ed. Reading, Mass., et al. (5th ed. 2013)

Siemens Nixdorf AG 1993. *Gestaltung von Benutzeroberflächen für Selbstbedienungsanwendungen: Ein Designbuch*. Munich and Paderborn (concept, text, and design: Martina Menzel and Frank Zebner)

Siemons, Mark 2012. "Ohne Apple verliert man sein Gesicht." *Frankfurter Allgemeine Zeitung*, November 2.

– 2014. "Die Roboter kommen." *Frankfurter Allgemeine Zeitung*, July 10.

Simmel, Georg 1890. *Über sociale Differenzierung*. Leipzig.

– 1900. *Philosophie des Geldes*. Leipzig.

– 1905. *Philosophie der Mode*. Berlin.

Sloterdijk, Peter 1999. *Wohin führt der globale Wettbewerb? Philosophische Aspekte der Globalisierung*. Berlin. (lecture at Bundesverband Deutscher Banken)

– 2001. *Nicht gerettet: Versuche nach Heidegger*. Frankfurt am Main.

– 2004. *Sphären III: Schäume*. Frankfurt am Main.

Snow, C. P. 1959. *The Two Cultures and the Scientific Revolution*. Cambridge.

Soentgen, Jens 1997. *Das Unscheinbare: Phänomenologische Beschreibungen von Stoffen, Dingen und fraktalen Gebilden*. Berlin.

– 1997. Die Faszination der Materialien. *Formdiskurs* 3 (2).

– 1998. *Splitter und Scherben: Essays zur Phänomenologie des Unscheinbaren*. Kusterdingen.

Spalt, Johannes, ed. 1987. *Klapptische*. Basel, Boston, and Stuttgart.

Sparke, Penny 1986. *An Introduction to Design and Culture in the Twentieth Century*. New York.

Spieß, Heinrich 1993. *Integriertes Designmanagement*, Beiträge zum Produktmarketing 23. Cologne.

Spiegel 2014. No. 49, December 1.

Spitz, René 2001. *Die Hochschule für Gestaltung Ulm – ein Blick hinter den Vordergrund*. Stuttgart

and London. (English: *The Ulm School of Design – A View behind the Foreground*. Stuttgart and London, 2001)

SpoKK, ed. 1997. *Kursbuch JugendKultur: Stile, Szenen und Identitäten vor der Jahrtausendwende*. Mannheim.

Spreenberg, Peter 1994. "Editor's Note." *Interact* (American Center for Design) 8 (1).

Stadler, Michael, and Heinrich Crabus, eds. 1999. *Wolfgang Metzger: Gestalt-Psychologie: Ausgewählte Werke aus den Jahren 1950 bis 1982*. Frankfurt am Main.

Steffen, Dagmar 1997b. "Zur Theorie der Produktsprache: Perspektiven der hermeneutischen Interpretation von Designobjekten." *Formdiskurs: Zeitschrift für Design und Theorie / Journal of Design and Design Theory* 3 (2).

– 1998. "Semantics in Design oder Die Sprachlichkeit in der Gestaltung." *Form online*, February 26.

– 2000. *Design als Produktsprache: Der „Offenbacher Ansatz in Theorie und Praxis"*, with contributions by Bernhard E. Bürdek, Volker Fischer and Jochen Gros. Frankfurt am Main.

– 2003. *C_Moebel: Digitale Machart und gestalterische Eigenart*, with a contribution by Jochen Gros. Frankfurt am Main.

– 2011. *Praxisintegrierende Designforschung und Theoriebildung: Analysen und Fallstudien zur produktiven Vermittlung zwischen Theorie und Praxis*. Wuppertal.

Steguweit, Christian 1994. "Typologie und Konsequenz einer Corporate Identity." In *Corporate Identity in Europa*, edited by Klaus Schmidt. Frankfurt am Main and New York.

Steiner, Urs 2014. "Das Ende des Designs." In *Neue Zürcher Zeitung*, September 27.

Stephan, Peter F. 2011. "im Interview mit Bernhard Krusche: Gestalterisches Denken ist viel umfassender – Forschung und Beratung im Design." *Revue für postheroisches Management*, no. 8.

Strassmann, Burkhard 2003. "Fühlen Sie mal ..." *Zeit*, July 7.

Sudjic, Deyan 2008. *The Language of Things*. London.

Sullivan, Louis H. 1896, revised 1918 [reprint 1955]). *Kindergarten Chats and Other Writings*. New York.

– 1896. *The Tall Office Building Artistically Considered*. Chicago. (cited from Wend Fischer, *Die verborgene Vernunft: Funktionale Gestaltung im 19. Jahrhundert*. Munich, 1971)

Terragni, Emilia, ed. 2002. *Spoon*. London and New York.

Terstiege, Gerrit 2013. "„Wir stehen noch am Anfang": Ein Gespräch mit Oliver Grabes." *Grid*, no. 1 (November/December).

Thackara, John, and Jane Stuart 1986. *New British Design*. London.

Tietenberg, Annette 2002. "Der Körper als Möglichkeit / Bodies of Evidence." *Form*, no. 185, (September/October).

Toffler, Alvin 1970. *Der Zukunftsschock*. Bern and Munich. (original: *Future Shock*. Cologne and Geneva, 1970)

– 1980. *Die Zukunftschance: Von der Industriegesellschaft zu einer humaneren Zivilisation*. Munich. (original: *The Third Wave*. New York, 1980)

– 1990. *Machtbeben*. Düsseldorf. (original: *Powershift*. New York, 1990)

Trüby, Stephan 2014. "Geldkulturen: Eine Einführung." In Geldkulturen, edited by Gerhard M. Buurman and Stephan Trüby. Bielefeld.

Tzonis, Alexander 1990. "Hütten, Schiffe und Flaschengestelle: Analogischer Entwurf für Architekten und/oder Maschinen." *Archithese*, no. 3.

U.F. 1987. "Keine Garantie für gut abgehangene Klassiker." Frankfurter Allgemeine Zeitung, August 20.

Ullrich, Wolfgang 2011. "Philosophen haben die Welt immer nur verschieden interpretiert – verändern Produktgestalter sie auch?" In *Warenästhetik: Neue Perspektiven auf Konsum, Kultur und Kunst*, edited by Heinz Drügh, Christian Metz, and Björn Weyand. Berlin.

Ulmer Museum and HfG-Archiv 2003. *Ulmer Modelle – Modelle nach Ulm: Zum 50. Gründungsjubiläum der Ulmer Hochschule für Gestaltung*, exh. cat. Ostfildern-Ruit.

Ursprung, Philip 2010. "Container: Rückgrat der Globalisierung." In *Global Design: Internationale Perspektiven und individuelle Konzepte*, edited by Museum für Gestaltung Zürich and Angeli Sachs. Baden, Switzerland.

VDI 1995. *Richtlinie 4500: Technische Dokumentation*, specifically "(d): Benutzerinformation." Düsseldorf.

Veblen, Thorstein 1899 [2005]. The Theory of the Leisure Class: An Economic Study of Institutions. Delhi.

Vegesack, Alexander von, ed. 1994. *Citizen Office: Ideen und Notizen zu einer neuen Bürowelt*. Göttingen.

Venturi, Robert 1966. *Complexity and Contradiction in Architecture*. New York. (German: Braunschweig, 1978)

Venturi, Robert, and Denise Scott-Brown 2002. "Wir sind ja für Unreine: Ein Gespräch mit Hanno Rauterberg." *Zeit*, October 17.

–, **and Steven Izenour** 1979. *Lernen von Las Vegas*. Braunschweig and Wiesbaden. (original: *Learning from Las Vegas*. Cambridge, Mass., 1972)

Veraart, Albert, and Reiner Wimmer 1984. "Hermeneutik." In *Enzyklopädie Philosophie und Wissenschaftstheorie*, vol. 2, edited by Jürgen Mittelstraß. Mannheim, Vienna, and Zürich.

Vershofen, Wilhelm 1959. *Die Marktentnahme als Kernstück der Wirtschaftsforschung*. Berlin and Cologne.

Vihma, Susann 1995. *Products as Representations: A Semiotic and Aesthetic Study of Design Products*. Helsinki.

Volli, Ugo. Semiotik 2002. *Eine Einführung in ihre Grundbegriffe*. Tübingen and Basel. (original: *Manuale di semiotica*. Rome and Bari, 2000)

Wagner, Christoph, ed. 2009. *Esoterik am Bauhaus: Eine Revision der Moderne?* Regensburg.

Waldenfels, Bernhard 1985. *In den Netzen der Lebenswelt*. Frankfurt am Main.

– 1992. *Einführung in die Phänomenologie*. Munich.

Walker, John Albert 1989. *Design History and the History of Design*. London.

Walther, Elisabeth 2002. *Zeichen: Aufsätze zur Semiotik*. Weimar.

Wang, Wilfried 1998. *Herzog & de Meuron*. Basel, Boston, and Berlin.

Warnier, Claire, Dries Verbruggen, Sven Ehmann, and Robert Klanten, eds. 2014. *Dinge drucken: Wie 3D-Drucken das Design verändert*. Berlin.

Weibel, Peter 1987. *Die Beschleunigung der Bilder.* Bern.

–, ed. 1994. *Kontext Kunst: Kunst der 90er Jahre.* Cologne.

– 2001. *Vom Tafelbild zum globalen Datenraum: Neue Möglichkeiten der Bildproduktion und bildgebenden Verfahren.* Stuttgart.

Weil, Michelle M., and Larry F. Rosen 1997. *TechnoStress: Coping with Technology @Work @ Home @Play.* New York et al.

Weinberg, A. J. 2014. "Wenn das Smartphone Teil des Körpers wird." Frankfurter Allgemeine Zeitung, September 3.

Welsch, Wolfgang 1987. *Unsere postmoderne Moderne.* Weinheim.

– 1990. *Ästhetisches Denken.* Stuttgart.

–, ed. 1993. *Die Aktualität des Ästhetischen.* Munich.

– 1996. *Grenzgänge der Ästhetik.* Stuttgart. (specifically: "Städte der Zukunft – Architektur-theoretische und kulturphilosophische Aspekte")

– 2012. *Blickwechsel: Neue Wege der Ästhetik.* Stuttgart.

Wewerka, Stefan 1983. *Tecta 1972–1982. Bericht einer deutschen Unternehmung.* Berlin.

Wick, Rainer 1982. *Bauhaus-Pädagogik.* Cologne.

Wilson, Mark 2014. "75% of Ikea's Catalog is Computer Generated Imagery." *Fast Company* website, August 29. http://www.fastcodesign.com/3034975/75-of-ikeas-catalog-is-computer-generated-imagery

Windsor, Alan 1985. *Peter Behrens: Architekt und Designer.* Stuttgart.

Wingler, Hans, M. 1962. *Das Bauhaus.* Bramsche. (3d ed., Cologne, 1975)

Christian Wölfel, Sylvia Wölfel, and Jens Krzywinski, eds. 2014. *Gutes Design: Martin Kelm und die Designförderung in der DDR.* Dresden.

Wolfe, Tom 1986. *Mit dem Bauhaus leben.* Frankfurt am Main. (original: *From Bauhaus to Our House.* New York, 1981)

Woodham, Jonathan M. 1997. *Twentieth-Century Design.* Oxford and New York.

– 2000. "Morris Mini." In *Design! Das 20. Jahrhundert,* edited by Volker Albus, Reyer Kras and Jonathan M. Woodham. Munich, London, and New York.

Yaneva, Albena 2012. "Grenzüberschreitungen: Das Soziale greifbar machen: Auf dem Weg zu einer Akteur-Netzwerk-Theorie des Designs." In *Das Design der Gesellschaft: Zur Kultursoziologie des Designs,* edited by Stephan Moebius and Sophia Prinz. Bielefeld.

Zänker, Jürgen 1981. "Utopisches Design oder Utopie des Design." In *Design ist unsichtbar: Forum Design Linz,* edited by Helmuth Gsöllpointner, Angela Hareiter, and Laurids Ortner. Vienna.

Zec, Peter 1988. *Informationsdesign: Die organisierte Kommunikation.* Zürich and Osnabrück.

Zimmermann, Monika 1989. "Die Tragik des Trabant." *Frankfurter Allgemeine Zeitung,* May 18.

Zumthor, Peter 2001. "Schutzbauten des Widerstandes: Ein Gespräch mit Hanno Rauterberg." *Zeit,* October 31.

Index of Names

A

Adorno, Theodor W. 58–59, 128, 130
Aicher, Otl 39–40, 48, 190, 209
Aisslinger, Werner 207
Akrich, Madeleine 237
Albers, Josef 28, 36–37, 40
Alexander, Christopher 45, 47, 59, 108, 110, 114, 116, 235
Alger, John R.M. 109
Ando, Tadao 207
Arad, Ron 64, 205, 222
Archer, Bruce 78, 109
Archimedes 81
Aristotle 81
Arnheim, Rudolf 157–158
Arnold, Florian 33
Arribas, Alfredo 207
Artschwager, Richard 66
Asa, Bruno 207
Asimov, Morris 109
Auger, James 223

B

Bacon, Francis 216
Bartels, Heiko 132, 222
Barthes, Roland 84, 141, 145–146, 172, 182
Baudrillard, Jean 63, 89, 97, 99, 172, 182, 212, 228–229
Baumann, Konrad 254
Behrens, Peter 23–24, 189–190, 196, 202, 207

Bellini, Mario 203
Bense, Max 45, 89, 94, 96, 129, 156
Berkeley, George 114, 154
Berndt, Heide 59
Bertoia, Harry 180
Beuys, Joseph 66, 234
Bill, Max 37, 39–40, 48, 151, 201, 249
Binazzi, Lapo 64
Blaich, Robert I. 178
Bloch, Ernst 58, 77, 128
Blum, Stefan 61
Bocheński, Joseph Maria 79
Böhme, Gernot 151, 231, 235
Bollnow, Otto Friedrich 103
Bonetto, Rodolfo 203
Bonsiepe, Gui 41, 44, 47, 91, 95, 111, 153
Borja de Mozota, Brigitte 198
Borkenhagen, Florian 64
Bortnik, Sandor 36
Botta, Mario 208
Boullée, Etienne-Louis 216
Bourdieu, Pierre 8, 173, 228, 231
Boyack, Kevin 153
Brancusi, Constantin 66
Brandes, Uta 60, 80, 174
Brandolini, Andreas 64
Branzi, Andrea 220
Braque, Georges 120
Braun, Erwin + Artur 4, 16, 26, 47–50, 52, 91, 137, 190, 197, 214
Braun, Max 4, 16, 26, 47–50, 52, 91, 137, 190, 197, 214

Breuer, Marcel 29, 32, 36
Bröhan, Karl 32
Bröhan, Torsten 32
Buck, Alex 198
Buckminster Fuller, Richard 209, 217
Bühler, Karl 142, 145, 157
Burckhardt, Lucius 242
Burkhardt, François 49, 233
Busse, Rido 47
Butter, Reinhart 41, 145, 178, 183
Buzan, Tony 117
Byrne, Bryan 252

C

Calatrava, Santiago 205, 208
Callon, Michel 236
Calvera, Anna 233
Campi, Isabel 233
Cassirer, Ernst 148–149
Castiglioni, Achille + Pier 203
Chauvel, Suzi 224
Chermayeff, Serge 36
Clarke, Alison Jane 252
Clarkson, P. John 186
Cole, Henry 19–20, 23
Colombo, Joe 220
Cooper, Alan 116–117
Coupland, Douglas 224
Crasset , Matali 207
Crilly, Nathan 186
Cross, Nigel 61, 110, 130, 133, 136, 201, 249

Csikszentmihalyi 141, 171
Curdes, Gerhard 43
Czemper, Achim 47

D

Da Vinci, Leonardo 11, 242, 259
Dalí, Salvador 66
Davis, Meredith 83
Deganello, Paolo 64, 203
Derrida, Jacques 165, 212
Descartes, René 81
Dewey, John 88
Diener, Horst 47
Dietel, Clauss 53–54, 56
Dilthey, Wilhelm 103, 155
Dörner, Volkhard 143
Douglas, Mary 144, 172, 224
Droysen, Johann Gustav 103
Duchamp, Marcel 66
Dunne, Anthony 223–224
Durkheim, Emile 172

E

Eames, Charles 180
Eckart, Peter 260
Eco, Umberto 84, 89–90, 93, 97,
    128, 145–147, 170, 172, 174, 209
Edelmann, Thomas 52
Ehmann, Sven 226, 256
Ehrenfels, Christian von 156–157,
    159
Eichler, Fritz 49
Eiermann, Egon 205, 209
Eiffel, Gustave 19
Eisenman, Peter 94, 205, 217
Ellinger, Theodor 136–137,
    139–140
Engels, Friedrich 82–83
Erlhoff, Michael 13, 41, 60, 64,
    80, 128
Escherle, Hans Jürgen 143
Esslinger, Hartmut 72, 92, 137,
    200, 246

F

Farr, Michael 196
Fassina, Giancarlo 162
Faßler, Manfred 119, 128, 148,
    242–243
Feierabend, Peter 32–33, 46
Feijs, Loe 185
Feininger, Lyonel 27
Feith, Michael 61
Feuerstein, Günther 164
Feyerabend, Paul 113
Fiebig, Wilfried 82
Fiedler, Jeannine 32–33, 46
Findeli, Alain 134
Fischer, Hardy 20, 23, 33, 41, 60,
    101, 131, 159, 164–165, 167, 173,
    205, 212, 222, 246
Fischer, Richard 20, 23, 33, 41,
    60, 101, 131, 159, 164–165, 167,
    173, 205, 212, 222, 246
Fischer, Theodor 20, 23, 33, 41,
    60, 101, 131, 159, 164–165, 167,
    173, 205, 212, 222, 246
Fischer, Uwe 20, 23, 33, 41, 60,
    101, 131, 159, 164–165, 167, 173,
    205, 212, 222, 246
Fischer, Volker 20, 23, 33, 41, 60,
    101, 131, 159, 164–165, 167, 173,
    205, 212, 222, 246
Fischer, Wend 20, 23, 33, 41, 60,
    101, 131, 159, 164–165, 167, 173,
    205, 212, 222, 246
Flatz, Wolfgang 61
Flierl, Bruno 55
Foerster, Heinz von 96
Foraita, Sabine 66
Foster, Norman 209–210, 246
Foucault, Michel 128
Freud, Sigmund 128, 149
Friedländer, Uri 177–178
Friedrich-Liebenberg 143
Frye, Annika 124

G

Gadamer, Hans-Georg 103–104,
    106

Galilei, Galileo 81
Gallé, Emile 83
Garnich, Rolf 129
Gehry, Frank O. 210, 241
Gell-Mann, Murray 253
Gerken, Gerd 224
Gershenfeld, Neil A. 223, 236, 255
Gessmann, Martin 98, 104, 127,
    165, 256
Gibson, James J. 159, 161
Giedion, Sigfried 12, 19, 24, 29
Ginnow-Merkert, Hartmut 183
Glaserfeld, Ernst von 96
Göbel, Lutz 135
Gombrich, Ernst 146
Gonda, Tomás 48
Gottlieb Baumgarten,
    Alexander 235
Gould, Stephen Jay 251
Grabes, Oliver 52
Graf, Annika 249
Groll, Sandra 139, 259
Gropius, Walter 23, 27–28, 33,
    36–37, 182, 202, 205
Gros, Jochen 131, 136, 143, 149,
    178, 252
Gucci 73
Gugelot, Hans 40, 49, 96, 164
Guggenberger, Bernd 9
Guixé, Martí 223
Gutenberg, Johannes 245–246

H

Habermas, Jürgen 58, 99, 107,
    138, 172–173, 245
Habermas, Tilmann 58, 99, 107,
    138, 172–173, 245
Hadid, Zaha 94, 210–211, 217
Hahn, Hans Peter 31, 105, 245, 252
Hase, Holger 143
Hauffe, Thomas 7, 17, 61, 226
Haug, Wolfgang Fritz 58, 130, 178
Häußling, Roger 230
Hays, Carl V. 109
Hegel, Georg Wilhelm Fried-
    rich 82, 105, 128

Heidegger, Martin 8, 33, 98–100, 104, 127, 191, 207, 215, 233, 260
Heine, Achim 222
Helmholtz, Hermann 155
Henseler, Wolfgang 128
Heqing, Yang 73
Herzog & De Meuron 94, 205
Heskett, John 17
Hesselgren, Sven 164
Heubach, Friedrich W. 174
Hirche, Herbert 49
Hirdina, Heinz 12, 53, 56
Hirsch, Sandra 93, 137
Hitchcock, Henry-Russell 59, 202
Hitzler, Jürgen 247
Hockney, David 66
Hoffmann, Josef 23, 61, 222
Höhler, Gertrud 224
Höhne, Günter 52–53, 57
Hollein, Hans 208, 211, 217
Holzer, Rainer Michael 208
Horkheimer, Max 58, 130
Horn, Klaus 59
Horx, Matthias 224
Hosokawa, Suhei 99
Hullmann, Harald 222
Husserl, Edmund 33, 98–100, 165

I

Ingenhoven, Christoph 205, 211
Iosa Ghini, Massimo 207
Ito, Toyo 211
Itten, Johannes 27–28, 32, 36–37, 40
Izenour, Steven 169, 203

J

Jacobsen, Arne 146, 162
Jacobsen, Jacob 146, 162
Jencks, Charles 83, 94, 136, 204, 241
Jobs, Steven P. 173, 245
Johnson, Philip 59, 202
Jonas, Wolfgang 137, 183

Jones, Allen 66, 109, 201
Jones, Christopher J. 66, 109, 201
Judd, Donald 66
Julier, Guy 17
Jungen, Patrick 175

K

Kahn, Hermann 118
Kaku, Michio 118
Kalow, Gerd 45
Kandinsky, Wassily 27, 32
Kant, Immanuel 82, 98, 128, 177
Karmasin, Helene 91, 144, 172
Karmasin, Matthias 91, 144, 172
Katz, David 156–157
Keller, Rudi 106
Kelley, David 201
Kelley, Jack 201
Kelm, Martin 53
Kicherer, Sibylle 143, 180, 197
Kiefer, Georg R. 94
Kiemle, Manfred 94, 129
Kienholz, Edward 66
Klanten , Robert 226
Klar, Michael 43, 130
Klavans, Dick 153
Klee, Paul 27, 31–32
Kleihues, Josef Paul 205
Klier, Hans von 193
Klotz, Heinrich 220
Kluge, Annalena 45, 201
Kluge, Alexander 45, 201
Knoll, Florence 180, 208, 212
Koffka, Kurt 157
Köhler, Wolfgang 156–158
Koolhaas, Rem 212, 217, 241
Koppelmann, Udo 143, 252
Kramer, Ferdinand 25
Krier, Leon 217
Krippendorff, Klaus 41, 47, 96, 145, 178, 180, 183
Krohn, Lisa 181
Kruft, Hanno-Walter 202, 204, 216
Kuby, Thomas 43, 130
Kuhn, Thomas S. 113

Kyffin, Steven 185

L

Langer, Susanne 148–149, 169
Lanier, Jaron 251
Lannoch, Hans-Jürgen + Helga 47, 178
Latour, Bruno 119, 236
Law, John 53, 70, 153, 236–237
Le Corbusier (Charles-Edouard Jeanneret) 23, 181, 202, 214
Ledoux, Claude-Nicolas 216
Lehnhardt, Jana-Maria 143
Leibniz, Gottfried Wilhelm 82
Leithäuser, Thomas 107
Leitherer, Eugen 142
Lévi-Strauss, Claude 141, 146
Lewin, Roger 252–253
LeWitt, Sol 220
Libeskind, Daniel 94, 217
Liebl, Franz 225
Lindinger, Herbert 38, 41, 44
Linn, Carl Eric 144–145
Lipps, Theodor 155–156
Lissitzky, El 26
Locke, John 82
Loos, Adolf 57–58, 213
Lorenzer, Alfred 59, 149
Lucchi, Michele de 162
Luhmann, Niklas 79, 97, 128, 152
Lux, Peter G.C. 191
Lyotard, Jean-François 203

M

Mackintosh, Charles Rennie 24
Magritte, René 66
Maldonado, Tomás 40, 44, 94–95, 111, 146
Malevich, Kazimir 26–27, 217
Mañá, Jordi 233
Mankau, Dieter 161
Marcks, Gerhard 27
Marcuse, Herbert 58, 130
Mareis, Claudia 78, 140, 147, 184, 259

Margolin, Victor 17
Mariscal, Javier 64
Marzano, Stefano 120
Maser, Siegfried 96, 111–112, 129, 131, 138, 153
Maturana, Humberto 96
McCoy, John 145, 178, 180, 182
McCoy, Katherine 145, 178, 180, 182
McCoy, Michael 145, 178, 180, 182
McLuhan, Marshall 246
Meier, Richard 197, 212
Meier-Kortwig, Hans Jörg 197
Meinong, Alexius 156
Mendini, Alessandro 203, 212, 220
Merz, Mario 66
Metzger, Wolfgang 157–158
Meyer, Hannes 30–31, 44, 96
Mies van der Rohe, Ludwig 23, 29, 31, 36, 50, 202, 205, 213
Mikosch, Gerda 33, 131, 164–165
Milev, Yana 93, 234
Mill, John Stuart 20, 102
Minx, Eckard P. 119
Mitscherlich, Alexander 59
Moggridge, Bill 201, 249
Moholy-Nagy, László 27–28, 30–32, 36
Moles, Abraham A. 45, 59, 129
Mondrian, Piet C. 24
Monö, Rune 145
Morris, Charles William 20, 23–24, 88–89, 109, 148–149, 218
Morris, William 20, 23–24, 88–89, 109, 148–149, 218
More, Thomas 216, 218
Moultrie, James 186
Muche, Georg 27
Mukařovský, Jan 88, 149–150
Muller, Wim 146–147
Müller-Krauspe, Gerda 59
Munari, Bruno 233
Mundt, Barbara 207
Muthesius, Herman 23
Mutius, Bernhard von 152, 243
MVRDV 218

N
Nadin, Mihai 111, 225
Naisbitt, John 74, 118
Nehls, Werner 59
Neumeister, Alexander 47
Nolte, Paul 174
Nonné-Schmidt, Helene 39
Norman, Donald A. 116, 167, 172, 201, 209–210, 253
Nouvel, Jean 94, 212–213
Nuttall, Mike 201

O
Oehlke, Horst 12, 56–57, 165, 182
Oevermann, Ulrich 230
Ohl, Herbert 129
Olbrich, Josef 23
Oldenburg, Claes 66
Onck, Andries van 47, 146
Oppenheim, Meret 66
Ortner, Laurids 217, 242
Oud, Jacobus Johannes Pieter 23–24

P
Palladio, Andrea 214
Panton, Verner 220
Papanek, Victor 130, 242
Paul, Bruno 23, 27, 32, 90, 113, 174, 205, 212
Paxton, Joseph 19
Peirce, Charles Sanders 86–89, 145
Pericot, Jordi 233
Pesce, Gaetano 220
Peterhans, Walter 37, 39
Picasso, Pablo 120
Pinter, Klaus 217
Piore, Michael J. 254
Plato 80, 86, 102, 164, 216
Plattner, Hasso 201
Plüm, Kerstin 69
Poelzig, Hans 23
Pohl, Herbert 56
Polo, Marco 69
Pombo, Fátima 233

Popcorn, Faith 224
Portoghesi, Paolo 241
Prix, Wolf D. 95, 204, 208

R
Raby, Fiona 224
Radice, Barbara 8, 242
Rams, Dieter 26, 49–50, 137, 157
Rashid, Karim 226
Ratzlaff, Jörg 61
Read, Herbert 65, 97, 127, 130, 162, 231
Reck, Hans-Ulrich 134
Reckwitz, Andreas 201, 236
Rehberger, Tobias 66
Reinmöller, Patrick 143, 184
Reitz, Edgar 45
Renzi, Guglielmo 64
Ricard, André 233
Riemerschmid, Richard 23
Rietveld, Gerrit T. 24, 65
Rittel, Horst 41, 108–109
Rochberg-Halton 141, 171
Rogers, Richard 209
Rossi, Aldo 213–214
Roth, Gerhard 61, 96
Roth, Jan 61, 96
Rudolph, Lutz 54
Rummel, Carlo 197
Ruppert, Wolfgang 91–92
Ruskin, John 20, 24

S
Saarinen, Eero 180
Saarinen, Eliel 180
Sabel, Charles F. 254
Sachs, Angeli 69–70
Santachiara, Denis 64
Sarasin, Wolfgang 192
Saussure, Ferdinand de 87–88, 142, 172, 181
Scharoun, Hans 23
Scheld, Christa 10
Scheuer, Winfried 177
Schinkel, Karl Friedrich 214

Schirrmacher, Frank 251

Schleiermacher, Friedrich Daniel
  Ernst 102–103

Schlemmer, Oskar 27, 31

Schmidt, Siegfried J. 39, 96–97,
  184, 193

Schmitz-Maibauer, Heinz 143

Scholl, Hans und Sophie 39

Scholl, Inge 39

Schönberger, Johanna 200–201

Schönhammer, Rainer 100, 247

Schultheis, Franz 134, 137, 147,
  153

Schulze, Gerhard 122, 175,
  228–233, 235

Schupbach, Stephan 120, 167,
  248

Schwer, Thilo 127

Schwitters, Kurt 128

Scott Brown, Denise 169, 203

Seckendorff von, Eva 38

Seeling, Hartmut 38

Segal, George 66

Selle, Gert 17, 92, 136, 140, 170,
  236

Semper, Gottfried 20

Sforza, Ludovico 11

Shneiderman, Ben 253

Simmel, Georg 227

Sloterdijk, Peter 8, 70, 128, 255

Snow, Charles Percy 102

Soentgen, Jens 100–101

Socrates 80

Sottsass, Ettore 64, 203, 242

Sparke, Penny 17

Spiekermann, Erik 184

Spieß, Heinrich 197

Spitz, René 38, 40–41

Spoerri, Daniel 66

Squires, Susan 252

Stam, Mart 12, 24, 202

Starck, Philippe 170, 205

Steffen, Dagmar 137, 146, 164,
  184, 254

Steiner, Urs 74

Stirling, James 214

Stölzl, Gunta 32

Straub, Christian 45

Sudjic, Deyan 186, 231, 238

Sullivan, Louis H. 57

Swiczinsky, Helmut 208

T

Tatlin, Vladimir 26

Taut, Max 23

Teherani, Hadi 214

Thomas, Bruce 7, 17, 52, 61, 107,
  113, 130, 216, 218, 245, 254

Thonet, Michael 21, 29, 92, 210

Thun, Matteo 121, 205

Toffler, Alvin 118

Trüby, Stephan 204

Tschumi, Bernhard 94, 217

Tusquet Blanca, Oscar 64

U

Uecker, Günther 66

Ullrich, Wolfgang 226

Ulrichs, Timm 66

Ungers, Oswald Mathias 215

Ursprung, Philip 69

V

van de Velde, Henry 23, 27

van Doesburg, Theo 24

Varela, Francisco J. 96

Vasari, Giorgio 11

Veblen, Thorstein Bunde 227

Venturi, Robert 50, 94, 169, 203,
  241

Verbruggen, Dries 226, 256

Verplank, Bill 249

Vershofen, Wilhelm 139, 143

Vihma, Susann 145–146

Virilio, Paul 212

Vitruvius 17–18, 94, 202, 213

Vogt, Oliver 198

Volli, Ugo 90–91

Volmerg, Birgit 107

Vostell, Wolf 66

W

Wagenfeld, Wilhelm 34

Wagner, Otto 23, 32, 205

Walker, John A. 17, 135

Walther, Franz Erhard 66, 89

Warnier, Claire 226, 256

Watson , Thomas 245

Watzlawick, Paul 90

Welsch, Wolfgang 13, 70,
  202–204, 233–236

Wendtland, Thomas 61

Wertheimer, Max 156–158

West, Franz 52–53, 56–57, 66, 70,
  230, 259

Wewerka, Stefan 60

Wick, Rainer 29

Winograd, Terry 201

Wippermann, Peter 224

Wittgenstein, Ludwig 180, 205,
  207, 233

Wolfe, Tom 203

Woodham, Jonathan M. 17

Woollatt, John 201

Wozniak, Stephen 173, 245

Wundt, Wilhelm 155–156

Wurm, Erwin 66

X

Xiaoping, Deng 71

Y

Yaneva, Albena 237

Young, Bob 29, 31, 61, 173, 176,
  185, 203, 207, 226, 250

Z

Zamp Kelp, Günter 217

Zanuso, Marco 203

Zebner, Frank 248

Zeischegg, Walter 39–41, 48

Zumthor, Peter 94, 99, 215–216

Subject Index

3-D printing 72, 226, 241, 255–257

A

ability to learn 251
absent structure 97
abstraction 158
accommodation 39, 44
acoustic body 216
act of creation 77
action 99, 107, 112, 118–119, 138, 149, 173, 200, 242
adaptation outputs 96
Adidas 171, 199
advanced design 72, 119
advertising 24, 56, 228, 236
advertising expert 24
AEG 24, 190, 196
aesthetic character 111
aesthetic production 32
aesthetic synthesis 32
aesthetics 5, 26, 56, 58, 88–89, 126, 128–130, 145, 148–149, 154, 156, 161, 164, 212, 233, 235–236
aircraft construction 162
AIF (Amt für industrielle Formgestaltung) 53, 55
Alchimia 177, 212, 220, 245
allusive qualities 252
alphabetization 252
Alessi 50, 210, 212, 214
analogy 103, 138, 144, 246
analysis 28, 33, 44, 46, 57, 80–81, 84, 89, 97–99, 104, 116, 119, 149, 172, 174, 180, 184, 198, 228–229, 248

anatomy 11, 104, 153
anthropology 128, 200, 223, 251
anthropometric 166
anticipation 225
antidesign 220
antifunctionalism 56
antithesis 83
apartment 24, 34, 172
Apple 72–73, 92, 137, 139, 151, 171, 173, 199, 227, 229, 231, 245–246, 249, 253
Apple community 139
application 11–12, 24, 36, 40, 58, 98, 106–107, 111, 116–117, 121, 134, 136, 155, 162, 166, 236
applied art 40, 65
architectural idiom 207
architectural theory 202, 205
architecture 5, 11, 17, 24, 31–32, 36–37, 44, 46, 50, 55, 58–59, 83, 90, 94–95, 108, 114, 129, 136, 151, 154, 159, 162, 164, 169, 182, 188, 190, 193, 202–205, 207–218, 220, 233, 236–237, 241–243
architecture as text 94–95
Archizoom Associati 222
art and technology 27, 33
art house 216
art nouveau 21
artifact 251
artificial intelligence 237
artisan craftsman 33
artist 17, 29, 37, 60, 66, 105, 151, 212, 217–218

artistic 11–12, 21, 23–24, 28–30, 32, 40, 45, 48, 63, 65, 77, 83, 120, 154, 190, 212, 222, 235
artistic adviser 24, 190
arts and crafts 13, 20, 23, 27, 46, 49, 61, 78, 111
arts and crafts museums 61
Asia 14, 69–74, 175
association 23, 53, 162, 169
assumption of constancy 157
attention 19, 29, 34, 38, 46–47, 77, 79, 83, 91, 101, 140, 142, 167, 181, 197, 199, 213, 216, 220, 222, 247, 253, 260
attitude 191, 198, 203
attribution of meaning 92, 96, 146
Audi 72
Austria 21, 23, 216, 242
author system 120
automobile (see car)
automobile manufacturer 115, 119
automotive industry 140
avant-garde 34, 40, 120, 142, 222, 237, 259
awareness of design 43, 259

B

basic elements 80–81
basic functionality 250
basic need 26, 31, 47
basic shape 251
Bauhaus 4, 16, 19, 23–24, 26–34, 36–37, 39–40, 43–46, 54–55, 58–60, 91, 111, 133, 142, 151, 169–170, 189, 202, 205, 215, 218, 241

Bauhaus classics 60, 142
Bauhaus style 34
Bauhaus tradition 40, 55
be or design 9
beauty 11, 18, 37, 94, 202, 227
behavior 50, 79, 88, 97, 100–101,
    116, 119, 121, 157, 171, 175,
    190–191, 193, 195, 228, 236, 245,
    249, 253
behavior of signs 88
behavior patterns 249
being at home 215
bel design 48, 142, 203
Biennale 66, 213, 241
BMW 140, 145, 183, 210
body 112, 133, 138, 143, 147, 166,
    173, 185, 216, 223, 234, 251
body of knowledge 133, 138, 143,
    147, 185
brand 115, 171, 174–175, 189, 191,
    199, 223
brand loyalty 115
brand products 174
Braun 4, 16, 26, 47–50, 52, 91, 137,
    190, 197, 214
bricolage design 7
brutalism 214
business schools 197

C
CAD (Computer Aided
    Design) 167, 242, 246, 250
car 115, 176, 255
carriers of function 177
Cartesian 44, 46, 81, 102, 110–111,
    113, 129
Cassina 34
cast iron 19
cell phone 241
cement 19
ceramics 208
changeability 166
changes of scenery 212
chaos research 252
Chicago 26, 36
China 32, 57, 69, 71–73, 78, 151,
    173, 175, 192, 205, 229–230
chip 245

civilization 8, 222, 245, 252
classics 53, 60, 99, 142, 176, 210
clothing 84, 172–173, 176, 228, 255
CNC 211, 254
cocooning 172, 224
code of conduct 192
co-evolution 128
coffee cup 24, 113
cognitive 28, 96, 144, 161, 164,
    167, 177, 253
collage 120
Cologne School (see Koppelmann
    School)
color 36, 156–157, 213, 220
commodity aesthetics 56, 58
communication 37, 44–45, 50,
    69, 89–91, 93–94, 96–97, 99, 119,
    121, 134, 137–141, 143–144, 146,
    152, 159, 170, 172, 184, 190–191,
    193, 198–199, 201, 236, 245, 248,
    254, 256
communicative function 5, 110,
    126, 138, 144, 148, 204
community 32, 46, 88, 133, 139, 174
communities of
    identification 173
company identity 191
complexity 7, 70, 91–92, 94, 113,
    135, 137, 155–157, 159, 203, 243,
    250–251, 253
composition 37, 110
computer 69, 128, 167, 181, 208,
    223, 242, 245–246, 249–250,
    253–255
computer technologies 255
concentration 27, 56, 207
conceptual art 220
concept cars 119
concept of design 8, 13, 79, 127,
    131, 152–153, 201, 233–234
concept of function 30, 88, 149
concept of functionalism 18
conceptual art 220
concrete 13, 33, 90, 99, 110, 131,
    152, 159, 182, 192, 207, 214–215,
    222, 233
configurability 166
connectibility 97, 144, 152
connotation 90, 144, 199

constants of design 195
constitution 105, 141, 192, 230
construct of meaning 144
construction 19, 24, 30, 34, 39,
    44, 55, 72, 78, 95, 97, 115, 143,
    162, 173, 177, 209–210, 254
constructive 56, 84, 252
constructivism 24, 26, 37, 96
consubstantiality 191
consumer 27, 48, 52, 69, 140, 175,
    223, 226, 252
consumer goods 27, 52, 69, 226, 252
consumption 14, 24, 122, 174–175,
    227, 234
contemplation 207, 216
convention 87, 101, 106, 147, 149,
    169, 171
core competency 132
corporate communication 190,
    193, 199
corporate culture 190, 199
corporate development 196
corporate identity 56, 140,
    189–193, 198, 210
corporate strategy 190, 193
corporate wording 190
craft trades 23, 27, 32
crafts 13, 20, 23–24, 27, 46, 49, 61,
    78, 111, 226, 255
craftsman 29, 33
creativity 39, 77, 113, 152,
    200–201, 236
crisis of meaning 80
critique of functionalism 41, 48,
    59, 129, 202
critique of society 58
critique of the aesthetics of
    commodities 130
cross-media dimension 249
cult brand 171
cultivation 141
cultural history 100
cultural revolution 245
cultural studies 91, 93, 141, 144, 245
cultural technique 145, 251
cultural theory 144
curriculum reform 47
curve theory 44
cybernetics 96, 112

D

Daimler 119, 139–140, 145, 199, 243

De Stijl group 24

death of modernity 204

developments 4, 10, 17, 19–20, 30, 36, 52, 74, 76–77, 104, 108, 118, 142, 157, 180, 197, 202, 220, 225, 247

decoding 170

decomposition 110

deconstructivist 208–210

deduction 81, 88, 110

deep simplicity 253

definition 12–13, 43, 45, 57, 80, 132, 137, 142, 175, 182, 234

dematerialization 220, 246–247, 252

denotation 90, 106

design bible 193

design boom 8, 233, 235

design classics 53

design concept 24, 41

design language 52, 137, 150

design management 5, 79, 135, 143, 188, 196–198, 243

design manual 193

design methodology 4, 46, 76, 78–80, 108–110, 112–114, 127, 133, 196, 201

design museums 9

design noir 224

design object 93, 105, 158

design or die 9

design practice 60, 91, 112, 116, 119, 129, 131, 133, 173, 235, 238, 249

design process 59, 77–78, 108–112, 116, 123, 171, 235, 254

design research 78, 80, 91, 122, 133–134, 172, 175, 234, 252

design strategy 50, 178, 248

design theory 5, 17, 43, 56, 77, 80, 93, 98, 103, 107, 112, 126–127, 130–132, 135, 138–139, 141, 145–147, 169, 172–173, 178, 182–184, 198, 227, 233–235, 238, 248, 251–252, 259

design thinking 201

design training 36, 113, 133

design science 8, 133, 185, 238

des-in 60

desire-needs 151, 218, 231, 235

desk lamp 162

Dessau 28, 31–32, 37, 151

Deutsche Lufthansa 190

development process 77, 112, 117, 131, 200

dialectics 105, 131, 165

differentiation 8, 70, 93, 140, 142, 199, 227, 230–231, 235

digitalization 7, 10, 69, 79, 116, 148, 241, 256, 260

dimension 88, 100, 129, 139, 141, 158, 175, 184, 204, 213, 235, 247, 249, 255

discipline 8, 10, 12, 14, 44, 46, 77–80, 83, 87, 95, 105, 113, 119, 127–128, 130–134, 136–138, 147, 151, 153, 155, 184–185, 197, 202, 205, 224, 226, 234, 241, 259

disegno 11

display 21, 45, 216, 247, 249

diversity 13, 94, 113

division of ideas 80

division of labor 18, 20, 259

DIY 7, 200, 255

DNA 115, 238

do-it-yourself movement 63

doctoral education in design 132–133

documenta 13, 64

domestic appliances 24, 247

domestic utensils 189

door handle 205, 208, 210–211, 215

double coding 136, 204

draft 11–12, 118

drawing 11, 20, 72, 140, 208–209, 215, 220, 250

E

eclecticism 204, 245

ecology 13, 69, 129, 132, 141, 234, 260

economics 40, 69, 132, 143, 196, 201, 234, 236, 238, 259

economy 52–53, 57, 73, 78, 91

eidetic inquiry 33, 182

eidetic marks 33

el buen diseño 48

electric shaver 146

electronic gadget 231

electroclimate 223

electronic 48, 100–101, 116, 159, 165, 173, 178, 181, 223–224, 231, 235–236, 247–248, 251–252, 254

electronic devices 101, 116, 178, 252

electronics 72, 116, 151, 171, 222, 227, 247, 253

elemental psychology 156

emblem 169, 227

empathy 155, 234

empirical 91, 107, 116, 120–121, 124, 141, 147, 171, 228, 237

engineer 17, 139

engineering sciences 134

England 19–21, 133, 209

envelopment technique 12

environment 8, 20, 53, 59, 94, 99–100, 114, 130, 137, 159, 161, 167, 186, 208, 216

environmental concerns 197

epistemology 77, 80, 89, 235

ergonomics 13, 40, 66, 131, 253

essence 33, 80, 86, 138, 155, 164, 191

ethics 80

ethnologists 171, 252

evaluation 88, 113, 123, 142, 196, 254

event design 9, 46, 92

exchange value 58

exhibition system 45

expanded functionalism 59, 131

experience society 9, 229

experiment 28, 81, 155

F

fashion 9, 46, 56, 59, 84, 172, 183, 212, 224, 235–236, 259

feature 97, 153, 189, 209, 211, 215

featuritis 159, 167

fiction 220

film 45–46, 118, 228

firmitas 18, 94, 202

form 8, 13, 20–21, 23, 27, 29, 33, 36–37, 44, 48, 53–55, 57, 59–61, 66, 72, 87, 90, 94, 98, 104,

110–112, 114, 116–117, 120, 131,
138–139, 142, 146–147, 150–152,
154, 156–157, 159, 161, 169–170,
173, 178, 180, 183, 185, 189, 200,
202–203, 215, 223, 225, 227, 229,
231, 234, 236, 242, 249, 254
form follows function 104, 147, 169
formal aesthetics 154, 161
formal device 154
formal element 26, 154
formal science 110, 112, 138
formalism 20, 154, 158
formation 8, 99, 148, 156, 175,
184, 249
Forum Design Linz 242
foundation course 28–29, 40,
43–44
France 21, 73, 133, 207, 214, 228
Frankfurt School 58, 107, 130
FSB 190, 205, 208, 210–211, 215
function 5, 9, 12, 20, 30, 57, 71, 84,
88, 90, 97, 104, 110, 113, 126, 130,
138–140, 142–144, 147–150, 157,
159, 164–167, 169, 171–173, 178,
181, 189, 202–204, 220, 222, 225,
228–230, 237, 242, 250
function overload 159, 167
functional design 20, 54, 91, 150,
182
functional furniture 29
functionalism 18, 37, 41, 48, 50,
52, 55, 58–60, 90, 110–111, 129,
131, 136, 159, 165, 169, 182, 189,
202
functionality 11, 18, 30, 55, 74,
141, 145, 159, 162, 189, 200, 227,
230, 251
fundamental design concept 24
fundamental design skills 28
furnishings 24, 170, 205, 207, 209,
211
furniture 7, 19, 23–24, 27, 29,
33–34, 58, 60–61, 65–66, 83–84,
95, 142, 170, 189–190, 205,
207–212, 214–215, 222, 224–225,
230, 242, 254–255, 260
furniture design 34, 211, 225
furniture industry 224
futurism 217

G
German Democratic Republic
(GDR) 12, 52–55
German Werkbund 19, 23
Germany 21, 31, 39, 45, 48, 52–60,
91, 95, 132, 164–165, 176, 182–184,
190, 196–197, 222, 229–230
Gesamtkunstwerk 24, 211–212, 214
Gestalt laws 44, 157–159, 165
Gestalt psychology 155–158, 203
Gestalt quality 156
Gestalt theory 143, 145, 151, 157–158
giving form 142, 151
Glashütte watches 57
glass 19, 29, 53, 213
globality 70
globalization 4, 50, 67, 69–74, 78,
91, 152, 199–200, 230, 241, 252,
256
goal 23, 26, 40, 43, 72, 81, 127, 138,
202
good design 4, 12–13, 16, 47–48, 53,
57, 74, 91, 164, 177, 182, 190, 222
good taste 23
graphic design 83, 139
grid formation 249
group membership 171
gute Form 48

H
habits 90, 122, 128, 175, 223–224,
253
handicrafts 111
handicrafts design 111
haptic design 139
hardware 8, 14, 116–117, 120–121,
152, 168, 181, 189, 222, 228, 242,
246, 249–250, 252–254
harmony 154, 214, 232
headphones 100
hermeneutic circle 105
hermeneutics 4, 76, 83, 98,
102–107, 171, 230
heuristics 81
high-tech 134, 162, 176–177, 209,
212, 214
history of architecture 169, 214
history of design 17, 93, 205

history of science 110
holistic 23–24, 79, 86, 145, 151,
157–159, 161, 165, 209, 215, 259
home 9, 34, 72, 84, 141–142,
209–210, 215, 254–255
horizon 99, 105, 121, 177
household 7, 52, 65, 89, 100, 108,
171, 174, 228, 255
human body 166, 251
humanistic 113
humanities 78–80, 83, 98–99,
101–104, 112, 116, 138, 153, 164,
170, 177, 204, 223
human-object relation 148, 150, 237
hypothesis 95

I
IBM 190, 199, 209, 245
icon 162
ICSID 132
identification 97, 171, 173, 199
identity 8, 32, 52, 56–57, 96, 105,
140–141, 172–174, 189–193, 198,
205, 210, 214, 230, 234, 249, 260
idle function 166
IDZ Berlin 130
Illumination 161
image 45, 49, 56–57, 100, 123, 145,
177, 183, 190–191, 193, 195, 199,
205, 209–210, 230, 243, 250
image transfer 145, 177, 205, 210
imaginary 216, 243
Imagineering 152, 199, 243
imparted by perception 148
implementation 49, 109, 203
importance 8, 19, 40, 46, 69,
78–79, 82–83, 92, 94–95, 98, 103,
123, 148, 156, 174, 177–178, 189,
192, 197, 204, 222, 227, 247
imposing shape 203
improvization 124
individualism 246
individuality 12, 23, 173, 175
induction 81
industrial 7, 9, 12–13, 17–20,
23–24, 27, 29–30, 33, 41, 43, 47,
53, 55, 58, 61, 66, 71–72, 78, 83,
93, 95–96, 108, 110–111, 124,

132–133, 135, 137, 139, 142, 170, 178, 182–183, 190, 198, 210, 213–214, 222–223, 234, 236, 238, 255–256
industrial design 7, 12–13, 17–18, 20, 47, 53, 55, 66, 72, 93, 96, 110–111, 132, 135, 137, 142, 182–183, 236, 258
Industrial Revolution 18, 20, 255–256
industrial traditions 7
industrialization 13, 20, 102, 220, 235, 259
industry 12, 23, 33, 41, 43–44, 48, 52, 69, 72, 78, 83, 111, 120, 135, 139–140, 151, 192, 198, 224, 226, 231, 250, 256
information design 150
information processing 112
information theory 45, 129
inline skates 173
innovation 74, 77, 92, 115, 117, 121, 137, 178, 197, 200–201, 229, 235
integralist 135
intellectual 34, 40, 44, 46, 58, 79, 81, 98, 103, 118, 136, 158, 169, 186, 212, 215–216, 222
intention 24, 43–44, 66, 106, 111
interaction 36, 69, 97, 111, 116, 120, 128, 147, 168, 183, 195, 200, 238, 246, 248–249, 251, 253–254
interaction design 168, 249, 253–254
interactive 117, 120
interconnectedness 255
interdisciplinarity 134–135
interface 111, 116, 123, 168, 184, 193, 199, 235, 242, 246–249, 252–253
interior 49, 66, 115, 140, 142, 148, 177–178, 193, 207, 209, 212, 214, 222
International Style 24, 50, 59, 94, 202–204
internet 10, 69, 119, 168, 255, 256
internet of things 69, 256
interpretation 59, 84, 87, 90, 96, 99, 102–106, 116, 164, 169, 230, 232
intuition 81, 149

J
jewelry 173, 211
joy of use 123, 254
Jugendstil 21, 24

K
Kahla 57
key competency 152
kitsch 63, 101
Knoll International 212
knowledge 18, 37, 40, 43, 69, 73, 78, 80–82, 87, 98, 101, 104–105, 112–113, 117, 127, 131, 133–136, 138, 140, 143, 147–149, 152, 155, 176, 185, 190, 215, 235, 259–260
knowledge design 152
knowledge interests 140
knowledge management 117
Koppelmann School 143
Kraftwerk 36–37

L
Lada 176
language 5, 9, 13, 21, 23, 33, 52, 56, 82–84, 87–89, 94–97, 100, 102, 104, 106–107, 111–112, 114, 116, 126–127, 131, 136–140, 142–143, 145–150, 152–154, 157, 165–166, 170, 175, 177, 180, 182–184, 186, 191, 198, 203–204, 220, 228, 233, 238, 248, 252, 254, 259
language of form 21, 23, 33, 111
language of things 96
language theory 157
laws of design 53
LCDs (liquid crystal displays) 247
legibility 209, 247
leisure 9, 52, 122, 227, 245, 254
leitmotif 173
life expression 148, 155
life philosophy 103
lifestyle 7, 72, 92, 115, 173–175, 189, 207, 226, 234
life-world 33, 99, 100–101, 104–105, 121–122, 138–139, 234, 245

lightning 114, 197, 205, 207, 211, 215
lightweight construction techniques 162
linguistic theory 145
linguistic turn 107, 182, 252
linguistics 87, 178, 203–204
list of requirements 113
logic 33, 80–81, 87, 110, 169, 180, 207
logic of semiotics 87
logo 195
logotype 193
London 8, 19–21, 64, 186, 205, 209–210, 222–223
loss of meaning 154
Lovegety 101, 237–238
luxury 45, 57, 73, 145, 176, 230

M
machine 11, 20–21, 24, 102, 197, 222, 245, 247, 256
machine tools 247
Magna Carta of functionalism 59
manufacture 7, 18, 24, 234, 256
Map of Science 153
mark 9, 17, 38, 118, 148–149, 165, 189, 255
market analysis 198
market launch 123, 180, 198
market niche 145
market segment 176, 224
marking function 150, 154, 158, 164, 167, 169–170, 246–248
mass communication 45, 140
mass culture 34, 116, 169–170
mass production 21, 29–30, 58, 169, 254, 256
mass products 24
material 20, 27, 55, 83, 94, 99, 103, 105, 111, 123, 139, 141, 144–146, 148, 152, 154, 165, 172, 184, 193, 195, 213, 220, 223, 236–237, 243, 249
material culture 105, 223
mathematical 40, 44, 81–82, 104, 109, 111, 129, 225
maturity 153, 205
Mayflower effect 46

meaning 9, 17, 19, 33, 71, 78–80,
84, 86–87, 90–97, 102, 106, 114,
136, 138, 141–142, 144, 146, 150,
154–155, 158, 162, 164–165, 169,
172, 180–181, 184, 198, 202–204,
216, 220, 225, 231, 242, 253
means 10, 23, 50, 56, 58–59, 69,
74, 77, 81, 84, 89–90, 92, 95,
100–102, 104–106, 110, 114, 120,
127, 134, 136–140, 143–144,
147–149, 151–152, 154, 158–159,
161, 169, 171–173, 175, 177, 183,
189–191, 215, 227–228, 236,
249–250, 252–253
means of communication 50,
144, 172
means of design 143
means of transport 84, 173
measuring device 166
mechanization 256
media 7–9, 65, 91, 93, 100, 120,
137, 150, 152–153, 195, 208, 213,
223–224, 226, 234, 236, 242, 246,
248–249, 255, 260
medical technology 118, 214
medicine 13, 86, 127, 134–135
medium 74, 84, 159, 161, 224–225
Memphis 7, 23, 60, 177, 207,
211–212, 242, 245
metamodernity 13
metaphor 145, 178, 216
metaproduct 145
method 21, 43, 45, 55, 79–83, 89,
93, 98–99, 104, 106, 108, 110,
113–114, 116–118, 121–122, 127,
129, 138, 155, 162, 165, 170, 178,
197, 201, 214, 224, 227
methodology 4, 38, 44, 46, 57–58,
75–80, 93, 96, 98, 108–114, 127,
133, 144, 172, 182, 196, 201, 254
micro-architecture 214
microchip 92, 223
microelectronics 5, 79, 102, 167,
223, 240–242, 245–247,
250–251, 254
Milan 7, 11, 120, 185, 212, 224
mind mapping 117
Miniaturization 243, 247
mobile 101

model 37–38, 40–41, 43, 48, 53,
60, 91–92, 97, 112, 121, 137, 140,
146, 148–150, 155, 180, 183, 198,
200, 203, 231, 236, 238, 254–255
model construction 255
modern 13, 18, 21, 24, 27, 33, 41,
70, 81–82, 100, 102, 136, 155, 162,
202, 204, 211, 222, 234–235, 238
Modern Style 21
modernism 18, 37, 46, 48, 50, 64,
208, 210, 212, 215, 222, 234–235
modes of behavior 97, 121
Monobloc chair 84–85
mood charts 120–121
Moscow 31
movement 20, 23, 27, 43, 47, 58,
60, 63, 78, 82, 129–130, 139, 147,
185, 201, 204, 212–213
Munich 8, 23, 59, 61, 142, 183, 190
Munich School 142
museum 8–9, 32, 38, 48, 61, 78,
115, 186, 202, 205, 207, 210–211,
213–216

N

nail design 14
natural science 102, 116, 138, 223
nature 8, 33, 37, 57–58, 81–82, 84,
103, 108, 116–118, 138, 149, 154,
162, 178, 182, 205, 207, 211, 216,
238, 247
navigation 249, 251
navigation systems 251
needs 12, 26, 29–32, 37, 47, 50, 54,
58, 72, 83, 89, 95, 104, 116–117,
144, 151, 176, 183, 191, 200, 204,
218, 220, 231, 235
net product 152
New Bauhaus 26, 36
new obscurity 64, 245
new simplicity 224
new technology 246, 255
New York 8, 202, 209, 212, 231
Nomos 57, 209
non-material 99, 103, 111, 145,
152, 172, 195, 213, 249
non-materiality 213
notion of function 204

O

object design 234
objective 8, 27–28, 33, 39, 53, 59,
81–82, 96–98, 100, 103, 108,
112–113, 122, 127, 129, 159, 175,
218, 230
objects of utility 172
objet-trouvé art 222
observation 77, 135, 142, 155, 165,
229, 234
Offenbach School of Design
(Hfg Offenbach) 33, 60, 82, 14,
127, 131, 136, 139–140, 147, 150,
159, 161, 164, 183, 246, 250
office chair 84
office communication 254
Olivetti 146, 190, 193, 196, 209, 214
ontic 112
operability 83
operating instructions 248, 250
operating structure 205
operation 14, 90, 123, 159, 166,
169, 247, 253
optics 11, 249
order of production 89
organic 59, 162, 208, 218, 225
orientation 12, 56, 93, 98,
100–101, 132, 139, 142, 161,
165–166, 175, 200, 228
overall visual appearance 50
overcoming 58, 60, 70, 92, 169

P

painting 11, 27, 29, 40, 53, 61, 228,
246
papiers collés 120
paradigm 108, 113–114, 116, 141
Paris 19, 47, 58, 198, 205, 213
Pattern Language 114, 116
perception 13, 43, 82, 96, 103,
106, 140, 142, 145, 148, 151,
153–159, 161–162, 186, 224
perception research 154
perception theory 151
personas 116–117
phenomena 69, 88, 98, 101, 138,
149, 155–156, 184, 186, 203, 214,
228, 231, 234, 246

phenomenology 4, 33, 76, 83, 98–101
Philadelphia 19
Philips 50, 120, 178, 185, 197
philosophy 18, 20, 32, 77, 80–82, 98, 102–105, 107, 142, 148, 165, 169, 174, 191, 209–210, 215, 220, 227, 233, 252
philosophy of life 32, 103
philosophy of technology 104
planning 10, 17, 30, 43, 46, 59, 69, 78, 90, 114, 117–118, 131–132, 159, 184, 196, 202, 211, 213, 217–218, 233
plastic 84
pluralism 13, 204
polyhedral geometry 44
pop 46, 50
porcelain 57, 226
post-alphabetic society 252
postmodernism 48, 53, 55, 60, 64, 83, 94, 110, 114, 121, 170, 204, 208, 211, 214, 226, 233–234, 241, 245
post-structuralism 182
potential for innovation 117
practice 1, 3, 8, 17, 24, 29, 33, 37–38, 54–55, 58–60, 80, 91, 105, 107–108, 110, 112–113, 116, 119, 121–122, 128–133, 137, 139, 145–146, 150, 155, 173, 191, 202, 209, 235, 237–238, 246, 249, 252, 260
pragmatism 87
precedents 146, 165
precision 44, 74, 127, 157, 166
principle of design 164, 209
probability 225
problem of design 114
problem structures 110
problem-solving 81, 113, 117, 135, 201
process 8, 18, 20, 59, 63, 70–71, 77–78, 88, 90, 92, 96–97, 105–106, 108–113, 116–117, 121, 123, 127, 129, 131, 134, 136, 138, 141, 148–149, 155, 164, 166–167, 169–172, 177, 180, 192, 196, 198, 200, 218, 223, 228, 235–236, 242, 247, 250, 254–256, 259–260
process of communication 97
process of construction 97
process of design 109, 127, 129, 170

process of interpretation 106
processing power 246
product aesthetics 145
product appearance 165, 183
product clinics 122–123
product concept 80, 223, 226
product culture 47–48, 50, 53, 92, 97
product development 72, 78, 93, 117–118, 120–122, 132, 144, 147, 159, 166, 171, 183, 196, 198–200, 228, 238, 241–242
product field 121, 254
product function 165
product graphics 159, 247
product group 99
product identity 52, 57
product information 139–140
product language 5, 13, 82, 95, 97, 100, 107, 126–127, 136–137, 139–140, 142–143, 145–150, 153, 165–166, 170, 175, 177, 182–184, 186, 198, 248, 252, 254, 259
product line 49
product sculpture 178
product semantics 5, 41, 52, 91, 95, 107, 126, 137, 145–147, 177–178, 180–184, 186, 259
product standardization 23
product system 247
product world 165, 249, 253
production 7, 12, 14, 18–21, 27, 29–30, 32, 44, 46, 58, 64–65, 69, 72–73, 77–78, 80, 89, 91–92, 124, 169, 182, 254, 256, 260
professional piracy 205
prognosis 86–87, 144
prognostic 87, 118
progress 14, 46, 54, 74, 92, 95, 102, 112–113, 127–128, 148, 152, 155, 169, 184, 202, 205, 246–247, 252
project management 196
promotion of design 53
prototype 201, 255
psychology 31, 40, 103, 144, 149, 155–159, 161, 167, 203
public design 148
public relations 195

R
radical constructivism 96
radical design 220
radio 45, 180, 222–223
rationalism 37, 40, 81–82, 109–110
rationalization 33, 111
ready-made 222
real sciences 112
reality 83, 94–95, 103, 112, 115, 122, 132, 138, 140–141, 183, 203, 213, 232, 235, 237, 255
reason 20, 80, 82, 94, 103, 106, 111, 117, 128, 135–136, 153, 162, 170–172, 177
recognition 77, 87, 91, 105, 107, 128, 175, 235
recognizability 77
recycling 14, 60, 256, 260
recycling design 60
Red Books 193
redesigning 108, 153, 189
reduction 24, 98, 252
reference to the human body 166
referential 87
reform movement 20, 27
relation 73, 86–88, 91, 141, 145, 149, 166, 171, 231–232, 235
relationship 13, 17, 53, 96, 105, 110–111, 140, 147, 149–150, 165, 180, 231
remote control 100
Renaissance 23
rendering 113
repertoire of methods 113
representation 43, 87, 92–93, 166, 234, 236, 249, 253
research 32, 36, 41, 78, 80, 91, 100, 102, 105, 108, 119, 122, 128, 132–134, 137, 139–141, 146–147, 153–155, 157–158, 172, 174–175, 185, 197, 218, 223–225, 230, 234, 243, 249, 252–253
retro wave 224
revolution 18, 20, 26, 73, 216, 245, 255–256
revolutionary milestone 169
Rio de Janeiro 47
rule 191, 254

rules of transformation 89
Russia 26, 122
Russian Bauhaus 27

S
satisfying needs 144
Scandinavia 53, 70, 144–146
Scenario 118–119
scholarliness 132
science 8, 11, 17, 28, 33, 40, 46,
    79–82, 86, 98, 101–103, 110–113,
    116, 122, 128, 131, 133–134,
    138–139, 141, 153, 155–156, 159,
    178, 185, 197, 220, 223, 236, 238,
    253
science fiction 220
science of design 28
science of mental life 155
science of perception 156, 159
science theory 131
scientific 11, 32, 40, 43–44, 54,
    59, 78–79, 81–82, 96, 103–104,
    109, 111, 113, 118, 123–124, 131,
    133–134, 138, 142, 144, 154–155,
    170, 218, 254
scientific community 133
scissor principle 222
scooters 173
Scotland 24
screen design 249
sculptural 161
SDN (Swiss Design Network) 134
seating furniture 214
Secession Style 21
semantic added value 140, 144
semantic transfer 178
semantic turn 96
semantics 5, 17, 41, 52, 56, 91–92,
    94–95, 106–107, 126, 137, 143,
    145–147, 149, 154, 177–178,
    180–186, 200, 259
semiology 87
semiotic terms 90, 95, 154
semiotics 4, 17, 40, 76, 83, 86–91,
    93–96, 100–101, 106, 136–137,
    141, 144–149, 164, 170, 182, 184,
    203–204, 231, 259
semiotics and architecture 90, 94

semiotization of the
    environment 94
sense 8, 13, 18, 33, 60, 70, 72, 77,
    87, 89–90, 92–95, 97, 102, 106,
    113, 131, 137, 139, 142, 148, 150,
    154, 158, 165–166, 183–184, 191,
    199, 214–216, 222, 228–229, 233,
    235, 237, 242–243, 250, 255
sense of space 216
sensory 82, 100–101, 103, 140,
    142, 145, 154–155, 158, 212
sensuality 136
series production 64
Shaker 189
shape 12, 57, 92, 114, 131, 141, 154,
    186, 189, 193, 195, 203, 213, 232,
    235, 243, 251, 259
sign 13, 45, 86, 90, 96, 101, 106,
    142, 144, 149, 151, 165, 169–170,
    173, 203, 231, 251–252
sign management 144
sign process 96
sign system 170
sign user 142
sign worlds 170
signal 136, 146
significance 19, 24, 38, 48, 56,
    147, 164, 186, 189, 199, 228, 230,
    251
simplicity 56, 189, 208, 224, 237,
    253
simulation 63, 120, 254
Singer 21
Slöjdforenigen 23
small series 7
smartphone 101, 151, 251, 255
sneakers 173
social networks 119, 173, 228, 256
social sciences 80, 107
socialization 141, 170
society 5, 9, 20, 23, 27, 54–55,
    58–59, 69–70, 84, 90–91, 116,
    118–119, 122, 130–131, 133,
    141–142, 172–173, 178, 188,
    217–218, 225–231, 234–235,
    237–238, 252
socio-cultural 97
sociology 40, 69, 122, 144, 230,
    234

software 8, 14, 116–117, 120–121,
    123, 128, 152, 167–168, 181, 189,
    222, 228, 242, 249–254
software design 222, 242, 252
sound design 139
space 9–10, 19, 66, 100, 104, 108,
    132, 178, 207, 211–212, 215–217,
    220, 222, 224, 235
space travel 9, 220
specifications 113, 115
speechlessness 205
sport 9, 171, 175–176, 224
stability 29, 166
stage design 46
stakeholder 183
standard 17, 33, 70, 84, 123, 146,
    155, 158, 251, 253
standardization 21, 23, 30, 89,
    250
status 9, 36, 46, 57, 70, 84, 133,
    137, 140, 142, 145, 171, 173, 175,
    192, 202, 208, 227, 233, 235, 253
status symbol 142
steel 19, 29, 34, 58, 208, 216
stewards of the disciplines 135
stone 101, 215–216
strategic design 5, 150, 188, 190,
    196, 199–200, 243
strategic management 225
strategic product planning 184
strategy 50, 72, 93, 99, 106, 137,
    178, 190, 193, 235, 248, 260
streamlined shape 12
stringency 50, 207, 215
structuralism 88, 149, 171, 182,
    203
structure 19, 36, 89, 97, 114, 139,
    141, 172, 180, 216, 256
student protest movements 58
Stuttgart 23, 43, 56, 59, 89, 94,
    115, 129, 134, 209, 211, 214
style 19–21, 24, 27, 34, 43, 50, 55,
    58–59, 94, 111, 169, 173, 183,
    202–204, 213–215
style element 50
style principle 111
styling 12, 174, 182, 234
Superstudio 217, 222
surface 59, 123, 139, 161, 253

SUV (Sports Utility Vehicle) 175–176, 224, 230
Swatch 57, 199, 230
Sweden 133
Swiss design 74, 134
Swissness 74
Switzerland 46, 74, 216
symbol 9, 58, 100, 142, 146, 148–149, 155, 169–170, 177, 216, 245
symbol theory 148, 155
syntax 94, 149, 154
synthesis 32, 46, 82–83, 191
system 41, 69–70, 88, 90, 94–95, 98, 107–109, 112, 119, 137, 166, 170, 183, 189, 208–209, 213–214, 222, 228, 247, 253
system design 41
systems theory 79, 196

T
tablet PC 119, 173, 247
talking furniture 83
tamagotchi 101
target 109, 112, 121–122, 130, 199, 201, 228, 233
target condition 109, 112
target group 121, 201
taste 23, 139, 173, 228, 232
techné hermeneutiké 102
technical 7, 11–12, 19, 26, 40, 45, 54, 77, 79, 83, 89, 96–97, 109, 116, 118, 129, 131, 134, 138, 148, 161–162, 164, 166, 173, 177–178, 199, 213, 230, 236–238, 247–248, 250–251
technical aesthetics 26
technical development 12
techno scene 173
technological revolution 245
technology 5, 27, 30, 33–34, 36, 40, 50, 77, 83, 90–91, 99–100, 102, 104, 110, 115, 118, 131–132, 137, 146–147, 153, 178, 190, 197, 200, 209, 211, 214, 217, 222–225, 234, 236, 238–239, 241–243, 245–247, 251, 255, 259
teen culture 173

telecommunications 96–97, 223, 254
telematic systems 140
television 45, 100, 190, 223
test procedures 113, 123
theoretical 8, 30, 40–41, 43, 52, 55, 58, 60, 79, 88, 93, 95, 98, 100, 103, 143, 146–147, 149, 157, 185, 198, 202, 204, 213
theoretical research 157
theory 1, 3, 5, 17, 28, 37–38, 40, 43–45, 54–59, 63, 77, 79–80, 82, 86, 88–89, 93, 96, 98–99, 102–104, 107, 111–112, 125–133, 135, 137–139, 141, 143–148, 150–151, 153–159, 165, 169–170, 172–173, 177–178, 182–184, 186, 196, 198, 202, 205, 225, 227, 231, 233–238, 242, 248, 251–252, 259–260
thesis 83, 96, 144, 152, 156, 183, 226, 235
things of nature 84
things that think 223
Thonet 21, 29, 92, 210
throne 33, 63–64, 84, 90
timeless design 177
tool 58, 120, 166, 197, 246
totality 13
trade fairs 8–9, 53, 224
trademark 34, 190, 199
trademark image 199
transcendental 98
trans-classical science 111–112
transcultural 70
transformation 33, 89, 136, 152, 226
transmitter 96, 180
transparent factory 115
trend 19, 44, 74, 173, 224–225
trend gurus 224
trend scouts 224
triadic relation 87, 141
tubular steel furniture 29, 58
TV 247
type furniture 34
typewriter 53
typography 45, 223, 253
typology 88, 149

U
ubiquitous computing 236
Ulm functionalism 111
Ulm School of Design (HfG Ulm) 26, 33, 37–49, 58–59, 78, 89, 91, 95–96, 108–109, 111, 127, 129, 130, 133, 146, 164, 177, 180, 196, 204, 218, 241
Ulm style 43
understanding 11, 28, 59, 81, 83, 95, 102–107, 116, 136–137, 145, 165, 170, 183, 218, 226, 234–235, 238, 242, 250
uniformity 161, 209
unity 24, 27, 33, 50, 55, 82, 87, 102–103, 106, 110, 114, 136, 155–156, 189–191, 195
universality 87, 102
urban planning 59, 159, 202, 213, 217, 233
usability 123, 250, 254
use 8–9, 11, 14, 26, 49, 56, 58–59, 66, 87, 90–92, 99–100, 119, 123, 127, 139, 147–148, 151–152, 165–166, 170–173, 177, 181–182, 186, 189, 198, 205, 214, 222–223, 227, 231, 233–235, 241, 245, 247, 249, 251–252, 254
use value 58, 91–92, 231
user 8, 12, 50, 83–84, 91, 96–97, 100–101, 105, 116–117, 119–121, 137, 143, 147, 150, 166–169, 176, 178, 181–184, 186, 222, 228, 235–236, 242, 247–251, 253–255
user interface 116, 168, 184, 253
utensil 96, 108
utilitarianism 20, 24
utilitas 18, 94, 202
utility objects 65–66
utility value 182
utopia 216, 218, 220

V
value 8, 56, 58, 70, 91–93, 97, 122, 137, 140, 144–145, 150, 154, 156, 169, 173, 180, 200, 215, 231, 250, 253, 256, 259–260
value creation 93, 137, 150, 200, 260

value orientation 12
variability 209
variety 13, 97, 100–101, 134, 146, 199, 204
velocity 210
Venice 66, 213, 241–242
video 100, 104, 247, 251
Vienna 19, 21, 23, 204, 208, 211, 252
Vienna Secession 23
virtual prototyping 122

vision 218
visual communication 37, 45, 89, 159, 190
visual design 36
visual methodology 44
visual turn 243, 252
visualization 120, 122, 152–153, 165–166, 182, 241–243, 247–249
VKhuTeMas 27
Volkswagen 115, 145, 198

W
Walkman 99–100, 224
way of life 40, 226
Weimar 24, 27–28, 32, 37, 55
Werkbund 19, 23, 241
Werkkunst 78, 111
work of art 11–12, 90
world-bettering 14
world of signs 95

Picture Credit

Bernhard E. Bürdek

Design
History, Theory and practice of product design

www.buerdek.info

Translation from German into English:
Meredith Dale, Susan Richter, Nina Hausmann

Copy editing: Julia Dawson

Project management: Katharina Kulke

Layout, cover design: Heimann and Schwantes

Typesetting: Sven Schrape

This publication is also available as an e-book
(ISBN PDF 978-3-0356-0394-;
ISBN EPUB 978-3-0356-0405-4)
and in a German language edition
(ISBN 978-3-0356-0404-7).

© 2015 Birkhäuser Verlag GmbH, Basel
P.O. Box 44, 4009 Basel, Switzerland
Part of Walter de Gruyter GmbH, Berlin/Boston

Printed on acid-free paper produced from
chlorine-free pulp. TCF ∞

Printed in Germany

ISBN 978-3-0356-0403-0

9 8 7 6 5 4 3 2 1
www.birkhauser.com